Collaborative Governance

A new era of public policy in Australia?

Collaborative Governance

A new era of public policy in Australia?

Edited by Janine O'Flynn and John Wanna

ANU
THE AUSTRALIAN NATIONAL UNIVERSITY

E PRESS

ANU
E PRESS

the Australia and New Zealand
School of Government

Published by ANU E Press
The Australian National University
Canberra ACT 0200, Australia
Email: anuepress@anu.edu.au
This title is also available online at: http://epress.anu.edu.au/collab_gov_citation.html

National Library of Australia
Cataloguing-in-Publication entry

Title:	Collaborative governance : a new era of public policy in Australia? / editors, Janine O'Flynn ; John Wanna.
ISBN:	9781921536403 (pbk.)
	9781921536410 (pdf)
Series:	ANZSOG series.
Subjects:	Public administration--Australia.
	Australia--Politics and government.

Other Authors/Contributors:
O'Flynn, Janine.
Wanna, John.

Dewey Number: 351.94

Cover design by John Butcher

Funding for this monograph series has been provided by the Australia and New Zealand School of Government Research Program.

John Wanna, *Series Editor*

Professor John Wanna is the Sir John Bunting Chair of Public Administration at the Research School of Social Sciences at The Australian National University. He is the director of research for the Australian and New Zealand School of Government (ANZSOG). He is also a joint appointment with the Department of Politics and Public Policy at Griffith University and a principal researcher with two research centres: the Governance and Public Policy Research Centre and the nationally-funded Key Centre in Ethics, Law, Justice and Governance at Griffith University. Professor Wanna has produced around 17 books including two national text books on policy and public management. He has produced a number of research-based studies on budgeting and financial management including: *Budgetary Management and Control* (1990); *Managing Public Expenditure* (2000), *From Accounting to Accountability* (2001) and, most recently, *Controlling Public Expenditure* (2003). He has just completed a study of state level leadership covering all the state and territory leaders — entitled *Yes Premier: Labor leadership in Australia's states and territories* — and has edited a book on Westminster Legacies in Asia and the Pacific — *Westminster Legacies: Democracy and responsible government in Asia and the Pacific*. He was a chief investigator in a major Australian Research Council funded study of the Future of Governance in Australia (1999-2001) involving Griffith and the ANU. His research interests include Australian and comparative politics, public expenditure and budgeting, and government-business relations. He also writes on Australian politics in newspapers such as *The Australian*, *Courier-Mail* and *The Canberra Times* and has been a regular state political commentator on ABC radio and TV.

Table of Contents

Contributors

Margaret Allison, Divisional Manager, Customer and Community Services, City of Brisbane

Shane Carmody, Deputy Chief Strategic Officer, Strategy and Support, Civil Aviation Safety Authority

Bill Eggers, Senior Fellow, Manhattan Institute for Policy Research and Global Director, Public Sector, Deloitte Research

Allan Fels AO, Dean, Australia and New Zealand School of Government

Carsten Greves, Professor, International Center for Business and Politics, Copenhagen Business School

Elaine Henry OAM, Chief Executive Officer, The Smith Family

Paul Hibbert, Research Fellow, University of Strathclyde Business School, United Kingdom

Graeme Hodge, Director, Centre for Regulatory Studies, Monash University

Rachel Hunter, Director-General, Department of Education, Training and the Arts, Queensland

Chris Huxham, Professor of Management, University of Strathclyde Business School and Senior Fellow of the Advanced Institute of Management Research

Ben Jupp, Director, Office of the Third Sector, Government of the United Kingdom

Evert Lindquist, Director, School of Public Administration, University of Victoria, Canada

Janine O'Flynn, Research Fellow, Research School of Social Sciences and Crawford School of Economics and Government, The Australian National University

Peter Shergold, Professor and Head, Centre for Social Impact, University of New South Wales and former Secretary, Department of the Prime Minister and Cabinet

Diane Smith, Research Fellow, Centre for Aboriginal Economic Policy Research, The Australian National University

Paul Smyth, Professorial Fellow in Social Policy, University of Melbourne

Louise Sylvan, Former Deputy Chair, Australian Competition and Consumer Commission

Jane Treadwell, Executive Director, Citizen Access and Transformation Department for Victorian Communities

Siv Vangen, Senior Lecturer, Open University Business School, United Kingdom

John Wanna, Sir John Bunting Chair of Public Administration, Australia and New Zealand School of Government, The Australian National University

Preface

Networked governance and collaboration to improve outcomes

In introducing this monograph, I would like to begin by emphasising the importance of collaboration to better governance. This involves collaboration within and across government and between government and the community. These are the central relationships we explore here.

It is clear today that governments across the developed world are preaching the gospel of collaboration, cooperation and coordination, and are realising that their objectives cannot be achieved without collaboration with others. The big question is: is the rhetoric matched by the reality or are governments merely mouthing platitudes? Do they really mean what they profess; do governments talk of collaboration genuinely and meaningfully or do they do so partially and largely with their own interests at heart? Do their actions indicate that they are serious and, if so, what cultural changes are necessary, what changes are under way and what changes will be required in the future? Questions of motivation and integrity are fundamental to the process of collaboration.

We also need to consider how we can translate collaborative engagement (inter-agency relations, community engagement, collaborative 'experiments') into more effective outcomes, better public policy and a better use of community and government resources. This raises questions such as how and when do we choose to collaborate? On what topics or issues? Are there policy matters on which we should not collaborate or on which it would be preferable not to do so? In short, how do we determine on what matters to collaborate?

These questions in turn raise the issue of the capacity to collaborate across the various sectors. Are the stakeholders and players prepared for the effort required, the investment in time and resources, the consequences of going down such a path and the 'loss of control' or shared control in most instances? Are governments geared up to collaborate and do they have real 'connections' with the community, or have the arm's-length cultures of contract management severed relations with providers and community representatives? Are community bodies themselves geared up to collaborate with government and with each other?

While it is imperative to find effective ways to engage with the community, it is not always clear 'who' represents the community. Governments often find themselves dealing with surrogates for the community: self-appointed, organised groups who profess to represent community interests as they see them. Some of these bodies could be doing useful work in the community, but does that mean they 'speak' for the community? The question, then, is with whom should we deal and why? How far can faith or charitable groups represent end users, 'real' consumers or ordinary citizens? Whose voice counts and who gets a say? How do we engage with those who do not really want us to engage with them or with those who have other priorities?

Governments tend to think that all forms of collaboration need to be effectively managed, but how do we effectively manage collaboration—as government officials or as community representatives? How do we establish meaningful processes, maintain enthusiasm and involvement, sustain the decision-making process and deliver better outcomes for society and the public interest? How do we manage collaboration between sovereign governments?

Finally, public collaborations need to be accountable—meaning the collaborative partners will have to find ways to deal with the changing accountabilities involved in collaborative government. For governments, this will involve fewer 'silo' authoritative structures and more shared accountabilities. Some might want to think of this in Mark Moore's terms as moving to an 'authorising-regime' notion of shared accountability in collaborative public-policy endeavours. What, however, would this mean in practice and how would things unravel if something went wrong?

In many ways, collaborative governance takes us beyond notions of responsible government and ministerial accountability. It takes us into the world of networked governance and governing by networks, in which collaboration becomes the dominant organisational culture and policymaking is by consensus and agreement. This is a world in which the skills of diplomacy are required: promoting dialogue, shared appreciations, participatory engagement and deliberative democracy. We will need new theoretical models of public policy and new understandings of how governance is going to work—not just by the active participants, but by parliament, by review committees, by auditors and evaluation teams and by the media and the general public.

Collaboration between governments could herald a new phase of federalism. If 'cooperative federalism' is about microeconomic reform and structural efficiencies, 'collaborative federalism' is about sharing intent, sharing goals and agreeing on delivery responsibilities. This new phase of federalism is likely to focus on social policies, national security and bio-security, the environment, infrastructure and communication. Above all, it is likely to dispense with the notion that 'government knows best', replacing it not just with intergovernmental agreements, but with community involvement in policy design and delivery. It could be more messy, but also more realistic and more results-based.

This monograph, *Collaborative Governance: A new era of public policy in Australia?*, draws from the best papers presented to the June 2007 conference on collaborative government held in Canberra. We invited senior executives from the public and non-government sectors to share their experiences of collaboration—and, in particular, to provide examples of what works, what does not work and why. We asked them to assess how we might be able to better achieve public-policy outcomes through collaborative arrangements. We asked them to provide a practical focus but also to raise theoretical issues to assist our thinking and policy frameworks.

I would like to thank Peter Shergold, the former secretary of the Department of Prime Minister and Cabinet (PM&C), for suggesting the topic and for his involvement in the planning of this Australia and New Zealand School of Government (ANZSOG) event. I also thank Professor John Wanna and his staff at The Australian National University and ANZSOG staff in Melbourne for organising and hosting the conference. Special thanks must also be given to the following for supporting the conference and identifying and suggesting speakers: the ANZSOG board, the New Zealand Government, and New Zealand State Services Commission, and Isi Unikowski and staff at PM&C. Finally, I thank Professor John Wanna, Dr Janine O'Flynn and John Butcher for their efforts in compiling this book.

ANZSOG's 2007 conference followed the successful 2006 conference on Improving Implementation: Program management and organisational change, which was subsequently published by ANU E Press in the highly successful ANZSOG monograph series. I recommend this series to all policymakers and those with an interest in public policy. The present publication provides a useful contribution to our continuing understanding about how to better deliver policy to the Australian community. I look forward to the further debates that will ensue.

Professor Allan Fels AO
Australia and New Zealand School of Government
Melbourne
October 2008

Editors' introduction

In this monograph, we present a collection of papers from the ANZSOG conference on collaboration held in 2007. We have been able to draw on a range of perspectives—practitioner and scholarly—to offer a collection focused on the issue of collaborative governance in Australia. Our contributors consider the drivers, challenges, prospects and promises of collaboration, from a conceptual and a practical perspective. We believe this provides a rich resource for readers who are interested in the issue of collaboration in the public sector, and more specifically in public policy.

Throughout the monograph, our contributors draw on their personal experience, their research and their visions for change to offer important insights into the potential of collaboration and the fiercely stubborn impediments to this ideal. You will note that there are differences of opinion, which, of course, are to be expected; we hope they will help in feeding the continuing debate about collaborative governance.

We have organised the monograph in four key sections. In the first, 'Setting the scene', there are six chapters, which provide an introduction for readers to a range of issues including the dimensions and drivers of collaboration, why governments are interested in collaboration, the Australian experience, the notions of collaborative advantage and collaborative inertia, what is meant by success in collaboration and the role of the community sector in collaborative governance.

In the second part, 'The reality of collaboration', we draw on the experience and research of experts to consider success, failure, challenges and questions that arise from attempts at collaboration. In the eight chapters in this section, a range of examples is provided by the authors and many point to traps and lessons that will be of considerable interest and value to readers.

In the third part, 'Collaboration abroad', there are two chapters that provide an international perspective. Drawing on experience and research in the United Kingdom and British Columbia, in Canada, the authors in this section give us a window into developments in other parts of the world, offering promise and words of warning.

In the final part, 'Collaboration: rhetoric and reality', the concluding chapter of the monograph seeks to examine the reality of collaboration in public policy. In this chapter, the author questions whether there is much evidence of true collaboration, raising the possibility that all the collaborative talk has yet to translate into much collaborative action.

Together, these sections offer readers the opportunity to consider collaborative governance in public policy from a range of perspectives, and to engage in the current debate about the value of collaboration.

One of the most important changes since the conference is, of course, the change of government and, along with many of our readers, we are keen to observe what will happen under the leadership of the new Prime Minister, Kevin Rudd. There is certainly a lot of talk, especially about intergovernmental collaboration, but will the Rudd Government be able to 'walk-the-walk'? Only time will tell.

We thank all of our contributors for their efforts in preparing their chapters for the monograph, in particular Peter Shergold, who was prepared to write a postscript after his move from the public service to academia. We especially thank John Butcher who, as usual, works tirelessly to ensure that the ANZSOG monographs are of the highest possible quality.

Janine O'Flynn and John Wanna

Part 1. Setting the scene: challenges and prospects for collaboration

1. Collaborative government: meanings, dimensions, drivers and outcomes

John Wanna

Collaboration means joint working or working in conjunction with others. It implies actors—individuals, groups or organisations—cooperating in some endeavour. The participants are 'co-labouring' with others on terms and conditions that, as we know, can vary enormously. The word 'collaboration' originally came into use in the nineteenth century as industrialisation developed, more complex organisations emerged and the division of labour and tasks increased. It was a fundamental norm of utilitarianism, social liberalism, collectivism, mutual aid and, later, scientific management and human relations organisational theory.[1] Explanations of collaboration could stress the descriptive/pragmatic side focusing on the practical realities of working with or through others, or the normative/intrinsic side emphasising participatory endeavour and the development of trust relations. For the most part, collaboration was portrayed at least as an essential imperative or more ideally as a highly desirable aspect of social, economic and political life.

Meanings and dimensions of collaboration

Collaboration usually attracts a positive 'spin'. It is often seen as a positive—to collaborate is better, it is creative, transformational and involves beneficial outcomes. There are, however, other dimensions to be considered. Collaborative endeavours can involve the achievement of some outcome or result or, alternatively, the negation or prevention of something happening. We can collaborate for 'good' ends and for 'bad' ends. The context in which collaboration exists is therefore important. The reasons for collaboration occurring are important—as are the means and practices involved, the motivations of the actors, the intended outcomes and the ends involved. To paraphrase Wildavsky, writing in 1973, collaboration and coordination involve several distinct dimensions. First, collaboration could involve cooperation to build commonality, improve consistency and align activities between actors. Second, collaboration can be the process of negotiation, involving a preparedness to compromise and make trade-offs. Third, collaboration can involve oversight roles, checking, pulling together and central coordination. Fourth, collaboration can involve power and coercion, the ability to force outcomes or impose one's own preferences on another, to some extent, with their compliance or involvement. Fifth, collaboration can involve future commitments and intentions, prospective behaviour, planning or preparation to align activities. Finally, collaboration can involve engagement, the development of internal motivations and personal commitment to projects, decisions, organisational goals or strategic objectives. It is apparent, even with a cursory glance, that these six dimensions are not necessarily either consistent or complementary with one another—indeed, some could be mutually exclusive.

Collaboration, therefore, is a complex phenomenon. Different aspects of collaborative relations can be evident or come into play in various examples of real collaboration. Different parties could also perceive the collaborative process with diametrically opposed views.

Conceptually, therefore, we have two distinct dimensions of collaboration that intersect continually and differentially: first, the scale or degree of collaboration, and second, the context, purpose or motivation behind collaborative activity. The scale or degree of collaboration categorises patterns of activity that are either evident or intended. It focuses on what levels of collaborative activity are apparent and how extensive are the dimensions of collaboration. In tabular form, the scale of collaboration can be depicted as an escalating ladder of commitment—from the lowest level of perfunctory collaboration to the highest and most elaborate level of integration (this would be similar to Arnstein's ladder of consultation). Table 1.1 lists the levels of collaboration relevant to the policy process and indicates what activities are involved at each of the various levels.

Second, collaboration does not occur in a vacuum. We also need to consider the context, purposes, choices and motivations of actors seeking to collaborate. Here, rather than an escalating ladder, we have a set of possible intentions and motivations that provides us with a range of alternatives or contrasting approaches. These options are listed in Table 1.2.

Table 1.1 The scale of collaboration

Degree of collaboration	What is involved—activities
Highest level: high normative commitment to collaboration; often highest political/managerial risks	Transformative interaction between network actors; substantive engagement and empowerment; search for high degree of stakeholder and inter-actor consensus and cooperation; coalition building by government and non-government actors
Medium–high level: strong normative orientation; high level of political/managerial risk	Strong engagement of stakeholders in decisions or policy process and implementation; devolving decision-making capacities to clients; more complex innovations in policy-delivery processes
Medium level: commitment to multiparty input and buy-in; moderate levels of political/managerial risk	Formal commitment to inter-agency consultation and collaboration; joined government strategies; formal joint involvement exercises and joint funding initiatives
Medium–low level: operational forms of collaboration to 'get job done'; some political/managerial risk	Forms of co-production; technical improvements in delivery chains; assistance to comply with obligations; direct consultation with clients over delivery and compliance systems; systematic use of evaluation data; public reporting on targets informed by client preferences
Lowest level: marginal operational adjustments, low levels of political/managerial risk	Incremental adjustments using consultative processes; client discussions and feedback mechanisms; gaining information on needs/expectations of others

Table 1.2 Contrasting context, purpose, choices and motivations of collaboration

Context & purpose	Choices or motivational possibilities	
Power dimension	Coercive and forced collaboration	Persuasive and voluntary involvement in collaboration
Commitment level	Meaningful and substantive collaboration	Meaningless and cosmetic collaboration
Cultural internalisation	Philosophical commitment to collaboration—development of collaborative cultures	Collaboration as a tool, an available instrument—no real commitment to collaboration as a *modus operandi*
Strategic dimension	Collaboration for positive and beneficial reasons	Collaboration for negative and/or preventive strategies
Means—ends dimension	Collaboration as a means and process; stages, due process	Collaboration as an end and outcome; shared results, outcome orientation
Goal dimension	Shared objectives; mutual intentions, consensual strategies and outcomes	Competing objectives; different reasons for participating in collaboration
Visibility and awareness dimension	Overt and public forms of collaboration; awareness of collaboration is high	Covert and behind-the-scenes collaboration; unawareness of collaboration
Problem applicability	Collaboration on simple problems; simple objectives and responsibilities	Collaboration on 'wicked' problems; defying description and solutions

Changing patterns of collaboration in public policy: historical eras

In public policy, we can identify different historical eras with distinct patterns of collaboration, perhaps indicating an evolution of practice. For example, from the outset of Australia as a nation, there was very little attempt to build collaboration into the design of Australian federalism and/or to practise it in the early years of Federation. Indeed, federalism can be interpreted from a Jeffersonian standpoint as an intentionally fragmented model of government with a high degree of decentralised autonomous powers. Jurisdictions retained separate responsibilities (sometimes misleadingly called 'coordinated federalism'). From this perspective, collaboration was not the essence of the chosen system of government, nor was it a particular priority of early governments. Attempts at collaboration would therefore have to work against the structural logic of federalism to succeed, and there would always remain a structural tension in such endeavours. This was characteristic of Australian governments in the first decades after Federation.

Postwar governments believing in Keynesian planning and demand management developed an interest in limited forms of collaboration. Infrastructure projects such as the Snowy Mountains Hydro-Electric Scheme involved multiple governments, inter-jurisdictional cooperation and shared commitments. The welfare state required some inter-agency collaboration and information sharing. Integrated forms of urban and regional planning (while often limited in effect) emphasised collaboration between various public and private entities. In such cases, collaboration often meant command and central coordination. The lessons from this period were mixed: joint action was complex and could stymie development; bad experiences with collaboration were notorious; collaborative projects had to be controlled and planned; and often governments did not learn from or build on their experiences of collaboration.

In the era of managerialism and rationalisation of the 1980s and 1990s, governments selectively used competition and forms of collaboration with market players to deliver their core business activities (Entwistle and Martin 2005). They separated roles and responsibilities, then coordinated delivery systems through contract management, funding arrangements and purchaser–provider relations. Governments believed they could improve delivery methods only by engaging in collaboration—which itself implied that they had also to specify outputs or results, control prices and select and monitor external providers. Collaboration occurred less across government than between government and third-party providers—involving individual government agencies and a myriad non-government providers (firms, charity-based and community providers). From the government's perspective, collaboration could involve a range of relationships, from arm's-length, hands-off contract management to close interaction and mutual partnerships. The rationale for greater collaboration was often given in terms of cost containment and economic criteria and/or providing client groups with greater accessibility to government programs. The lessons from this era tended to stress the value of market testing and provision while avoiding incurring new dependencies or capture. Collaboration was often on the government's terms or not at all.

By the turn of the century, governments were becoming interested in higher levels of collaboration—especially in vertical and horizontal collaboration, in whole-of-government integration, joint solutions and in various active partnerships. Governments began to redefine themselves as 'facilitators' engaged in 'value chains' and working through markets, rather than autarkic 'doers' who owned, operated and produced things themselves. They realised and accepted that they were reliant on a host of other actors in order to deliver effective outcomes. These other actors were potentially able to deliver better services because they had special knowledge and skills, had market access or specialisation or concentrated their efforts in key parts of the delivery chains. Four types of collaborative relations between actors became apparent:

- collaboration within government, involving different agencies and players
- collaboration between governments, involving agencies from different jurisdictions
- collaboration between governments and external third-party providers of goods and services
- collaboration between governments and individual citizens/clients.

Policymakers began to recognise new dependencies, the role of extensive policy networks in implementation and the need to reach out to other bodies with interests in shared outcomes. Collaboration was now a widely used policy instrument across the fields of public policy. Governments relied on collaboration to improve policy formulation (using such bodies as consultants and think tanks). They used collaboration to improve implementation and provide more integrated services (using firms, charity organisations and community associations). Governments could extend access regimes and widen the reach of policy using a matrix of local players, incentive payments and one-stop shops. Collaboration became an essential *modus operandi* for coping with crisis management and emergency situations, involving the coordination and mutual assistance of diverse specialist agencies. Collaboration now took on the mantle of managing mutual dependencies using diplomacy, dialogue and deliberation. Collaborators on all sides, however, questioned the effort–value equation and searched for ways to predict the ingredients of successful collaboration.

The vocabulary of governments also changed. They began to talk of engagement, connected government and collaboration as a new era of public administration ('public administration of the future'). In part, the language change was strategic and transformational, but in part it was also exhortatory (encouraging administrators to attempt collaboration to assist them in doing their jobs better). Collaboration was not framed within the mind-set of bureaucracy, but was beyond bureaucracy. Collaboration was by now the next wave of public-sector reform (after hierarchy, managerialism, 'new public management' and outsourcing and market delivery). It allowed governments to reconsider where they could best direct their strategies and energies to achieve desired outcomes. Governments sometimes chose to keep selected services or assets in public hands (for example, the benefit-payments system, the national rail track, regimes of safety regulation), but such decisions were made because governments felt they then had the appropriate springboard to build collaborative arrangements to deliver preferred outcomes. Governments began to build networks, coalitions and partnerships, but these arrangements were not meant as ends in themselves; rather, the investment in such collaborative arrangements was intended to improve services and government-to-citizen relations. Collaboration began to mean working with and through others for greater effectiveness.

If we look internationally at which nations are leading the way in the promotion of collaboration as an issue of good governance, we find the discourse is strongest in the Anglo-American nations that have undergone new public management reforms—especially in Westminster systems with strong executive governments. Why do we detect this trend? Reasons could include that the public sector in these nations is 'post-managerialist', there is a reduced role for and belief in hierarchies, governments have attempted to de-silo their administrative organisations and have introduced contractualism and commercial principles in policy implementation and delivery. US and Westminster-style systems have also tended to display less emphasis on ministerial autonomy in departments (compared with continental European or Asian governments), and have stronger traditions of coordination through and across cabinet. Central and line agencies in these countries overtly recognised the need for collaboration across government jurisdictions and agencies (and eventually collaboration with business and community organisations).

Drivers of collaboration today

We can cluster the drivers of collaboration under three headings: external drivers, internal drivers and volition in relation to the roles and responsibilities of government. External drivers include the pressures of globalisation, greater international connectedness and travel, knowledge of other cultures, information technology (IT) and technological sophistication. Economic pressures have also played a crucial role—with the push to develop world markets, global trade, international investment patterns, business aggregations and demand for uniform regulation, competitive neutrality and specialisation. Terrorism and national security concerns (including immigration and people movement) have also crystalised these global pressures in ways that go to the heart of the authoritative nature of the State. Global environmental, physical and resource pressures have forced governments to engage in international dialogue and action to manage these problems. Community demands, education, changing demographics and social structures have also changed expectations and understandings.

Internal drivers and preconditions within government include the political demands for public officials to be 'responsive' to community needs. Policy reach and accessibility are powerful drivers, as are policy orientations towards mutual obligation and reciprocity. Making policy outcomes more effective is also a major factor. This can include responsive resource systems, flexible budgetary frameworks and the managerial focus on outcomes and performance results. The growing preference for and greater reliance on contract provision necessitates basic forms of collaboration with external providers and the management of relations. Capacity issues inside government agencies and the changing composition and skills base of the public sector (from an operational focus to an emphasis on policy and management roles, with staff recruits shifting from school-leavers to graduates) have made collaboration a necessary imperative of modern management.

Volition factors include political strategies for shared goals and understanding of problems across the community—building consensus among players and coalitions of support for particular action. Part of the impetus behind volition is the desire for a new activism in government, to develop new policy agendas, take on wider responsibilities and remake policy frameworks to suit the changing times. Governments have declared their intentions to deliver 'seamless government', wired-up services, joint policy solutions and integrated services. Their public commitment to new performance-reporting regimes underscores these strategies.

Advantages and opportunities versus disadvantages and weaknesses

The advantages of collaboration are that it often assists policymakers to identify and target problems and achieve stakeholder agreement or acceptance of directions or decisions. It can be a means to better policy solutions that have greater traction in the community. It can contribute new visions or perspectives on problems and thus offer new opportunities to implement strategies for change. It can allow governments to take the initiative and get on the front foot. For public officials engaged in policy formulation, it can be either a way of genuinely opening up the policy process to wider ideas and suggestions or a way of road-testing ideas and collating responses before implementation. For non-government players, it allows them to understand better the thinking and practices of government and to exert some influence on policy determination or amendment.

Collaboration can lead to mutual learning and shared experience. It can provide direction for capacity building inside and outside organisations (either through the recruitment of different profiles and skills or the development of networks of supportive/dependent contributors). Many government agencies now work jointly with private-sector providers to the mutual benefit of both parties. A commitment to collaboration is also likely to drive organisational change and affect resource reallocation. It can spawn new organisational and interactive forums—from dedicated task forces to reference groups and advisory bodies, or from new authorities and policy forums to new intergovernmental bodies.

Collaboration in implementation has the advantages of clarifying roles and responsibilities, combining relevant skills and capacities, allowing specialisation and enabling public bureaucracies to be far more effective in delivering policy to the ground. It can be used to develop markets and bring into the policy process additional players who were not previously involved. It can also make governments conscious of the real value-for-money issues involved in delivering policy effectively (specifying outputs, prices, reporting requirements, and so on).

The disadvantages or weaknesses that could be experienced with collaborative activities include the difficulties of ensuring political or ministerial buy-in to arrangements of additional complexity. Ministers could show little interest in such initiatives or ask why they should volunteer to extend their political accountabilities, especially when they are likely to have less and less control over the outcomes. Politicians could regard collaboration as a way of losing control, not of gaining greater leverage over policy options. They could also fear that collaboration increases the political risks for them as politicians but not for others in the system.

Collaboration can blur lines of accountability even further than their current state. This raises questions about who is responsible for what and who is ultimately accountable for decisions taken, if problems emerge or if things go wrong. Collaboration can increase the blame game and excite complaints when the expectations of stakeholders are not met or are frustrated. Indeed, the promise of collaboration can heighten expectations that are likely to be dashed in practice.

Collaboration can frustrate rather than expedite decision making. Interdepartmental committees once had the reputation of being the graveyard of decision making; the combatants of such committees went along to meetings to defend their turf and prevent decisions being taken contrary to their interests. Many considered a successful outcome of such meetings was that no decision was taken or that potential action was averted.

Non-government actors can have other problems. From the viewpoint of business and community associations, they could feel that they are not necessarily bound by collective processes or consensual agreements—or cannot speak for their sector or ensure compliance with collective agreements. Governments can impose formal or informal constraints on their behaviour—imposing 'gag' conditions in legal contracts, insisting on vetting public comments or presentations and vetoing the selection of staff working for non-governmental organisations. Conversely, non-government actors can disengage and disrupt policy delivery at times of their own choosing, and have no real accountability for any final outcome.

Collaborative exercises can run at cross-purposes if the objectives and incentives of the participants are not aligned or compatible. Shared preferences can be the exception rather than the rule. For some technical purists or expert specialists in the policy process, collaboration can be perceived as leading to second-best solutions (or even to lowest common denominator solutions) if participants possess veto rights or can sway decisions (even if such outcomes are workable).

Governments have attracted criticism for not being entirely genuine in collaborative engagements. Collaboration can be undertaken for ulterior political motives. It can be cosmetic or a smokescreen for action. It can be used to 'sell' decisions decided elsewhere or taken previously by departments. Collaboration then becomes an exercise in the dissemination and promotion of government policy. Such examples of perfunctory collaboration can undermine trust in government and in the policy process more generally.

Lessons from collaboration

One of the main aims of this monograph is to identify and debate the substantive lessons from real experiences of collaboration in the public sector but involving the private sector and the wider community—to enable policymakers to better understand the processes and the range of possibilities available. We aim to analyse the 'black box' of opacity that often characterises the practice of collaboration (Thomson and Perry 2006). Already from experiences and from the literature, we know that collaborative arrangements are costly in time and resources, are inherently fragile, need to be constantly managed and nurtured, involve trust and reciprocal obligations and are *sui generis* or uniquely distinct (Huxham 2005; Entwistle and Martin 2005; Agranoff 2006; Bardach 1998; and, for the private sector, see Simonin 1997). We know that successful collaboration requires commitment, trust, leadership, clarity of objectives and planning stages, developing understanding and mutual working relations (Huxham and Vangen 2000). From within government there is a belief that collaboration works best when responsibilities are clear and when a lead agency or 'champion' has been selected. Is this empirically valid? Can responsibilities be clearly separated in collaborative ventures and can leadership be successfully anointed in an *a priori* manner? How can the momentum for collaboration be generated and sustained?

In this monograph, many of the contributors speak from years of practical experience engaged in collaborative endeavours. Many identify general lessons from their specific if diverse experiences. Some of the lessons highlight the perspectives of the individual players (the official, the community representative, the business manager, or the end user) about what collaboration entails, how it impacts on them and how players can collaborate better. Others present collaboration as a new organising principle of government and policymaking—a structured set of collective choices from which new policy possibilities develop and germinate—feeding into policy formulation, implementation and evaluation. Others tend to see collaboration as a new form of democratic engagement bringing substantial deliberative benefit to the development of good public policy and quality services. Others disseminate comparative policy learning from overseas indicating how other jurisdictions have gone about the journey of collaboration in policy setting, encouraging policy transfer or emulation and illustrating how beneficial outcomes have been achieved in their particular context.

We hope that the sharing of this combined learning, experience and understanding will inform governments and policy processes into the future—and give non-government participants and policy networks a realistic if not sanguine view of the potentialities and implications of collaborative government. Governing through collaboration will change not only how we make policy, it will change what policy is made and who cooperates in its delivery. Collaboration poses a major challenge to the traditional ways of making policy and to the conventional departmental cultures of 'government knows best'. Governing though collaboration throws out many challenges to all players in almost all policy fields; it poses challenges but also opens the possibility of truly sustained improvements in the quality of implementation and service delivery.

References

Agranoff, R. 2006, 'Inside collaborative networks: ten lessons for public managers', *Public Administration Review*, December.

Bardach, E. 1998, *Getting Agencies to Work Together: The practice and theory of managerial craftsmanship*, Brookings Institution, Washington, DC.

Entwistle, T. and Martin, S. 2005, 'From competition to collaboration in public service delivery: a new agenda for research', *Public Administration*, vol. 83, no. 1.

Huxham, C. 2005, *Managing to Collaborate: The theory and practice of collaborative advantage*, Routledge, New York.

Huxham, C. and Vangen, S. 2000, 'Leadership in the shaping and implementation of collaboration agendas', *Academy of Management Journal*, vol. 43, no. 6.

Simonin, B. 1997, 'The importance of collaborative know-how: an empirical test of the learning organisation', *Academy of Management Journal*, vol. 40, no. 5.

Thomson, A. M and Perry, J. L. 2006, 'Collaboration processes: inside the black box', *Public Administration Review*, December.

Watt, I. and Dangerfield, G. 2007, *Arrangements for Facilitating Trans-Tasman Government Institutional Co-operation*, Australia New Zealand School of Government, Carlton, Victoria.

Wildavsky, A. 1973, 'If planning is everything, maybe it's nothing', *Policy Sciences*, Volume 4, no.2, pp. 127-153.

ENDNOTES

[1] Thomson and Perry (2006:20) state that collaboration in the United States has its roots in two competing political traditions: classic liberalism (market individualism requiring preferences and exchange) and civic republicanism (community integration of shared preferences).

2. Governing through collaboration

Dr Peter Shergold

There are new and exciting changes occurring in the processes of governance, which have profound implications for public services. The provision of policy advice is becoming more contested. The views of officials now compete with those of political advisers, advocacy organisations and policy think tanks. The implementation of policy is increasingly contracted out and delivered through third parties, with the Public Service taking responsibility for oversight, evaluation and accountability.

At the same time—and significantly extending these developments—broader networks of policy influence are emerging. They demand new ways of doing things and new forms of leadership behaviour. At the heart of these changes lies the growing importance of collaboration—across government agencies and jurisdictions and between the public, private and not-for-profit sectors.

In Australia, these trends are evolving within a Westminster form of government, set within a federal system, much (but not all) of it articulated in a written constitution. The Australian systems' sovereignty, majority-party control of the Executive, ministers accountable to parliament, the cabinet as the basis of collective responsibility, institutionalised opposition and parliamentary conventions and rules of debate.

This system of representative and responsible government provides an institutional framework for managing political debate in democratic ways. Within this structure, the Australian Public Service (APS) plays a key role. Much of its influence is hidden, in that it provides advice to the government of the day in confidence. It works, however, within an environment of political contest in which decisions are subject to parliamentary questioning and intense media scrutiny. The delicate balance between responsiveness to government direction and Public Service independence is a matter of continuing public debate.

Public servants provide support to ministers. They put forward non-partisan policy advice, but, sometimes after robust behind-the-scenes discussion, they accept the directions set by government. They implement the policy decisions of government whether or not their advice has been taken. They draft the legislation, deliver the programs and services and provide the regulatory and compliance framework for government.

The APS remains a professional, merit-based, career service. By that I mean that its senior public servants continue to be selected on the basis of competence and experience. They serve through changes in ministers and government. They are not recruited or promoted on the basis of party affiliation or political allegiance. The APS serves successive governments with equal commitment. It accepts the right of the Executive to set directions and make decisions. It is accountable, through ministers, to parliament.

There have been some fundamental developments in the past 30 years, such as the emergence of ministerial advisers (employed outside the *Public Service Act*) and the growth of a panoply of mechanisms to provide administrative review of decision making. At the same time, in a form often characterised as 'new public management', the Public Service has increasingly assessed its performance against the achievement of explicit outputs and outcomes—not just the ethical deployment of inputs. Nevertheless, until now the traditional structures of Westminster have continued to frame the relationship between the government and the APS. Greater change could beckon.

Let me tell a personal story. My job seems to be getting harder. In part, that's because government gets ever busier. The volume of legislation is rising. The number of policy measures is increasing. Here's one example: whereas there were 353 individual budget items in 2001–02, there were 532 items in 2006–07. At the same time, my job is becoming more intense. I discern that the speed with which government expects programs to be delivered is intensifying. New forms of technology are adding immediacy to decision making and public communication.

Concurrently, new, more complex institutional structures of governance are emerging, which take many forms. Within the Public Service, much authority has been devolved to individual agencies. The number of these organisations has increased with time and many wield various levels of statutory independence. To some extent, specialist agencies have assumed the power that was traditionally the provenance of departments of state. Consequently, the need for inter-agency, cross-jurisdictional involvement is rising. So, too, is the requirement for contracts, memorandums of understanding, partnerships and alliances to establish continuing relationships across the public–private divide.

I find that the pressures of devolution, the proliferation of government agencies and involvement of non-government parties present significant challenges to the way I work. Increased organisational demarcations present the danger of territoriality at the same time that political issues are broadening beyond the ambit of single agencies. The increased number and authority of agencies across governments need to be harnessed to a single purpose—namely, the making and executing of good policy. That demands collaboration. It is now a requirement of my job. I spend much of my time trying to overcome bureaucratic barriers in pursuit of whole-of-government, joined up approaches to policy development and more seamless policy delivery.

Partly in response, I have established a Cabinet Implementation Unit (CIU) in my department (Prime Minister and Cabinet, PM&C) to oversee the delivery of government programs. Today, 16 per cent of the programs the CIU is monitoring in its 'traffic-light' implementation reports to cabinet involve three or more Commonwealth agencies in delivery or are based on agreements between the Commonwealth and the states. The challenges of inter-agency and/or inter-jurisdictional cooperation are each responsible for one-quarter of the reasons given by agencies for programs accorded 'amber lights' (indicating potential delivery problems).

At the same time, more stakeholders are being given an opportunity to contribute to the processes of governance. An emerging trend is for policy to be progressed through task forces. My department has hosted no fewer than 62 individual task forces since 1999–2000. Many are internal to the Public Service, effectively operating as a full-time interdepartmental committee (IDC), brought together for a specific purpose. Increasingly, however, they are being widened to include participation from the private and not-for-profit sectors, often with secretariat support. They are being given the opportunity to provide advice to government on specific issues.

Typical is the Task Group on Emissions Trading, which I chaired (as Secretary of PM&C) from its establishment in December 2006 until it presented its report to the Prime Minister in May 2007. It comprised a group of seven private-sector business leaders and five Public Service secretaries, supported by a high-level secretariat drawn from a range of agencies. Innovatively, the secretariat was also widened to include outside representation (from the Business Council of Australia and the Australian Industry Greenhouse Network). Its conclusions—to support the introduction of an Australian cap-and-trade emissions trading system—were accepted by the government. The APS is now tasked with implementing that decision.

Such task forces are taking an increasingly significant role, including even the oversight of the implementation of government policy. I have just become a member, for instance, of the Northern Territory (NT) Emergency Response Taskforce. Its key role will be to provide advice to government on the diverse operational issues associated with Commonwealth intervention in remote Indigenous communities. It will require a high degree of collaboration between Commonwealth departments, the Australian Defence Force, the Australian Federal Police, NT government agencies and non-governmental organisations.

Another emerging role is for third-party agents. Private-sector and community institutions now deliver services to and on behalf of the government outside the traditional structures of governance. The key characteristics involve the allocation of government business, by Public Service tender, with conditions set by contract. The goal is to harness market competition. Payment is made on the basis of outcomes and procurement decided on the criterion of performance. The contracted organisations enjoy greater autonomy with respect to delivery processes than is normal in public-sector agencies. Crucially, the Public Service (the purchaser) remains accountable as manager for the ethical conduct of the contracted body (the provider).

Let me again give a personal instance. The Job Network was established in May 1998 to replace the 50-year-old government provider, the Commonwealth Employment Service (CES). I had responsibility for the network while I was secretary of the Department of Employment, Workplace Relations and Small Business from 1998 to 2002. Indeed, in 1999, I was the decision maker on a tender for the reallocation of business, which, controversially, saw the dominant public provider (Employment National) lose most of its work. It had found itself unable to compete effectively on performance with private and community-based organisations. Today, the network has more than 100 competing providers, predominantly from the private and not-for-profit sector, operating from 1100 locations around Australia. It delivers job placement, job-search training and customised assistance to job-seekers, worth about $1.2 billion annually.

Outsourcing began as a competitive form of procurement. It used the market to secure the best value for money in achieving required government outcomes. It required Public Service contract management to meet required standards and to assess performance. The rationale of third-party delivery is, however, now changing. Increasingly, it has become clear to me that the Job Network's success depends on continuing collaboration between the APS and delivery agents. It calls for relationship management in order to facilitate innovation and continuing improvement in the long term.

A contractual relationship, based initially on compliance, has the potential to be transformed by collaboration. Third-party delivery has the capacity to evolve into a partnership in which public and private goals and values become ever more similar.

Stakeholders are also increasingly important. Again, let me inform my remarks by personal experience. In 2002, when I was secretary of the Department of Education, Science and Training, I launched an 'Open for Business' initiative, which was designed to make the department more externally focused. It sought to recognise formally as stakeholders those organisations and individuals who shared the department's interest in university, vocational and school education, skills training and science policy.

A 'Stakeholder Charter' was drafted and used as the basis for informing expectations and assessing the extent to which they were met. It has proved an important vehicle for building and maintaining levels of trust across the 'network' of those who engage with government. The third *Stakeholder Perception Survey* was conducted in June 2007. It indicated that perceptions about the quality of the relationship between public servant and external advocate had progressively improved. Indeed, overall satisfaction levels have risen since my time and are now at more than 85 per cent. The goals of accessibility, engagement and inclusiveness have largely been met.

Challenges remain. The department receives considerable positive feedback on the opportunities it now provides for networking, general discussion and helping stakeholders to understand government policies and programs. Perceptions, unfortunately, are less satisfactory in terms of the department consulting stakeholders early in the process of policy development and facilitating their influence on policy. Here, too, is a relationship, originally premised on notions of consultation and communication, that has the potential to be transformed through collaboration into participatory governance.

Other structures of governance are already evolving into partnerships. I take as my personal example the Area Consultative Committees (ACCs), which were established in 1994 to generate support for the government's labour-market programs. Today, there are 54 ACCs. They take particular responsibility for promoting and facilitating projects under the Regional Partnerships Program. With time, the ACCs have also played a growing role in promoting government programs and helping small business to respond to them. To this end they have hosted Indigenous employment policy officers (to promote training and job opportunities for Aboriginal and Torres Strait Islanders), goods and services tax (GST) support officers (to advise and assist small business on changed tax arrangements), sugar resource officers (to facilitate the restructuring of the Queensland sugar industry) and AusIndustry/Austrade outpost officers.

The ACCs remain volunteer-based organisations whose administration is funded by government and supported by the Public Service. They have provided a vital conduit between regional areas and the Australian Government. They have proved an effective means by which to link government to business and the community at the local level, to facilitate public–private dialogue, to promote access to government programs, to advise on government projects and to build stakeholder networks. Here, again, is the potential for greater collaboration.

There is also greater interest from governments, through their public services, in engaging directly with communities. Perhaps the best instance of this approach—of which I have personal experience—relates to the delivery of policy to Indigenous communities, particularly in remote Australia. The Office of Indigenous Policy Coordination initiated Shared Responsibility Agreements (SRAs) in 2004 with my active encouragement. They have expanded during the period I chaired the Secretaries' Group on Indigenous Affairs. SRAs are based on the negotiation of joint responsibilities between the government and the community. Today, there are 240 SRAs with Indigenous communities around

Australia. Initially, they focused on the funding of discretionary projects, but they have become progressively more complex.

The goal is not just to provide a vehicle for delivering publicly funded initiatives tailored to local need, or even to establish a mechanism for channelling whole-of-government effort: beyond that, SRAs serve to articulate in concrete terms the government ethos of mutual obligation. Success clearly requires a commitment to consultation and negotiation. Even more effective would be government–community collaboration.

This variety of new network arrangements—many still in the early stages of development—suggests an evolutionary process is under way. Government, it would appear, is being transformed into an 'enabling state'. Sources of authority and influence are becoming more diffused. A 'shared-power world' beckons. Some argue that the State is becoming weaker and 'hollowed out'. Sovereign decision making, it is argued, is increasingly constrained by the growing importance of international regulatory and legislative frameworks and by the impacts of globalisation. Both serve to weaken national autonomy.

At the same time, it is suggested, government is reducing the scope of its public interventions, leaving more to the market. The commercialisation of government enterprise continues apace. Accompanying this, the Public Service is becoming enmeshed in a series of horizontal networks that limit (or crowd out) its influence. It is left with only 'rubber levers' to achieve government objectives. Its influence is concomitantly weakened.

I am not persuaded by this interpretation. While the State certainly appears to be changing its mode of operation, I see no indication of a diminution in the government's desire to shape society. Rather, government appears to be embracing new interventions. It now seeks to extend its influence to private behaviour (for example, smoking, the use of alcohol, sexual conduct, obesity and respect for the rights of others).

Whether or not the State is weakening, the structures of governance are widening, influenced by a complex interrelationship of organisations. A 'differentiated polity' is emerging, distinguished by governance characteristics and institutional features. Table 2.1 summarises the key elements.

Table 2.1 The differentiated polity

Governance characteristics	Institutional features
Functional devolution	Privatisation of government enterprise
Agency specialisation	Market competition
Policy fragmentation	'New public management'
Delivery outsourcing	Alternative delivery systems
Greater use of	
• markets	Special-purpose state agencies
• networks	Involvement of non-state actors
More interdependence	Professionalisation of advocacy

What we are witnessing appears to be the emergence of a 'centreless society' in which public policy is made and delivered by an interdependent mix of government, markets and networks. Institutional networks in which sources of influence are fragmented are replacing the traditional hierarchical procedures, formal organisation and rules, procedures and conventions. The exercise of power is becoming more diffuse and opaque.

More players get to play a part, including advocacy groups and lobbyists. For this reason, I sometimes argue that this represents the democratisation of governance. More organisations are engaged with the political process, even as the number and influence of individual members of political parties wane. It is a new process of governing, involving non-state actors, in which the boundaries between the public, private and voluntary sectors are becoming more opaque.

This is exciting. It opens new prospects. I do not, however, want to exaggerate the speed or substance of change. The Public Service remains the key to coordination. It retains positional authority. In exercising government will, the bureaucracy still dominates.

A public service remains at the political heart of governance networks. It retains extensive powers. There are many reasons for this: its resource capability; its collective experience and knowledge; its legislative and regulatory authority; the financial control it wields through grants, loans and contracts; its access to influence; and its exercise of covert power (by which I mean nothing more sinister than the provision of advice on the basis of confidentiality).

The processes of public-sector collaborations often continue to reflect implicit hierarchical relationships between the actors. The government (or its public service) often externally imposes the structure of public-sector collaborations. It decides on representation. Bureaucracy can exert covert power through access to information and its capacity to marshall resources. It benefits from direct access to government ministers.

Structures tend to maintain public service dominance. The real work of collaboration is generally done in committee or through a secretariat, usually provided by the bureaucratic 'host'. Decision making continues to reside with the government, not with networks (although it is now subject to more contest, wider scrutiny and greater 'outside' influence). While the deliberative processes of networks result in agreements, conclusions or recommendations, most decisions are still taken outside the collaborative group. In short, neither the Public Service nor the government operates within the network of governance as 'just another organisation'.

The Public Service also retains a distinctive role. That is appropriate. It has to discern and understand the nature of particular interests and advise the government of its own assessment of the national interest (while accepting that it is the responsibility of the government to decide that interest). The environment in which it wields its influence is, however, changing. The Public Service is playing out a traditional role in contemporary circumstances. Increasingly—outside or within government—its power is that of persuasion.

Certainly, the coordinating mechanisms are changing—so are the modes of achieving outcomes. At the risk of gross simplification, I discern a move from command, through coordination and cooperation to collaboration (Table 2.2).

Table 2.2 The transformation of process

Command	The process of centralised control—with clear lines of hierarchical authority
Coordination	The process of collective decision making—imposed on participating institutions
Cooperation	The process of sharing ideas and resources —for mutual benefit
Collaboration	The process of shared creation—brokered between autonomous institutions

Increasingly, governance outcomes (the development and delivery of public policy) require the collaboration of a diversity of interested parties. They possess varying degrees of influence, autonomy and capability and often exhibit competing interests, expectations and values.

At its best, collaboration adds public value to the process of governance. It allows participants to learn alternative modes of behaviour and new ways of doing things. It provides mutual benefit to participants, stimulates the development of a mutual inter-agency or inter-organisational culture and helps create and manage knowledge.

Genuine collaboration in governance involves recognition of interdependence within the network of institutional structures. It depends on accepting mutuality of interest. It should not naively assume consensus. The parties will often come to the table with competing interests. Their different perspectives will be resolved—indeed, they will be properly understood—only by interaction and negotiation. The entire process of seeking solutions needs to be iterative: not just reaching agreement on answers, but jointly framing the questions and identifying the problems.

Through a process of integration, collaboration can bring a network of interested parties to mutually beneficial outcomes, sometimes in unexpected ways. I have been fortunate enough on occasion to be present at meetings during which collective deliberation has added creative value. It has fired imagination beyond the capacity of any single participant. When collaboration works, the whole can be greater than the sum of its parts. The process of governance is improved. The key to success is to appreciate these characteristics and seize the opportunities they provide. To build collaboration requires the Public Service to recognise the innate differences in power and to consciously modify its approach to mitigate these imbalances.

The success or failure of collaboration lies not in the emerging network structures of governance or even in the evolving systems by which influence is wielded. It requires new forms of leadership behaviour, particularly on the part of the public servants who remain central to most discussions of public policy and administration. Instead of agendas being imposed, they need to be negotiated. Collaboration demands public servants who can stand in the shoes of those with whom they deal, who can understand their particular perspectives and interests and, by doing so, can build trust. Collaboration can also be enhanced by a clear indication that public servants will champion the collective decisions of the group—using their disproportionate power on behalf of the collaborative venture.

Genuine collaboration will not come about simply as a result of evolving networks of democratic governance or the changing role of the nation-state. It requires public servants who, with eyes wide open, can exert the qualities of leadership necessary to forsake the simplicity of control for the complexity of influence. More explicitly, they need to operate outside the traditionally narrow framework of government, which they have for so long worked within.

Public Service leadership has always been premised on the ability to influence. The challenge now is to extend that capacity from government structures to governance networks. While it will not be an easy path to travel, the prospect is alluring.

References

Agranoff, R. 2006, 'Inside collaborative networks: ten lessons for public managers', *Public Administration Review*, December.

Entwistle, T. and Martin, S. 2005, 'From competition to collaboration in public service delivery: a new agenda for research', *Public Administration*, vol. 83, no. 1.

Huxham, C. and Vangen, S. 2000, 'Leadership in the shaping and implementation of collaboration agendas: how things happen in a (not quite) joined-up world', *Academy of Management Journal*, vol. 3, no. 6, December.

Kirkpatrick, L. 1999, 'The worst of both worlds? Public services without markets or bureaucracy', *Public Money and Management*, vol. 19, no. 4.

Mandell, M. P. 1999, 'Community collaborations: working through network structures', *Policy Studies Review*, vol. 16, no. 1.

Rhodes, R. A. W. 1997, 'From marketisation to diplomacy: it's the mix that matters', *Australian Journal of Public Administration*, vol. 56, no. 2.

Sullivan, H. and Skelcher, C. 2003, *Working Across Organisational Boundaries: Collaboration in public services*, Basingstoke.

Thomson, A. M. and Parry, J. L. 2006, 'Collaboration processes: inside the black box', *Public Administration Review*, December.

3. The changing nature of government: network governance

William D. Eggers

Governing by network is at the heart of numerous major Australian Federal Government initiatives.

In the twentieth century, hierarchical government bureaucracy was the predominant organisational model used to deliver public services and fulfil public-policy goals. Public managers won acclaim by ordering those under them to accomplish highly routine—albeit professional—tasks with uniformity but without discretion. Today, increasingly complex societies force public officials to develop new governance models.

In many ways, twenty-first-century challenges and the methods of addressing them are more numerous and complex than ever. Problems have become both more global and more local as power disperses and boundaries (when they exist at all) become more fluid. One-size-fits-all solutions have given way to customised approaches as the complicated problems of diverse and mobile populations increasingly defy simplistic solutions.

The traditional, hierarchical government model simply does not meet the demands of this complex, rapidly changing age. Rigid bureaucratic systems with command-and-control procedures, narrow work restrictions and inward-looking cultures and operational models are particularly ill suited to addressing problems that often transcend organisational boundaries.

The hierarchical model of government is in decline, pushed by governments' appetites to solve ever more complicated problems and pulled by new tools that allow innovators to fashion creative responses. This push and pull is gradually producing a new government model, in which executives' core responsibilities no longer centre on managing people and programs but on organising resources—often belonging to others—to produce public value. We call this trend 'governing by network'.

Complex public–private, network-to-network collaboration models now operate, with varying degrees of success, in nearly every area of Australian government. As outsourcing, partnerships and network models multiply, scores of Australian public agencies have become de facto contract-management agencies.

In the private sector, customer-oriented corporations and corporations that are directly in contact with the public have changed their product and service-delivery systems in recent times. In the public sector, we are now finding that service delivery by government is also adapting to a new context by relying on various partnerships with others. In such circumstances, networking becomes a critical skill for public-sector managers.

Whether the challenge is responding to natural disasters such as the South-East Asian tsunami or protecting Australia's citizens and critical infrastructure from terrorism, there is a growing recognition that the traditional, hierarchical model of government is inadequate

Governing by network: a new model of achieving results

The fundamental issue facing many Australian government executives today, across the various levels of government, is how to conceptualise, configure and manage a network of public, private and non-profit providers in a way that generates increased value for citizens.

In the past year, I have spent time with dozens of senior Australian government officials and leaders from the private sector and Australia's fledgling non-profit community, talking about the future of government. We have met with chief executives from many of the largest federal agencies in Canberra, senior public servants in Victoria, New South Wales and Queensland, and numerous local government officials. The purpose of these meetings has been to discuss the ways in which modern governments are changing to meet today's challenges.

Governing by network cannot succeed without robust knowledge sharing. Cross-sectoral knowledge sharing can help develop new knowledge, flesh out solutions to daily problems, enhance learning across the network and build trust and aid in learning from one another's successes—and mistakes. These capabilities, in turn, can help government better integrate and align its own strategic objectives with those of its partners.

A fundamentally different approach

These discussions have convinced us that hierarchical government bureaucracy—the principal organisational model used for more than a century to deliver public services in Australia and most of the developed world—is beginning to give way to a fundamentally different approach.

Governing by network is at the heart of numerous major Australian Federal Government initiatives. The Department of Employment and Workplace Relations' welfare-to-work program relies mostly on a network of hundreds of private and non-profit organisations to move individuals from dependency to independence. Different commercial and contractual arrangements and relationships exist across the different sub-national jurisdictions and regional markets.

Meanwhile, the Australian Business Entry Point, a government business portal, partners with more than 160 individual businesses and associations to syndicate government information and transactions relevant to business. Partners such as Westpac, CPA Australia (the sixth-largest accounting body in the world) and NineMSN (Australia's top web site) are just a few of the active companies that use the Business Entry Point's reverse portal service to offer value-added resources to their customers.

At the state level, Gary Tweedlie, the chief executive of Victoria's WorkCover Authority—the state accident fund that insures about three million workers and oversees workplace safety—has used a networked model to dramatically improve the agency's performance. Performance-based contracts with four major insurers and two third-party claims administrators have helped to reduce the agency's liabilities by more than $1.5 billion. On the safety side, workplace injuries have been cut through a bevy of partnerships with trade unions, businesses and professional associations.

Challenges posed for governments by working through networks

The movement from command government to networked governance is not just a recent phenomenon in Australia. It is a global development driven by various business and societal forces. It was led by the public's growing demand for personalised and integrated services, the plummeting costs of engagement and collaboration (thanks to the Internet and other new technologies), the enhanced level of outsourcing and the growing number of complex problems that demanded cross-governmental and cross-sectoral responses. Network governance has also enabled governments to extend their influence and responsibilities into areas of community need and value. These expectations and societal forces have in turn confronted governments with other difficult choices.

As local, state and federal governments and agencies in Australia continue the journey to more networked governance, it is important to recognise that while government by network offers vast benefits (including greater reach and specialisation), it also poses serious challenges and policy dilemmas. It is not always a 'win-win' or 'costless' transition.

One such dilemma surfaced prominently during the planning debates for Sydney's Cross-City Tunnel and its associated toll roads. The issue revolves around how governments should protect public values. Should public side roads or exit roads be closed, diverted or narrowed to force local traffic onto a toll road? Should governments use their authoritative powers to attempt to make public–private partnership (PPP) schemes profitable for the partners—and guarantee the planned volumes of users? Or, in another PPP example that we know of, what if the private partner in a major urban redevelopment project with by far the best financial offer nevertheless refuses to increase its share of minority and women subcontractors? Should the government accept this or intervene? Should contracts be let to such providers in the future? Network governance places traditional and new forms of accountabilities on elected governments.

Safeguarding the public interest

Sometimes the public purpose or public value line blurs or becomes distorted. This is one reason why public officials must be careful to protect important values at every stage of the process. In many collaborations that involve a great deal of necessary messiness, it means asking questions such as: what are the core values that governments must protect; how can public officials maintain the integrity of these values; what is the best and most appropriate role for the government in the delivery of desired services; and how will accountabilities and potential risks be managed? Answering these questions requires working through issues such as access to services, citizen costs, fairness and equity, financial accountability, sustainability and stability and quality of service.

Networking also involves human-resource challenges for traditional governments

Another daunting challenge for networked governance is dealing with the people issue. Managing in a networked environment requires a whole set of competencies and capabilities separate to and beyond those expected of hierarchical government. In addition to knowing about planning, budgeting, staffing and other traditional government duties, networked management requires becoming proficient in tasks such as collaboration, engagement skills, negotiating deals as well as working with and managing third-party service providers. These skills are not currently uppermost in government—and many of these skills defy or confound the traditional emphasis on due process and conventional control orientations. Such skills will also tend not to flourish in agencies in which a self-protective mentality reigns or in which a culture of turf ownership is prevalent. Networking means letting go to some extent in order to achieve better outcomes for citizens.

Today, government agencies need senior public officials who can see through restrictive government walls and defensive practices into the potentiality of relationships that might produce value. They need to develop agile managers with sophisticated skills in team building, project management and risk analysis.

They need frontline and middle-management employees who can collaborate with outside partners and quickly adapt to rapidly changing environments. They need staff prepared to take risks and to explore opportunities. Unfortunately, according to the Australian Public Service Commission, these kinds of skills are also the ones of which there is the most profound shortage in Australian government. They are also the skills governments typically find hardest to encourage.

Employees today need much more mobility and opportunity to move from project to project without sacrificing career advancement. Highly restrictive human-resource and public-sector regulations need updating to enable employees to bring broad skills to their assigned projects, unrestricted by the narrow 'bands' or grades in which they are employed.

Lynelle Briggs, Australia's Public Service Commissioner, recently argued that government leaders must look for people with broader skill sets and more flexible deployment patterns. She argued that 'the future will be one of greater diversity in careers...more movement in and out, with more part-time and different working patterns'. The question is: is the sector prepared for this change and can it anticipate and deal with the consequences?

A final summary

Sometimes networked governance fails not because of how a particular venture is managed, but because of what was delegated to the private sector in the first place. All too often, precious little thought is given to what policy goals an agency is trying to accomplish and how they relate to what is contracted out. Instead, agency officials pick up their organisational chart, look for something they are not doing very well and then get the private sector to do it for them.

Before federal executives think about how they should do something, they need to figure out what they are trying to do in the first place. The government executive, hamstrung by precedent and reinforced by well-intentioned bureaucratic practices, often will find it difficult to step into the larger, more important and more exciting role of conceptualising new models and solutions.

I have argued that thriving in the networked age requires governments to change the way they think and operate. Governments in the future will not simply be bureaucratic providers of a narrow range of public goods. They will no longer merely occupy the space traditionally promulgated and occupied by governments to act as monopolist service owner and direct service provider. Instead, governments will act as aggregators of networks, managers or partnered arrangements and buyers of diverse services and new forms of value. In this transformation, they will need to refashion their systems, practices, structures and skill sets in a way that reflects the government's new roles in service delivery and working through network governance models.

It is important to understand that today's complex problems often require carefully integrated solutions. In certain instances, governments can act as their own 'general contractor', but that role requires the federal executive to think creatively across product lines and agencies, build an intergovernmental network before the procurement process starts and find internal management talent that can creatively configure the best possible solution. When the capacity to do this is absent, executives must recognise that the ability of the private sector to properly integrate the parties into a solution might, in fact, be the most important asset to be procured.

The day-to-day business of working in networks is infinitely more complex and more difficult than managing a traditional bureaucracy. It requires a whole different set of skills. In addition to knowing about planning, budgeting, staffing and other traditional government duties, networked management requires proficiency in a host of new tasks, such as business process re-engineering, negotiation, mediation and network design.

Unfortunately, such skills aren't exactly plentiful in the public sector, nor are they typically recognised or rewarded. The way to get ahead in government has been to be an adviser on policy issues or demonstrate a solid ability to manage government employees, not to show proficiency in negotiating deals and managing third-party service providers. As a result, some agencies don't even have effective contract-management capabilities, much less the capacity to handle the vastly more sophisticated requirements of network management.

Building such capacity requires not only far-reaching training and recruitment strategies, it requires a full-blown cultural transformation. What is required is nothing less than changing the definition of what it means to be a public employee.

Contracting and relationship skills can no longer be the province only of acquisition employees. People with these skills—skills that currently are not highly valued in government—need to be recruited, rewarded and promoted.

The reflexive opposition on the political left to all things outsourced, and the failure of those on the right to acknowledge that far too many contracting endeavours fail to measure up to expectations, are symptomatic of a stale debate that is still stuck in a 1980s ideological box. To succeed in an age of networked government, we need not only to update our approach to government, we need to update our thinking.

References

Eggers, William D. and Goldsmith, Stephen 2003, 'Networked government', *Government Executive*, June.

Eggers, William D. and Goldsmith, Stephen 2004a, 'Governing by network: CIOs and the new public sector', *Public CIO Magazine*, 10 November 2004, <http://www.govtech.com/pcio/92107?id=&story_pg=1>

Eggers, William D. and Goldsmith, Stephen 2004b, *Governing by Network: The new shape of the public sector*, Brookings Institution Press, Washington, DC.

4. Doing Things Collaboratively: Realizing the Advantage or Succumbing to Inertia?[1] [2]

Chris Huxham and Siv Vangen

> The project has worked out, but oh boy, it has caused pain.
>
> – senior health promotion officer, health promotion partnership
>
> Decisions are made by the Alliance Executive, but they keep procrastinating over big decisions ... you can't afford to procrastinate over spending a million pounds.
>
> – information manager, retail property development alliance
>
> Multi-agency work is very slow ... trying to get people moving collectively rather than alone is difficult.
>
> – project officer, young offender community organization
>
> I am under partnership attack from my colleagues.
>
> – operations manager, engineering supply chain
>
> The long catalogue of failed JVs—lcatel/Sharp, Sony/Qualcomm, Lucent/Philips—demonstrates the enormous difficulties in pulling companies like these together.
>
> – a Gartner analyst quoted in the *Financial Times*, 10 December 2002, p. 8

Not everyone who works daily in collaborative alliances, partnerships or networks reports such negative experiences as those quoted above. Indeed the *Financial Times* (24 June 2003, p. 14) reports a Nokia executive as saying that their linkages are paying off. Others talk similarly enthusiastically about their partnership experiences:

> When it works well you feel inspired ... you can feel the collaborative energy.

However, very many do express frustration. There has been much rhetoric about the value of strategic alliances, industry networks, public service delivery partnerships and many other collaborative forms, but reports of unmitigated success are not common. In this article we explore the nature of *the practice of collaboration*, focusing in particular on some of the reasons why collaborative initiatives tend to challenge those involved. Two concepts are central to this exploration. The first is *collaborative advantage*. This captures the synergy argument: to gain real *advantage* from collaboration, something has to be achieved that could not have been achieved by any one of the organizations acting alone. This concept provides a useful 'guiding light' for the purpose of collaboration. The second concept, *collaborative inertia*, captures what happens very frequently in practice: the output from a collaborative arrangement is negligible, the rate of output is extremely slow, or stories of pain and hard grind are integral to successes achieved.

Clearly there is a dilemma between advantage and inertia. The key question seems to be:

> If achievement of collaborative advantage is the goal for those who initiate collaborative arrangements, why is collaborative inertia so often the outcome?

To address this question, and the question of what managers can do about it, we will present a set of seven overlapping perspectives on collaborative management. This is extracted from the theory of collaborative advantage, which has derived from extensive action research over 15 years. We have worked with practitioners of collaboration, in the capacity of facilitators, consultants and trainers, in a wide variety of collaborative situations. We have kept detailed records about the challenges and dilemmas faced by managers, and of comments they make in the course of enacting their collaborative endeavours. Many such statements are reproduced as illustrative examples in this article.

PERSPECTIVE 1: WE MUST HAVE COMMON AIMS BUT WE CANNOT AGREE ON THEM

Agreement on aims is an appropriate starting point because it is raised consistently as an issue. *Common wisdom* suggests that it is necessary to be clear about the aims of joint working if partners are to work together to operationalise policies.

Typically individuals argue for common (or at least compatible), agreed, or clear sets of aims as a starting point in collaboration. *Common practice*, however, appears to be that the variety of organisational and individual agendas that are present in collaborative situations makes reaching agreement difficult. For example, a board member of an alliance of 120 charities commented on the difficulty of reconciling members' interests. Invariably someone would call to say, 'We don't want you to do that.'

The reasons behind the struggles for agreement may not be obvious. Organisations come together bringing different resources and expertise to the table, which in turn creates the potential for collaborative advantage. Yet organisations also have different reasons for being involved, and their representatives seek to achieve different outputs from their involvement. Sometimes these different organisational aims lead to conflicts of interest. Furthermore, for some organisations the joint purpose for the collaboration is perceived as central to achieving organisational purposes, whereas others are less interested and perhaps only involved (reluctantly) as a result of external pressure. Tensions often arise, therefore, because some organisations are very interested in influencing and controlling the joint agenda, and some are reluctant to commit resources to it, and so on. Similarly, individuals too will join the collaboration with different expectations, aspirations and understandings of what is to be achieved jointly. It follows that whilst at first glance it may appear that partners only need be concerned with the joint aims for the collaboration, in reality organisational and individual aims can prevent agreement because they cause confusion, misunderstanding and conflicts of interest. In addition, while some of these various aims may be explicit, many will be taken for granted (assumed) by one partner but not necessarily recognized by another, and many will be deliberately hidden:

My company is really most interested in having access to, and experience of, the Chinese business environment and cares little for the formally declared purpose of the alliance.

On reflection then it is not so surprising that reaching agreement can be very difficult.

Figure 1 – A framework for understanding aims in collaboration

(one participant's perspective)	Explicit	Assumed	Hidden
Collaboration Aims	The purpose of the collaboration		By definition, these are perceptions of joint aims and so cannot be hidden
Organisation Aims	What each organisation hopes to gain for itself via the collaboration		
Individual Aims	What each individual hopes to gain for him/herself via the collaboration		

Managing Aims in Practice

Fig. 1 is a simplified version of a framework of aims in collaborative situations. Its purpose is to facilitate a better understanding of the motivations of those involved, and the ways in which multiple and (sometimes even) conflicting aims can prevent agreement and block progress. In turn, this sort of understanding can help in finding ways of addressing the concerns of all involved.

The framework distinguishes between the various types of aims mentioned above and emphasizes that some aims will be assumed rather than explicitly acknowledged, and many will be deliberately hidden. This framework can be used as an effective tool for gaining insight about the motivations of members of a collaboration—even of one's own! Obviously it is not possible to know others' hidden agendas, but it is possible to speculate on the possibility that they might have some—and even have a guess at what they might be. Trying to 'fill in' each of the cells of the framework for each other partner can be enlightening, whether it is done quickly, 'back of an envelope' style, or as a major investigative exercise. Gaining this kind of insight into partners' expectations and aspirations can be very helpful in understanding and judging how best to work with them.

At the general level, the obvious conclusion to be drawn from the framework is that it is rarely going to be easy in practice to satisfy fully the common wisdom. Therein lies the dilemma—clarity of purpose provides much needed direction, yet open discussion can unearth irreconcilable differences! Difficulties that arise out of the need to communicate across different professional and natural languages and different organisational and professional cultures are unlikely to assist the negotiation process. Likewise, concerns about accountability of participants to their own organisations or to other constituents are unlikely to make it easy for individuals to make compromises. Often, the only practical way forward is to get started on some action without fully agreeing the aims. In the words of the manager of an urban regeneration partnership engaged in writing a bid for funding, the task for managers can be to:

> find a way of stating the aims so that none of the parties can disagree.

PERSPECTIVE 2: SHARING POWER IS IMPORTANT, BUT PEOPLE BEHAVE AS IF IT'S ALL IN THE PURSE STRINGS

As with the previous perspective, the 'pain' associated with issues of power is often raised by practitioners of collaboration. *Common wisdom* is that 'the power is in the purse strings,' which suggests that those who do not have control of the financial resource are automatically deprived of power. Viewed dispassionately, these perceptions quite often seem at odds with 'reality' since most parties do, minimally, have at least the 'power of exit.' A manager in an automotive industry joint venture commented:

> The balance of power was seemingly with the U.K. company, who had a majority shareholding, but in reality it was with U.S. company, who knew how closely the investment analysts were watching the joint venture. The threat of pulling out was always in the background.

However, the *common practice*, unsurprisingly, is that people act as though their perceptions are real and often display defensiveness and aggression.

Looking more closely at where power is actually used to influence the way in which collaborative activities are negotiated and carried out, it is possible to identify different *points of power*. Many of these occur at a micro level in the collaboration, and would often not be particularly obvious to those involved. One example of a point of power is the naming of the collaboration, since this is likely to influence what it does. Those who are involved in the naming process are therefore in a powerful position at that time. Other examples concern invitations to join a collaboration; those who choose who to involve are obviously powerful, but those who choose the process of whom to involve are even more so.

Many points of power relate to communication media and processes. One set of examples concerns the arrangements for meetings. Clearly, any person taking the role of chair or facilitator in a meeting is in a position of power whilst the meeting is in place, but those who get to choose which facilitator to appoint are more subtly and perhaps more significantly powerful. Those who choose the location of a meeting may be in a powerful position, particularly in terms of determining whether it will be on the premises of one of the participants. Those who choose the timing of the meeting are also powerful. It is possible to identify many more points of power that typically are present during collaborative activities.

An important characteristic of points of power is that they are not static. In collaborative situations, power continually shifts. At the macro level, for example, in a pre-startup phase those who get to draw up contracts, write bids for funding or who have direct access to a customer may be powerful. In a start-up phase however, once money is available, those who are given the task of administering the collaboration may be highly powerful in determining many parameters concerned with direction and ways of working. It may only be at later stages that the actual members become active and have the chance to exert power.

Less obvious, but very significant, are the continuous shifts of power at a micro level during all phases. For example, network managers are often in powerful positions between meetings because they are the only people formally employed by the network— and hence the only people who have its agenda as their main concern. They may also have access to the network funds. During meetings, however, members can shift many of the points of power in significant ways, often determining new members, times and locations of meetings as well as influencing agreements about action. Those less centrally involved, such as facilitators or consultants, can be in powerful positions for short periods of time. External influences, such as those from government, can sometimes be extremely powerful in a short-term way as they make demands for reports or responses to initiatives.

Managing Power in Practice

Issues concerned with control of purse strings are significant, but there are many other points at which power is, in practice, enacted in collaborative settings. All participants have power at one time or another and may frequently have the option to empower themselves. Understanding and exploring the points of power can enable assessment of where and when others are unwittingly or consciously exerting power, and where and when others may view them as exerting power. It also allows for consideration of how and when deliberately to exert power. Responding to these insights, however, requires a willingness to accept that manipulative behaviour is appropriate, which some would argue is against the spirit of collaborative working. We will return to this point later.

Figure 2 – The trust-building loop

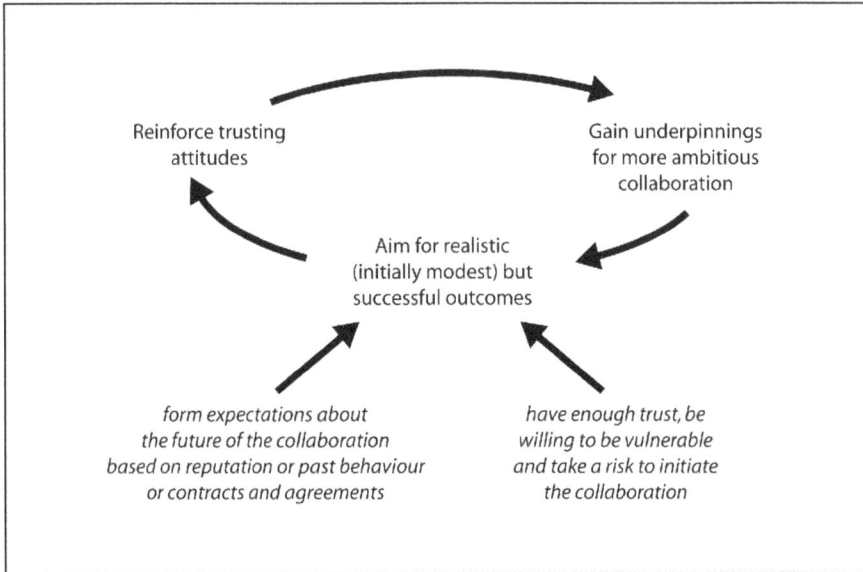

Reinforce trusting attitudes

Gain underpinnings for more ambitious collaboration

Aim for realistic (initially modest) but successful outcomes

form expectations about the future of the collaboration based on reputation or past behaviour or contracts and agreements

have enough trust, be willing to be vulnerable and take a risk to initiate the collaboration

PERSPECTIVE 3: TRUST IS NECESSARY FOR SUCCESSFUL COLLABORATION, BUT WE ARE SUSPICIOUS OF EACH OTHER

Issues relating to trust are also commonly raised by participants. The *common wisdom* seems to be that trust is a precondition for successful collaboration. However, while the existence of trusting relationships between partners probably would be an ideal situation, the *common practice* appears to be that suspicion, rather than trust, is the starting point. Often participants do not have the luxury to choose their partners. Either imposed (e.g. government) policy dictates who the partners must be or, as expressed by the business development manager of the Far East operation of a major oil producer below, the pragmatics of the situation dictate that partners are needed where trust is weak:

> You may have to jump into bed with someone you don't like in order to prevent a competitor coming into the market.

This suggests that it is appropriate to pay attention to trust *building* between partners.

One way of thinking about trust building is through the loop depicted in Fig. 2. This argues that two factors are important in getting started in a trusting relationship. The first is concerned with the formation of expectations about the future of the collaboration; these will be based either on reputation or past behaviour, or on more formal contracts and agreements. Given the earlier remarks about the difficulty of agreeing on aims in collaborative settings, this in itself is a non-trivial starting point. The second starting point involves risk taking. The argument is that partners need to trust each other *enough* to allow them to take a risk to initiate the collaboration. If both of these initiators are possible, then the loop argues that trust can gradually be built through starting with some modest but realistic aims that are likely to be successfully realized. This reinforces trusting attitudes between partners and provides a basis for more ambitious collaboration.

Managing Trust in Practice

The practical conclusion from the trust-building loop is very similar to that concerning the management of aims: sometimes it is better to get started on some small but tangible action and then to allow trust to develop slowly. This incremental approach to trust building would obviously not be relevant if an immediate need to attain a major objective is paramount. In those situations, expectation forming and risk taking would have to be managed simultaneously and alongside other trust-building activities. However, in other situations building trust incrementally is, in principle, appealing. We shall return to it later.

PERSPECTIVE 4: WE ARE PARTNERSHIP-FATIGUED AND TIRED OF BEING PULLED IN ALL DIRECTIONS

In this perspective it is not so much the common wisdom but the *taken for granted assumptions* that are to be challenged. One of the most surprising observations about collaborative situations is the frequency with which clarity about who the collaborators are is lacking. Different members often list different partners from each other, and staff who are very centrally involved in managing collaborations often cannot name partners without referring to formal documentation. Reasons for this include the different statuses or commitment that people or organisations have with regard to the network:

> They were only involved to provide the financial support ... (rather than as a proper member);

and ambiguity about whether people are involved as individuals or on behalf of their organisations:

Members were invited to join because of their ethnic background, but the organisations they worked in (which were not specifically concerned with ethnicity issues) then became partners.

The lack of clarity about who partners are is often compounded by the complexity of collaborative arrangements in practice. The sheer scale of networking activities is one aspect of this. Many organisations are involved in multiple alliances. One major electronics manufacturer, for example, is said to be involved in around 400 strategic alliances. Clearly, even with the most coherent alliance management practices, no individual manager is likely to know which partner organisations are involved. Clearly also, multiple alliances must pull the organisation in a variety of different directions. As one senior manager in a division of a multinational computer hardware manufacturer put it:

We have separate alliances with two companies (worldwide operating system providers) that are in direct competition with each other ... there is a lot of conflict within the company over these alliances ... the people involved try to raise the importance of theirs.

The same issue arises in the public sector context, with ever increasing numbers of partnerships and inter-agency initiatives appearing in localities. In this case, however, the problem that is most commonly voiced is 'partnership fatigue,' with individuals often regularly attending meetings of five or six collaborative schemes. More extreme cases occur in this sector too. For example, a manager from a community- based careers guidance organisation commented:

When I heard of the person attending meetings of five partnerships, I thought 'Is that all?!' ... My organisation is involved in 56 partnerships.

There are many other consequences of these multiple initiatives apart from fatigue. One is that some participants try to link agendas across the initiatives, but the links they see relate to the particular combinations of initiatives that they are involved in, which generally do not overlap precisely, if at all, with involvements of other members. Another is that it is hard for any individual to judge when another is inputting the views of their employing organisation or bringing an agenda from another partnership.

In addition to the volume of relationships, there is frequently complexity in the networks of relationships between organisations. For example, the complexity of interacting supply chain networks—in which every supplier has multiple customers, every customer has multiple suppliers, and suppliers have suppliers and customers have customers— is potentially infinite. Many networks of collaborations are, in addition, hierarchical in the sense that collaborations are members of other collaborations. For example, a local government organisation may be a member of a regeneration partnership but also a member of several community collaborations which are in turn members of a community 'umbrella group,' which is in turn a member of the regeneration partnership. Similarly, joint ventures may be members of strategic alliances, trade associations may represent their members in policy networks, and so on.

Managing Ambiguity and Complexity in Practice

Clearly, it is hard for managers to agree on aims, build mutual understanding and manage trust and power relationships with partners if they do not unambiguously know who their partners are. Equally, it is difficult to manage collaborative working in complex systems in which different elements must be affecting each other but there is little clarity on the nature of the inter-relationships.

Diagramming techniques can help in mapping the structure of partnerships. Fig. 3 provides two possible ways of doing this. Obviously this cannot remove the ambiguity and uncertainty completely, but it is generally enlightening at the point of construction and useful as a long-term reminder. As with the aims framework, this exercise can be done in more or less detail.

At a general level, learning how to identify, live with and progress despite ambiguity and complexity is probably the key challenge of this perspective. A careful approach to nurturing relationships must be an essential aspect of this.

PERSPECTIVE 5: EVERYTHING KEEPS CHANGING

Collaborative structures are commonly talked about as though stability of membership can be *taken for granted*, at least for a tangible period. The ambiguity and complexity indicated in the previous section would be difficult enough for participants to cope with if that were the case. In practice, however, policy influences, which may be internal but are frequently imposed externally, often generate restructuring of member organisations. Merger and de-merger, new start-ups and closures, acquisitions and sell-offs, and restructurings are all commonplace. In turn, these imply a necessary restructuring of any collaboration in which they participated.

Equally, policy changes in the individual organisations or the collaboration affect the purpose of the collaboration. These may be generated internally—for example, as the result of a revision of strategic direction. Or they may be generated externally—for example, as a result of government policy or major market disturbances. Either way, this in turn implies a shift in the relevance of the collaboration to its members. New members may join and others may leave, and sometimes such changes are imposed:

> The problem isn't that their collaboration is not working, but that because of the new policy we are asking them to work differently, which means breaking up established successful and effective working relationships and building new ones.

Another source of dynamic change comes with individual movements. The manager of a company that was delivering a major service for an alliance partner, for example, commented that the relationship with the partner organisation had been both helped and hindered because:

> ... the chief executive in the partner organisation was, until recently, my boss in my own organisation.

The relationships between individual participants in collaborations are often fundamental to getting things done. This makes collaborations highly sensitive to changes in individuals' employment, even if these are simply role changes within one of the participating organisations. Finally, even if all of the above stood still there is often an inherent dynamic. If an initial collaborative purpose is achieved, there will usually be a need to move to new collaborative agendas, and these are likely to imply different membership requirements.

Figure 3 - Example diagramming methods for mapping the complexity of collaborative structures

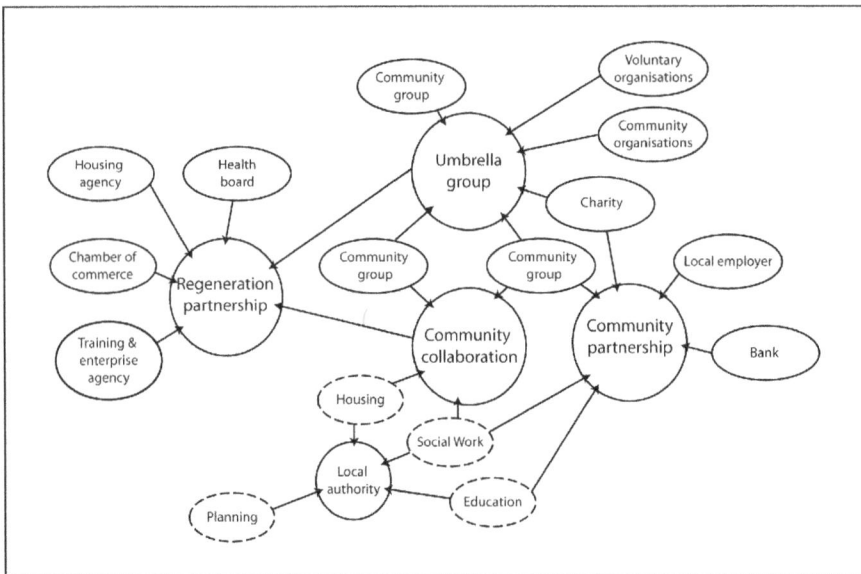

All organisations are dynamic to the extent that they will gradually transform. However, collaborations are sensitive to transformations in *each of* the partner organisations and therefore may change very quickly. In one example, a collaborative group with an ambiguous structure involving many partners went through three identifiable reincarnations over a three-year period and ended up as a very controlled partnership between two organisations. Its final stated purpose was related to, but definitely not the same as, the original one. It would be reasonable to argue that the final partnership was a different one from the original collaborative group, but it is possible to trace a clear lineage from one to the other.

Managing Collaborative Dynamics in Practice

One obvious conclusion that derives from recognition of the dynamic nature of collaborations is that the appealing trust-building loop (Fig. 2) is inherently extremely fragile. Effort put into building mutual understanding and developing trust can be shattered, for example, by a change in the structure of a key organisation or the job change of a key individual. A practical conclusion, therefore, for those who want to make collaboration work is that *the nurturing process must be continuous and permanent*. No sooner will gains be made than a disturbance, in the form of a change to one of the partners, will shatter many of them.

PERSPECTIVE 6: LEADERSHIP IS NOT ALWAYS IN THE HANDS OF MEMBERS

Given the inherent difficulties with collaborative forms that have been discussed so far, the issue of leadership seems highly relevant. Because traditional hierarchies do not exist in collaborative settings, it is appropriate to consider leadership in a general sense, rather than as specifically the realm of senior executives or prominent public figures. Here, we consider leadership as being concerned with *the mechanisms that lead to the actual outcomes of a collaboration*. Put simply, we are concerned with what '*makes things happen*' in a collaboration. More formally, this concern is with the formation and implementation of the collaboration's policy and activity agenda.

Looked at from this perspective, leadership, interestingly, becomes something that is not only enacted by people. Structures and processes are as important in leading agendas as are the participants involved in the collaboration. Thus, for example, a structure in which two organisations only are involved in partnership should allow both organisations good access to the agenda, but clearly excludes others. To take an extreme contrast, a collaboration in which any organisation that wants to be a member may send a representative allows wide access to the agenda in principle, but it can be difficult for any individual to have much influence in practice. Similarly, in the context of collaborative processes, a collaboration for which a major form of communication is through open meetings is going to allow a very different form of access to the agenda from one whose principal mode of communication is through e-mail and/or telephone. Thus, agendas may be led by the type of structure that is in place and the type of processes used. Once again, this challenges a *taken for granted* presumption about the nature of leadership. Agendas can, of course, also be led by participants, though generally these are emergent, informal leaders rather than those who lead from a position of authority.

Structures, processes and participants can be thought of as different *media* through which collaborative leadership is, in practice, enacted. An important point about these media is that all three are largely not controlled by *members* of the collaboration. Structures and processes are sometimes imposed externally, for example, by government, a corporate headquarters or a funding body. Even if this is not the case, they often emerge out of previous action rather than being explicitly designed by members. Even in the context of 'participants' as the leadership medium, leadership is not solely the role of *members* of the collaboration. External stakeholders such as customers or local public figures often strongly direct the territory of a partnership or alliance. A strong lead is often also given by support staff who are not strictly members. For example, the information manager of a retail property development alliance commented about his role in moving the alliance members towards agreement about action:

I find that attrition helps ... I am a stubborn old devil.

Managing Leadership Media

This perspective demonstrates the ease with which collaborations can move out of the control of their membership. Recognizing the at least partial inevitability of this and working around it is part of the practical response required. Diagramming techniques such as those in Fig. 3 may be helpful in exploring the nature of the structure as a first step towards gaining an understanding of its leadership consequences.

For managers who wish to lead more actively, the implication appears to be that part of their activity must be concerned with the design of structures and processes that are effective for the particular purpose, and with monitoring their performance and evolution. We look further at active leadership in the final perspective.

PERSPECTIVE 7: LEADERSHIP ACTIVITIES CONTINUALLY MEET WITH DILEMMAS AND DIFFICULTIES

Despite the strong contextual leadership derived from structures and processes, participants (whether or not they actually are members) do carry out *leadership activities* in order to move a collaboration forward in ways that they regard as beneficial. In carrying out these activities, they do affect the outcomes of collaborative initiatives. However they are frequently thwarted by difficulties, so that the outcomes are not as they intend. For example, despite his war of attrition, the information manager quoted above was continuously thwarted in his attempts to create events in which key members of the partnering organisations would jointly consider their modes of thinking and working. Several dates set aside for group workshops were ultimately used for other kinds of meetings, as issues needing immediate attention emerged.

In practice, much of what is done by those who aim to take a lead in moving a collaboration forward may be said to be fundamentally *within the spirit of collaboration*. Activities of this sort are highly facilitative and are concerned with embracing, empowering, involving and mobilizing members. However, the same people are also engaged in activities that, on the face of it, are much less collaborative. Many of them are adept at manipulating agendas and playing the politics. We have characterized these kinds of activities as being *towards collaborative thuggery* after the member of a city partnership who told us that a partnership that he was involved with had been successful:

> ... because the convenor is a thug ... if people are not pulling their weight
> he pushes them out.

He appeared to be arguing that this was a positive and effective mode of leadership.

Managing Leadership Activities

Does this, then, suggest a dilemma between the ideology of collaborative working and the pragmatism needed to get things done? Not necessarily. One way of thinking about this is to consider the nature of nurturing. Nurturing is often talked about in the context of the gentle care required for fragile plants. However, rather more decisive tactics have to be taken if the object is to nurture an overgrown garden back to health. Chopping down of excess growth and pulling up of weeds are likely to be key activities, in addition to the nurturing back to health of individual plants that have become overpowered by others. Whilst it is not possible to produce hard evidence of this, those who lead more successfully seem to operate from both perspectives—the *spirit of collaboration* and *towards collaborative thuggery*—and to continually switch between them, often carrying out both types of leadership in the same act.

REALIZING COLLABORATIVE ADVANTAGE

Our aim here has been to convey some of the complexity that underlies collaborative situations in a way that should seem real to those involved. Obviously the set of seven perspectives does not, in itself, provide any precise recipes for managerial action. It does, however, provide a dual basis for thoughtful action.

The first basis is through legitimizing the pain and addressing the isolation that people often feel when trapped in collaborative inertia:

> I have been working in a health-education partnership ... for about a
> year, and it is a relief and a reassurance to see that the 'pain and grind'
> of partnership work exists in other partnerships, not just my situation.

Like this person, many managers are empowered simply by understanding that the problems they are experiencing are inevitable. This is partly because this awareness increases self-confidence, and partly because it immediately highlights the need to tackle the problem at a different level. Legitimizing a degree of manipulative and political activity through the notion of *collaborative thuggery* can also be helpful in this respect.

The second, and perhaps more significant, basis for action is through the conceptual handles that the perspectives provide. As presented here in summary, the combined picture gives a sense of the kinds of issues that have to be managed (a more detailed version of each perspective is available). Like the summary, the detailed perspectives do not provide a recipe for good practice, because to do so would be to over-simplify. Rather, they are intended to alert managers to challenges of collaborative situations that will need active attention and nurturing if problems of collaborative inertia are to be minimized. Each perspective provides a particular view on this, and can be used in isolation to stimulate thinking about that in particular. However, the issues raised by each perspective overlap with those raised by others, so the combination of perspectives always needs to be in the background, even if the focus at a particular time is a specific one. Many of the challenges are inherent, and there are often tensions between directly opposed possible ways of tackling them. This approach to practical support regards the action to be taken as a matter for managerial judgement. This includes making informed judgements about the resource that needs to be available to support the nurturing activities.

DON'T WORK COLLABORATIVELY UNLESS YOU HAVE TO

One definite conclusion can, however, be drawn. That is, that making collaboration work effectively is highly resource-consuming and often painful. The strongest piece of advice to managers (and policy makers) that derives from the above perspectives, therefore, is 'don't do it unless you have to.' Put rather more formally, the argument is that unless potential for real collaborative advantage is clear, it is generally best, *if there is a choice*, to avoid collaboration. It is worth noting, however, that collaborative advantage sometimes comes in non-obvious forms and may be concerned with the process of collaborating—for example from the development of a relationship with a partner— rather than the actual output.

SELECTED BIBLIOGRAPHY

This article draws on the *theory of collaborative advantage*, which we have developed gradually from extensive research with practitioners of collaboration over the last 15 years. The notions of Collaborative Advantage and Collaborative Inertia are central to this theory. *Collaborative Advantage* was first used in this way in the early 1990s. See for example, C. Huxham and D. Macdonald, 'Introducing Collaborative Advantage,' *Management Decision*, 1992, 30(3), 50–56. Rosabeth Moss Kanter used the term differently in her 1994 article 'Collaborative Advantage: The Art of Alliances,' *Harvard Business Review*, 72(4), 96–108. *Collaborative inertia* was introduced in C. Huxham, 'Advantage or Inertia: Making Collaboration Work,' in R. Paton, G. Clark, G. Jones, and P. Quintas (Eds.), *The New Management Reader* (London: Routledge, 1996, 238–254). Theory relating to the aims framework of perspective one can be found in C. Eden and C. Huxham, 'The Negotiation of Purpose in Multi-Organisational Collaborative Groups,' *Journal of Management Studies*, 2001, 38(3), 351–369. A detailed discussion on the points of power in perspective two can be found in C. Huxham and N. Beech, 'Points of Power in Interorganisational Forms: Learning from a Learning Network,' *Best 10%, Proceedings of the Academy of Management Conference*, 2002. The development of the trust-building loop and its implication for the management of trust in perspective three is explored in S. Vangen and C. Huxham, 'Nurturing Collaborative Relations: Building Trust in Inter-organisational Collaboration,' *Journal of Applied Behavioral Science*, 2003, 39(1), 5–31. A detailed exposition of perspectives four and five can be found in C. Huxham and S. Vangen, 'Ambiguity, Complexity and Dynamics in the Membership of Collaboration,' *Human Relations*, 2000, 53(6), 771–806. For a detailed discussion on the conceptualization and enactment of leadership in perspectives six and seven see C. Huxham and S. Vangen, 'Leadership in the Shaping and Implementation of Collaboration Agendas: How Things Happen in a (Not Quite) Joined Up World,' *Academy of Management Journal (Special Forum on Managing in the New Millennium)*, 2000, 43(6), 1159–1175; and S. Vangen and C. Huxham, 'Enacting Leadership for Collaborative Advantage: Dilemmas of Ideology and Pragmatism in the Activities of Partnership Managers,' *British Journal of Management*, 2003, 14, 61–74.

Chris Huxham is a Fellow of the (UK) Advanced Institute of Management Research and a professor of management in the University of Strathclyde, Graduate School of Business. (chris@gsb.strath.ac.uk)

Siv Vangen is a senior lecturer in management at The Open University Business School.

They have developed the Theory of Collaborative Advantage through an action research programme spanning 15 years. During this period they have worked with a large number of individuals and organisations involved in partnerships, alliances, networks and joint ventures across all sectors.

ENDNOTES

[1] This paper was originally published in *Organizational Dynamics*, Vol. 33, No. 2, pp. 190–201, 2004. It is reprinted here by permission of the publisher.

[2] *Acknowledgments*: Colin Eden and Nic Beech have been involved in developing specific elements of this theory. Their perspectives and styles of researching have provided invaluable insights. We would also like to thank Murray Stewart and Robin Hambleton for the research collaboration that led to our work on collaborative leadership. Many, many practitioners have been wittingly and unwittingly involved in the development of this theory; they are too numerous to name, but our thanks are due to them all. We would like to acknowledge the support for this research of the U.K. Economic and Social Research Council (ESRC) and Engineering and Physical Sciences Research Council (EPSRC) under ESRC grant numbers 000234450 and L130251031 and the ESRC/EPSRC Advanced Institute of Management Research grant number RES-331-25-0016.

5. Hit or myth? Stories of collaborative success[1]

Chris Huxham and Paul Hibbert

Partnering is notoriously difficult; success rates as low as 20 per cent are often quoted. So, is success achievable or are the benefits to be gained from partnering just a myth?

What does 'success' mean in partnerships, alliances and other collaborative ventures? The answer might not be as straightforward as you expect. We talked to partnership managers and their colleagues about the collaborations that they were pleased with. Naturally, they were concerned to tell us that they had achieved the objectives that they and their partners had jointly agreed to pursue. Their stories also told of other types of achievement; we identified five main categories of these. All seem to be important and need to be recognised as elements of positive collaborative progress.

We also found, however, that success was always qualified. Getting some sort of positive outcome was never completely straightforward. We think it is essential that people have a realistic idea of the costs and compromises necessary when seeking success in partnerships, so these caveats need to be recognised, too. Let us start, however, with the positive and review the five categories of achievement that we found in stories of success.

Five types of collaborative success

1. Achieving outcomes

People often point to particular outcomes for their shareholders, customers, clients or other stakeholders, but these can be outcomes of radically different types.

> 'Everyone was gaining from it all the way along. Pounds, shillings and pence on the bottom line.'
>
> Banking Partnership Manager
>
> 'We have a robust ante-natal screening program and none of the babies (to HIV positive mothers) have proved positive.'
>
> Drug Abuse Project Manager

The important lesson we draw from this is that outcome success in partnership can be characterised in a number of very different ways. This is a particularly important consideration in cross-sectoral partnerships, in which different notions of success might be at odds with each other. For example, what some people might see as a successful social project, others might consider a revenue drain. There is a need to see the situation from all sides, and temper our expectations.

2. Getting the processes to work

People don't just value the 'end result'; they are proud of getting the processes right, too. The 'how' seems to matter at least as much as the 'what'.

> 'A significant success on the organisational side and inter-organisational process side was that 10 pharmaceutical companies, who were natural competitors, learnt to work with each other.'
>
> Health Industry Partnership Manager

We were given many examples of process success, and these could be things that worked at the individual as well as the organisational or inter-organisational levels. Clearly, processes are important to partnerships at all of these levels, and capturing the learning from process successes could be helpful in the future. The first step is to take the time to look for, and recognise, them.

3. Reaching emergent milestones

Good project planning in partnership—setting plans and milestones—is standard practice for many. Emergent milestones are, however, different. These are not events planned from the start, but semi-serendipitous achievements as particular circumstances come together in a helpful way. They are signals that the partnership has really achieved something, however great or small, and they are important indicators of success for many.

> '... they both needed new premises. The cost was monstrous. So they decided.'
>
> Banking Partnership Manager'
>
> 'It was quite a landmark ... getting such a public statement published and properly printed and distributed.'
>
> Public Health Partnership Manager'

These emergent milestones can be the outcomes of large or small initiatives but even relatively small achievements can be important to participants—especially if they mark points at which 'hostilities cease' and the partnership starts to work effectively.

4. Gaining recognition—from others

People seem to value partnership processes that work and outcomes that make a difference to the people they are serving not simply as ends in themselves. Often, they or their organisations receive something that they value just as much: recognition.

> 'We have been able to show a major client that we are able to operate as mature and sensible partners when they might perhaps suspected that wasn't the case.'
>
> Manager in an Oil Industry Joint Venture
>
> 'I don't get treated like shit anymore ...'
>
> Drug Abuse Project Manager'

Personal recognition seems to be the type of recognition that people mention most often, but they do like to see their organisations recognised too. Both of these seem quite legitimate aspirations, so perhaps the lesson is to not lose the people under the umbrella of the partnership.

5. Acknowledging personal pride in championing a partnership

As we have mentioned, people do seek recognition and therefore, perhaps understandably, they are often not shy about highlighting their role in 'making things happen'.

> 'Part of the reason I was successful was that I spent lots time getting to understand other parts of the business.'
>
> Airline – Car-Rental Alliance Manager
>
> 'I willed it to happen and put an awful lot time in ... Health had initially been very suspicious of the partnership.'
>
> Health Industry Partnership Manager

To be motivated, people have to be able to identify with the success that is achieved and see it as their own. Reaching the point at which individuals are willing to acknowledge overtly—and even promote—their own role in a partnership is therefore significant. If people portray themselves as heroes in a collaboration story, it is a sure indicator of some of the other four types of success, as well as being a positive outcome in itself.

It seems, from our research, that you are most likely to hear about collaborative successes from project 'champions'. What is interesting about them is that they do not generally display or behave as some sort of 'transformational leader'. It is difficult to suggest a common set of behaviours for champions, but stubborn determination seems to be important in most cases, often balanced with a concern for relationships.

> 'I was always having an uphill struggle to get people to push the things I wanted to get pushed.'
>
> Airline – Car-Rental Alliance Manager
>
> 'It became apparent within two or three years that we had a family … we worked, played and got drunk together.'
>
> European Regional Partnership Manager

But it's never straightforward...

Stubborn determination seems to be central in achieving some success from partnerships and collaborations—for a very good reason. Even in the stories of success that we heard, there were four kinds of clear indication that it wasn't easy to get to the good stuff. As in most good stories, there are always challenges and setbacks that the heroes must overcome.

1. It's usually an epic tale—definitely not a short story...

For many, partnership seems to be intrinsically more difficult than other organisational situations. Even informal, emergent milestones take time to achieve.

People commonly talk about taking two years or more to get a partnership functioning well. Many people, however, who champion partnerships treat collaboration as their 'day job', so for them this is 'situation normal'.

2. There's always a twist in the tale...

Although a partnership has been successful—or at least functioning—for a prolonged period, that is no guarantee that it will remain so. In most cases, the good times come and go, and what works well at one time might not achieve results at another.

> 'Some times are better than others – for example, we had two attempts at building the joint site.'
>
> Banking Partnership Manager

It would be easy to become complacent in the good times, but that would obviously be unwise.

3. It's rarely a happy ending for all the characters...

Even when a partnership seems to be robustly successful for one partner, it's possible that others might disagree.

> **Three Participants in a Youth Development Partnership**
>
> 'a really good forum for bringing services together … It works – there are clear outcomes.'
>
> Youth Development Worker
>
> 'a forum around a few individuals – don't feel it's working that well … the housing department shift the goalposts to suit themselves.'
>
> Charity Worker
>
> 'at one time we used to be able to be able to refer kids (to the charity) but we can't now because of their lack of resources.'
>
> Housing Manager

It is impossible to judge, in such cases, whether the success is or is not 'real'. While there can be clear substantive outcomes for one partner (and the first speaker in Figure 5.8 describes some), other partners might view the outcomes as sub-optimal, as achievable by other means or of no value to their organisation.

4. The genie is apt to stay in the bottle...

Our fourth and final caveat, which emphasises the risky nature of collaboration, is that luck seems to play a part in most successful partnerships.

> 'My organisation was also involved in a similar – on paper – partnership with a transport company but [it wasn't successful in that case because] the client was less committed to the partnership philosophy than the traditional contracting philosophy.'
>
> Manager in a Utilities Partnership

The stories we were told included many examples in which the speaker's organisation was involved in other partnerships that were not as successful as the one being described. Often a critical part of success seems to involve being in the right place at the right time, or having the right set of characters involved. Being able to tempt the genie out of his—or her—bottle to charm those circumstances into place is a significant part of the art of managing collaboration. We think of this as 'enhancing serendipity'.

Is successful collaboration just a myth?

The answer to this question is no! The collaborations we heard about were definitely hits. They were success stories for at least some—and probably many—of the participants. They were, however, stories told with hindsight and at a moment in a partnership's life when success was tangible. When you are in the thick of normal partnership life the story is likely to involve a lot of suspense and it might not be clear whether the plot involves a happy ending.

In those situations, it can be useful to think about the five types of success. They can be useful landmarks, ways to acknowledge the progress that is being made. Remembering that progress might not be on a single dimension is important, as well as the fact that partners can find different things to celebrate in each dimension. The 'five types' can form a useful basis for discussion between partners about past and future progress. They can also be useful in demonstrating value to external stakeholders.

How to seek successful partnership

First, take courage! The newcomer to partnership working can find their optimism quickly eroded, and 'battle-scarred' wisdom can drift over into calculating cynicism—with devastating consequences for the partnership. You need to have a clear sense of the benefits and a willingness to live with process pain and a level of risk in order to achieve the desired ends. All of this can be minimised through active management of the collaboration. There will always be a need to manage the complex balance between processes, substantive outcomes and recognition if commitment and energy are to be kept alive. Perhaps the likelihood of being able to have a story of successful partnership to recount depends on the expectations that you bring to the enterprise.

ENDNOTES

[1] Reproduced from The Partner 2007 by kind permission of Partnership Sourcing Ltd (PSL), <www.pslcbi.com>. This chapter is based on research carried out by the authors as part of a program of research on the management of collaboration undertaken within the ESRC/EPSRC Advanced Institute for Management Research.

6. Collaborative governance: the community sector and collaborative network governance

Paul Smyth

Introduction

This chapter presents a view of the potential role of the community sector in the emerging forms of social governance within Australia's social-policy regime. This regime is currently in a state of transition and contest and the view here is based on an understanding that before looking at the nuts and bolts of collaboration it is essential to ask the question 'collaboration for what?'. As writers such as Newman (2004) indicate, it is not at all clear what direction the mooted transition from hierarchical and market to network forms of governance will take in different countries (see Considine 2001). Hess and Adams (2002) are persuasive that future organisational forms should not be thought of in terms of more of what we have now; while McDonald and Marston (2005) show how the apparently day-to-day business of governing is shot through with contested understandings of what should be the appropriate 'ends and means' of welfare.

Inevitably, any regime of collaboration will be conditioned by what Salamon and Anheier (1998) have referred to as the 'social origins' of the sector, or what might also be thought of as its 'path dependency'; while others (Evers and Laville 2004) emphasise the importance of understanding the role of the third sector in relation to the configuration of the first and second sectors—namely, the State and the market. Australian history has in fact seen the roles of community organisations, government and business shaped and reshaped several times, which is why it is important to consider the changing configuration of what we call here the three pillars of social governance.

The three pillars of social governance

The first pillar, the community welfare sector, was assigned a key role in Australian social policy until World War II. A 'welfare society' sustained by wage-earners' welfare was preferred to the welfare state. This model placed great value on what today we would call the voluntary principle, with individuals and community groups trusted to manage their own affairs rather than be managed by government. The 'Australian way' has clearly privileged the contribution of voluntary organisations and is likely to continue to do so.

The second pillar was founded on the hard-won wisdom of the Great Depression—that often what voluntary groups could do by the 'tens' needed to be done by the 'hundreds' by governments. To guarantee the 'fair go' of Australian social policy, voluntary effort had to be underpinned by government guarantees to all citizens.

These two pillars were synthesised in the 1970s and 1980s in the Keynesian-style welfare state. The government oversaw the macro-social development of its citizens and the community sector provided a complementary role: filling gaps, innovating, being an ombudsman and bringing effective local knowledge into policy development. An older sectarian competitiveness in the sector gave way to collaboration between agencies and with government (Smyth and Wearing 2002). Many of the community-development practices generated in this period still have relevance today. The central aim of including all citizens more directly in the decisions that affected their lives was nicely described in terms of welfare by R. G. Brown's (1975) phrase of developing a 'constituency of the poor'. What was missing in this model was any connection between social and economic development.

The role of the sector changed radically with the switch to free-market economics in the 1990s. The broad aim of social development based on citizenship entitlement was replaced by 'conditional welfare for the few'. In a climate of fiscal austerity, governments turned to contracting out public services via the mechanism of quasi-markets with the aim of achieving greater 'value for money'. Collaboration in the sector was replaced by competition and, for many welfare agencies, growing 'market share' became the central organisational driver. Peak bodies were destabilised and the old ombudsman or advocacy role was compromised. In the literature, this became known as the era of the 'industry model' and it is this model that is slowly being abandoned as governments and the community sector reach for more joined up collaborative models.

The failings of the industry model—epitomised in the Job Network—have been canvassed in the literature (McDonald and Marston 2005; Mwaiteleke 2007). It is said to be unsuited to the people and places with multiple disadvantage, which are increasingly becoming the core clientele of the Job Network. It is said to be overly centralised with excessive regulation, which hinders responsive professional practice. It is also said to overlook unique local circumstances and directs activity away from collaboration, advocacy, lobbying and networking.

The central failing was the problem identified in the literature as isomorphism—that is, the dynamics of competitive contracting tended to turn the sector into an image of government departments. The sector's 'first-pillar' role with its 'voluntary' character and community-based features was compromised as agencies took on the characteristics of semi-state agencies. The community sector found itself constrained by excessive centralisation and regulation and less and less able to respond to human and local complexity. Its ability to exercise local discretion became shackled and capacities for collaboration, advocacy and lobbying seriously impaired.

It is notable that the arguments for an 'industry' model for the community sector are primarily economic and this highlights the importance of the 'third pillar' in social governance—namely, the role of the market. In the welfare-state model, the community sector's role was constructed as social—that is, based on advancing social or human rights. This function was thought to have nothing to do with the economy or indeed was seen as being inherently against the capitalist economy. In the industry-model phase, the goal of economic efficiency often appeared to be opposed to the social-development goals of earlier times.

Today, we see a reconfiguring of this third pillar—the market economy—and in ways that indicate a new convergence of economic and social goals. This is witnessed in part by the continuing expansion of the social responsibility of corporations, but also by the recognition by governments that the primary aim of economic policy today is to create a 'third wave' of productivity growth that will simply not happen without the effective engagement of certain people and places currently excluded from mainstream economic and social participation (Productivity Commission 2007).

For the three sectors to enter a new era of collaborative governance, due attention needs to be paid to this emerging policy framework. It is no longer useful to think of social policies in terms of 'ending welfare dependency' or 'ending welfare as we know it' with the sub-goal of ensuring conditional welfare only for the few. Not only will there be a participation and productivity penalty for allowing continuing social exclusion, there will be a growing economic cost in terms of services needed to address the fallout of social neglect.

The third sector: social investment, capabilities and a new service model

In this time of transition it is paramount that we ask afresh just what is distinctive about the contributions the three sectors should make to the new forms of collaborative governance. The third sector's contribution was not well conceived in terms of the industry model, in which differences between the sectors became blurred as each was cast as a competitive player in what were styled 'quasi-markets'. In the new, networked collaborative model of governance that we see as desirable, a premium needs to be placed on what is distinctive about the roles and products that each agency brings to the ensemble.

While the focus here is on the third sector, this needs to be considered alongside the other two sectors. While it cannot be developed here, there appear to be significant shifts in thinking about the roles of government, for example, from the 'new public management' to the 'strategic-governance' model as discussed by Gallop (2006), and of the economy, from the pure market exchange model of the 1990s to a more Schumpeterian political economy, which highlights the importance of evolving key institutional networks that foster innovation, knowledge transfer, research and development.

As already mentioned, this understanding of the economy has been overlaid increasingly by a sense of the importance of its social foundations. The human-capital agenda of the Council of Australian Governments (COAG), for example, has been increasingly linked to the wellbeing agenda. Therefore investments in the early years, for example, or in the 'long tail' of under-performing Australian youth are seen to be as much economic as social in value.

Of course, simply acknowledging the need for a greater role for social policy does not tell us a lot about how to reconfigure the governance roles of the three sectors. Clearly, there are no hard and fast rules, but as noted above it is likely in view of our history that in Australia there will continue to be a mixed economy of welfare based on the public and for-profit sectors with governments seeking to sustain an underlying commitment to a 'fair go' for all citizens. More specifically, however, we need to revisit the role of the third sector and review what has been its historically proven, different and indispensable role in engaging with those least able to access either government or private services.

The literature expresses this role in terms of addressing market and government failures (Bowles and Gintis 2002). It suggests that the community sector, because of its local reputation, respect and connectedness, is likely to be the initiator of community-based economic activity and to understand local community dynamics, needs and possibilities. It is also likely to be able to generate the trust and cooperation that local initiatives require to succeed (Teague 2007; Halpern 2004; Arrow 1999).

Often this capacity to engage is linked to an ability to generate 'social capital'. While this is possibly valuable, it remains a vacuous way of capturing what the third sector along with its network partners is likely to be aiming to achieve. Here it is arguably more useful to think in terms of the specific social and economic objectives around which the sectoral collaboration is organised. Following the United Kingdom and the European Union, for example, it would appear to make more sense to have a set of explicit objectives for growth, employment, social inclusion and sustainability by which to benchmark and measure the efforts of the networks.

It is arguable that Sen's notion of 'capability' provides, rather than social capital, a more robust way of thinking about the economic and social purposes of public investment. It cannot be developed here (see Bonvin and Farvaque 2006), but the Sen framework also suggests the kind of capacities that will be needed in the third sector if it is to make its distinctive contribution to the new collaborative models. Under the industry model, third-sector agencies have tended to become suppliers of centrally packaged services to passive consumers. This is what is funded and there is little spare for developing different services for people not well served by what has become a 'one-size-fits-all' approach. A capabilities model suggests that effective services will flourish when there are engaged communities and that new funding arrangements ought to have a premium paid for community-building work as an end in itself.

With the Sen approach, the focus shifts to the sets of entitlements people ought to have if they are to be able to choose the life they value—or to convert 'capabilities' into 'functionings'. This imposes obligations on governments to ensure opportunities are real. In terms of service delivery, it suggests a model in which service users have an effective voice with real freedom to negotiate their pathway in a fair and reasonable way. The model also advances that central authorities are important for resourcing and accountability and that local, reflexive regulation is needed for local actors to have autonomy, with the institutional environment able to listen.

These principles would allow the development of a new kind of local network of government, business and third-sector agencies, which could create an institutional environment with the capacity to tap into local aspirations and exercise the autonomy necessary for effective responses.

Conclusion: the whole is more than the sum of its parts

This chapter has emphasised the importance of locating discussions about how to collaborate within a wider consideration of the ends and means of social policy and with particular reference to the national context. It has been proposed that the postwar period has seen a shift from a welfare-state collaborative model to a contract state–industry model and that the evolution of collaborative or network governance signals that we are in the midst of a third major transition.

Within these shifts we have identified the changing goals of social administration. The welfare state was identified with promoting citizenship-based social development. The market model rejected positive state intervention for social purposes and sought to restrict welfare to the deserving few. Now a new set of goals is forming around social investment in an inclusive society in which all people have the opportunities to realise their capabilities.

Achieving these goals, especially those for engaging the excluded, presents new challenges for social governance. Whereas the industry model blurred the differences between the sectors, collaborative governance requires a heightened sense of what makes the sectors distinctive and of what is required to maximise their unique contributions.

In this regard, the negative views about the role of governments characteristic of the 1990s need to give way to a view of government as the strategic agency responsible for overall outcomes but working through relevant networks. Governments need to develop this role in ways that include facilitating information sharing, research, development and innovation within relevant networks. Government has a key role to play in bringing the sectors together and enabling them to achieve shared, inter-sectoral policy and program goals.

We have seen that the community sector has historically played an elevated role in the nation's social governance and will undoubtedly play an indispensable role in terms of maximising workforce participation and productivity improvements as much as social cohesion and inclusiveness. From the third sector's perspective, a key issue will be whether it will be resourced in a way that enables it to achieve these functions. In this regard, it will be important that those responsible for collaboration as a whole ensure that the third sector has the resources and the political independence it requires to make an effective contribution.

References

Arrow, K. 1999, 'Observations on social capital', in P. Dasgupta and I. Serageldin (eds), *Social Capital: A multifaceted perspective*, World Bank, Washington, DC.

Bonvin, J. and Farvaque, N. 2006, 'Promoting capability for work: the role of local actors', in S. Deneulin et al. (eds), *Transforming Unjust Structures: The capability approach*, Springer, Amsterdam, pp. 121–42.

Bowles, B. and Gintis, H. 2002, 'Social capital and community governance', *Economic Journal*, vol. 112, no. 4, pp. 419–36.

Brown, R. G. 1975, *The Management of Welfare: A study of the British Social Service Administration*.

Considine, M. 2001, *Enterprising States: The public management of welfare-to-work*, Cambridge University Press, Melbourne.

Evers, A. and Laville, J. (eds) 2004, *The Third Sector in Europe*, Edward Elgar, Cheltenham.

Gallop, G. 2006, Strategic planning: is it the new model?, Address to the Institute of Public Administration, New South Wales, November.

Halpern, D. 2004, *Social Capital*, Polity Press, Cambridge.

Hess, M. and Adams, D. 2002, 'Knowing and skilling in contemporary public administration', *Australian Journal of Public Administration*, vol. 61, no. 4, pp. 68–79.

McDonald, C. and Marston, G. 2005, 'Workfare as welfare: governing unemployment in the advanced welfare state', *Critical Social Policy*, vol. 25, no. 3, pp. 374–401.

Mwaiteleke, P. 2007, The influence of national competition policy in reshaping human service delivery, PhD thesis, Murdoch University.

Newman, J. 2004, 'Modernizing the state: a new style of governance?', in J. Lewis and R. Surender (eds), *Welfare State Change: Towards a third way?*, Oxford University Press, Oxford, pp. 69–88.

Productivity Commission 2007, *Potential Benefits of the National Reform Agenda*, Report to the Council of Australian Governments, Canberra.

Salamon, L. and Anheier, H. 1998, 'Social origins of civil society: explaining the nonprofit sector cross-nationally', *Voluntas*, vol. 9, no. 3, pp. 213–48.

Smyth, P. and Wearing, M. 2002, 'After the welfare state? Welfare governance and the communitarian revival', in S. Bell (ed.), *Economic Governance and Institutional Dynamics*, Oxford University Press, Melbourne, pp. 226–43.

Teague, P. 2007, 'Developing the social economy in Ireland?', *International Journal of Urban and Regional Research*, vol. 31, no. 1, pp. 91–108.

Part 2. The reality of collaboration: success, failure, challenges and questions

7. What works and why: collaborating in a crisis

Shane Carmody

The fundamental premise of this chapter derives from my experience as a practitioner of cross-government collaboration. We must seek ways to improve the processes of governing through collaboration if we want to successfully manage crises. To do so we need to be more effective in managing others and in making maximum use of their individual capacities to deal with the common threat or crisis situation. The lessons from crises involving the Federal Government, statutory organisations, emergency authorities, other governments and non-governmental organisations (NGOs) are that effective leadership is essential, as are clear identification of responsibilities and effective implementation of decisions.

My use of the term 'collaboration' is in its benign meaning: a context of cooperation and working or acting together, being helpful and doing as one is asked for the wider public good rather than cooperating or working with the enemy. With hindsight, however, I might observe that many of my pre-2000 experiences in intergovernmental collaboration often felt a lot more like trying to negotiate with the enemy than a helpful dialogue among friends.

I was a deputy secretary in the Department of Defence from 2001 to 2006. Defence is a large and immensely complex organisation of some 90 000 military and civilian staff, with elements in all Australian states and territories, operating day and night throughout the year. It is a tough organisation to manage internally. Most senior managers have large personnel and financial accountabilities—and of course they need to negotiate successful outcomes across and outside the organisation.

While Defence 'operates' in all Australian states, it is worth noting that this is not really what Defence is set up to do. Defence is set up to fight wars, it is to be hoped, far offshore. And, like the Australian Federal Police's 'Fight crime together and win' mantra, the Australian Defence Force is above all established to 'fight wars and win'.

From 2000–06, I was a member of Defence's Strategic Command Group, chaired by the Chief of the Defence Forces and comprising the secretary, the Vice-Chief of the Defence Force, service chiefs and key senior civilian appointments. The group was established to deal with all operational matters. During my time there (under three successive Chiefs of the Defence Force), we were involved in numerous exceptional operations or crises. These crises included: the original

Defence deployment to East Timor (which began in 1999 but was still in full flight in 2000); the aftermath of the 11 September 2001 attacks, including the Australian deployment to Afghanistan; the planning, negotiation, development and continuation of operations in Iraq after 2003; problems in Fiji; the Bali bombing of 2003; the Jakarta bombing of 2004; the second Bali bombing in 2005; the Asian tsunami in 2004; the Solomon Islands deployments one and two; Afghanistan again; East Timor again. This is not a comprehensive list but merely the main situations we dealt with in that period.

Fighting wars and undertaking military interventions are multidimensional. To be successful, it is important to understand the aim, to conduct detailed planning and to have good organisation and effective logistical support, including good sustainment for long and often unspecified periods. Anyone who has been in the military will know that there must also be—particularly in times of peace—constant training, repetitive development of doctrine and endless rehearsal. These three are in themselves features of military operational planning. These three—in contexts other than the one I am using here—will often be referred to as 'mere process'. The military knows, however, that this attention to the intricacies of preparation is what makes for effective military operations. Effective preparation wins wars. The military also knows that there is little discernable difference between the initial phases of a combat operation and the initial phases of a national crisis. In fact, in Australia, international crises are frequently allocated Defence operational names partly for that purpose, such as 'Bali Assist', 'Pakistan Assist' or the 'Regional Assistance Mission to Solomon Islands' (RAMSI, from 2003).

Objectives in crisis management

A decade ago there was much less understanding of the management of crises than is apparent today. Maybe that was because we did not perceive that there were many crises. Maybe it was also because, by and large, any such crises were considered more as local issues—or even state issues—than national issues.

Things have changed remarkably in the past decade. One of the great consultative trend-setting endeavours was the so-called Y2K threat (the supposed meltdown of computers and information technology systems at the turn of the past century). Of course, we all recall that nothing significant happened. What many people do not recall with equal clarity, however, is the level of cooperation and coordination engendered in the management of and approach to the impending crisis. In some ways, it was a unique experience across government and across the nation. It represented a transition to a more 'shared' sense of common accountabilities.

To most outside observers, nothing resulted except a lot of expenditure, empowerment of our information technology (IT) people and a realisation that we were critically dependent on systems we could not hope to understand. The reality is that since 2000, and in a process that started well before then, crisis planning and management have moved from the ad hoc to a highly sophisticated, evolved and coordinated process. While not without its faults, crisis management is now well past the 'let's just do something' mentality in the hope that it will deliver a result and ensure that we 'look like' we are contributing.

From pre-existing arrangements to what works and why

Crisis management in the late 1990s was an ad hoc and generally under-prepared system. The few standing institutional arrangements that did exist tended to be of recent origin. For example, the Strategy Policy Coordination Group began only in the 1990s, and the departments of Prime Minister and Cabinet (PM&C), Foreign Affairs and Trade (DFAT) and Defence used this mechanism to manage immediate crises on a case-by-case basis (before the Secretaries' Committee on National Security and the National Security Committee of cabinet took on these responsibilities more formally). In these circumstances, PM&C had some moral suasion; DFAT had access and networks overseas; and Defence had the means and the human-resource capabilities.

We did not seem to need much more. Furthermore, there were a number of broader whole-of-government, interdepartmental committees (IDCs). IDCs, however, had a reputation for being the graveyard of good outcomes and the bastions of the protection and preservation of individual agency powers; this reduced their effectiveness.

My recent experience of collaborating across government organisations to manage crises has been one of sustained growth and increasing professionalism. There has been significant evolution in management processes, their sophistication and frequency, a broadening of involvement and, as a result, better outcomes. In the past few years, it would appear that almost everyone in these collaborative networks has worked out why they are there and what they need to be ready to do.

In the past few years, however, there has been a real change in the institutional architecture of crisis management. What has caused this could be the subject of debate: perhaps national security issues became bigger and more pressing, crises became more real and more numerous, perceptions of vulnerability were more pronounced or the need for greater preparedness in the face of national security threats was more imperative. Whatever the proximate cause, we experienced a large growth in specialist task forces charged with specific missions and objectives.

Drawing from this experience, I want to reflect on what has worked in this recent time frame and why. In particular, I will extract the objectives of effective crisis management—the opposite to just doing something (anything!) and hoping for the best.

As indicated earlier, the prime objectives of good crisis management mirror those for sound military operations. First, we must define the problem and identify what needs to be done. This sounds simple and logical but is often far from simple in the early stages of a crisis. How do the multiple agencies involved define the scale of a problem as it first appears or as initial information is channelled back to government? To illustrate with real cases, it was days after the Asian tsunami or the first Bali bombing when the scale and magnitude of the crisis was eventually apparent to policymakers at the centre of government. By then, much of the response work was well under way.

Second, clear, strategic leadership is necessary to identify the best organisation or organisational mix to progress the response or resolve the crisis. This involves dispassionately asking who is best placed to resolve the crisis or, alternatively, who should perform the lead agency role among the constellation of agencies likely to become involved. We should then identify the most efficient arrangements to establish effective command and control and make it happen in reality. Such control has to be effectively maintained as the situation develops—if for no other reason than to ensure that resources are not squandered. We need to constantly ask what sort of activity is required, when and how it is best managed and controlled. In collaboration with the main players, we need to identify and allocate resources to the two principal tasks emanating from the crisis: the 'understanding' and the 'doing'. Not all such considerations will be known at the start, so some inter-agency agility is required to meet the challenges as they unfold.

Third, the urge simply 'to do something' to indicate action or intent must be avoided. Such urges are generally wasteful of effort and expertise. Rather, the participants should look to building long-term capacity—or sustainment—so they can still manage the crisis when it slips to the routine, and to have better capacities with which to address future situations. Practical examples of this investment in long-term capacity include the long-running consultative measures in Iraq and East Timor.

Finally, we need to learn and apply lessons as we discover them in each new scenario. Crisis-management experience is, above all, evolutionary in nature.

I summarise the key practical activities that work well in crisis management across agencies, governments and organisations thus:

- early action, meetings or planning intervention
- well-established initial communications protocols
- a clear perspective and clear identification of the aim
- well-established, documented and rehearsed processes

- clear accountabilities for those brought into the collaborative venture
- a commitment to resource sharing across agencies and to special initiatives
- a willingness by agencies to contribute staff (the Tsunami Task Force was a perfect example of this commitment, where staff external to the department were up and running in the DFAT Crisis Centre within hours)
- promoting and developing a feeling of 'we are all in it together'
- having only contributors present—no passengers
- individual agendas need to be sacrificed for the common agenda
- actively manage the media
- thinking about the 'end' at the 'beginning' and planning for it: repatriation, disengagement and a return to the pre-crisis status quo.

What inhibits effective crisis management? When responsibilities are not clear and no formal lead agency in charge has been selected, there is a lack of direction and the potential for inter-agency tensions. Collaboration does not work purely by consensus or when the scope of responsibility is uncertain. There is no room for excessive ideology in addressing crises. Crisis management is about clarity of understanding of the problem and clarity about what is needed to resolve it. Attempts to resolve the crisis will be impeded in the absence of a strategic perspective.

It is worth noting that some, but not all, of these inhibitors can be countered in advance. For example, it is imperative to define the problem accurately and early to avoid blurred objectives. It is also important to depoliticise problems, build trusting relations between agencies and put turf wars to one side. As indicated earlier, we can develop sound crisis-management arrangements and processes in leadership development. We can also seek to establish procedures in the absence of consistency.

For a long time, collaboration in a crisis was all about getting there and visibly doing something. More recently, we have taken on board more policy learning and adopted a much more sophisticated approach.

Conclusions: lessons across government

There are numerous important but often simple ways to improve collaboration across government. Knowing them and invoking them will lead to better overall outcomes not only in crisis management, but in all forms of collaboration.

In terms of continuing process and management responsibilities, we need to work out and identify the key organisational players who will attend most crises, most often, and be regularly at the centre of things, and ensure that they can speak with authority and act quickly. This line of authority and accumulated experience is not to be taken lightly. Officials in these organisations need to develop simple procedures and templates that suit different scenarios. If we rely on such accumulated experience and structured processes to start with, the chances are that the management of a specific crisis will start off well. Experience counts.

We also need to broaden responsibilities and accountabilities to take into account the expertise and local knowledge of specialised agencies. This is likely to include inter alia the Emergency Management Authority, the Australian Federal Police, health departments, Customs, state police, Coastwatch and the Attorney-General's Department. We cannot 'do' things from Canberra alone.

Emergency agencies need to regularly engage in simulated exercises and practise for the real event. They should routinely run realistic exercises, planning workshops, rehearsals, tests of capacities and inter-agency cooperation in order to reveal glitches. They need to document their learning and seek explicitly to apply the lessons of practice.

At the whole-of-government level, we need to embrace a multi-jurisdictional, multi-agency approach. This builds capacity across agencies, drills learning into agencies, develops individual skills and promotes thinking across disciplinary approaches. If we adopt this broader multi-agency focus, we begin to develop an effective network governance to deal with crises and similar situations.

8. Collaboration in education[1]

Rachel Hunter

Australia's education and training system is founded on multiple models of collaboration. In Queensland, we collaborate with three school sectors (state, Catholic and independent), three education sectors (schools, vocational education and training and higher education), seven other states and territories, the Commonwealth Government, innumerable statutory authorities, local government, communities, parents, students, industry and, importantly, our workforce and their industrial representatives.

The Queensland Department of Education, Training and the Arts (DETA) was formed in September 2006 and is Queensland's largest government agency. DETA employs more than 62 000 full-time staff and supports almost one million students in state and non-state schools and in the Queensland technical and further education (TAFE) system. We are directly responsible for the funding, operations and performance of more than 1250 state schools and support a further 460 non-state schools with financial assistance, educational partnerships and a framework of regulation and quality assurance.

Our vision is for a smart, skilled and creative Queensland—a goal that is shared by our many collaborative partners. The African proverb 'It takes a village to educate a child' succinctly sums up our philosophy. Education is a shared responsibility and partnerships within our education and training systems and beyond are crucial. Without collaboration, our schools and training institutions cannot hope to meet the human and social capital needs of a modern and prosperous state and ensure that the social and economic benefits of education and training are shared more equally than is currently the case.

How we collaborate is also important. Here I examine collaboration within and across governments, particularly the nexus between education policy and funding in the federalist model in which we operate.

Human and social capital

Around the world, there is a growing research and policy consensus that investment in education and skills is critical to a nation's future prosperity and social wellbeing. Many developed nations are facing the challenge of sustaining and increasing productivity without the benefits of large-scale population growth and in the face of an ageing workforce. Our capacity to compete in the global knowledge economy depends on the strength of our response to this human-capital challenge.

In Queensland, the tightest labour market in years means that young people are finding employment readily available and in the short term more attractive as an alternative to education. The labour-market participation rate of Queensland's young people aged 15–17 years is almost 60 per cent, compared with about 46 per cent for the rest of Australia.[2] This can be explained partly by Queensland's larger than average share of youth working part-time in retail, tourism and hospitality. The additional job opportunities due to the strength of the economy are placing pressure on retention rates, as students weigh up the costs of continuing schooling or gaining readily available employment.

Despite the current strength of the labour market, seldom has the need to invest in education and skills been more crucial, to remain competitive with the booming economies of our Asian neighbours, which are investing more and more in education and skills development.

In Queensland, we are looking to innovative collaborations between the public and private sectors to help us meet the skills demands of a productive economy. One example is the Aerospace Project, involving Education Queensland, Boeing Australia, Aviation Australia, Australian Aerospace, Smiths Aerospace and the Brisbane Airport Corporation. Developed at the aerospace industry's request, the initial project started in 2004 with joint funding from Boeing, which contributed $600 000, and the Queensland Government, with a $300 000 investment. The project now involves 17 'gateway' schools—state and non-state—which incorporate aerospace into their regular subjects. Boeing offers up to 12 traineeships and 30 work-experience placements to gateway students annually. Ten students each year will be offered direct entry into new double-major bachelor degree programs at the University of Queensland in electrical, mechanical or software-system engineering coupled with aerospace engineering. Additionally, the new Aviation High, a former gateway school, was officially launched in 2007. It offers specialist aviation education and training to students in Years 8 to 12, providing them with a direct path to careers in the aviation industry.

Equity

Collaborative projects of this kind are designed to best match the skills of the state's young people with industry needs. Across Queensland, teachers, leaders, schools, students and parents contribute every day to the achievement of outstanding educational performance and to the current strength of the Queensland economy. The benefits of education are, however, not being realised to their fullest extent, and are not being shared equally.

Despite the fact that Queensland students perform well on average when benchmarked internationally, Queensland has persistent inequalities in achievement for students from disadvantaged backgrounds. National research shows high levels of social exclusion for school-age young children in Queensland. Of the 10 per cent of the most disadvantaged children in Australia, it is estimated that half live in Queensland (NATSEM 2006).

One of the key lessons we have learnt is that collaboration between agencies can make a difference to individual lives. An exemplary case is that of a nine-year-old Indigenous boy—a victim of abandonment, sexual abuse and domestic violence. He was receiving one-to-one care and was isolated because of his history of dangerous and unpredictable behaviour. Obviously, he faced very substantial barriers to education. Thanks to a committed, flexible, multidisciplinary team of caring professionals, the child's situation is changing. Professionals from the Department of Child Safety, the Department of Disability Services Queensland, Queensland Health and DETA joined forces to provide emotional, therapeutic and educational support to meet the complex needs of the child. Led by DETA, together these dedicated professionals have helped support the boy to successfully join the regular Year 4 program three mornings a week. This is a positive example of collaboration between government agencies at the state level, but one that illustrates the intensity of effort and resources required to make a positive difference to one child's life.

The reality is that disadvantaged students are often over-represented in state schools, as well as geographically concentrated in remote and rural areas. In the provision of education services to students with disabilities, Indigenous students and students in remote and rural areas, it is state schools that bear the majority of responsibilities and the higher associated costs.[3] When you take into account recent research that suggests that density of disadvantage at the school level is a significant contributor to poor outcomes, the consequences of this stratification of students begin to look even more significant (Holmes-Smith 2006).

The current state of stratification is at least partly attributable to a deliberate policy on the part of the Federal Government to subsidise school choice, understood simply as a choice between government and non-government schools. For example, in Queensland, the state government provides 91 per cent of the public funding for Queensland state schools and the Federal Government provides 9 per cent. For Queensland non-state schools, the Federal Government provides 70 per cent of the public funding and the Queensland Government provides 30 per cent.[4]

This federal funding regime has as its first principle who owns the schools, rather than what the students need. In a sustained period, the impact has been to divide the school sectors and feed the increasing stratification of government and non-government schools. An education system thus divided in its responsibilities for students in need operates in nobody's interests. It is wastefully inefficient, creates diseconomies of scale, encourages false forms of competition and prevents all schools from contributing fully to the creation of human and social capital.

American social theorist Robert Putnam (2004) has addressed the social purposes of schooling and the role of schools in forging social capital and social cohesion. He describes two forms of social capital that schools help create: bonding capital and bridging capital. Bonding capital refers to connections between like social groups, while bridging capital is the development of connections between different social groups. Following Putnam, Barry McGaw (2006) has used these concepts to consider the current state of schooling in Australia. Schools that emphasise accessibility, inclusion and collaboration must create bonding and bridging capital in order to be successful.

Continuing to divide schools through funding regimes that inadequately reflect student need, enrolment practices that produce concentrations of disadvantage and competing regulatory and policy regimes at different levels of government can create strong forms of bonding capital within some schools, but will not contribute to the creation of bridging capital.

The cost of losing that opportunity will be felt in the performance of all our schools and in the entrenched educational, socioeconomic and geographical disadvantage that it will continue to create in sections of the student cohort. If we are to ensure that schools contribute fully to the development of human and social capital, every school must be expected—and resourced—to provide high-quality education for each of their students.

A new federalism

To meet this challenge will require genuine collaboration between both levels of government that regulate and financially support our schools. It will require a new federalism. As John Wanna (2007) suggests, early federalism was not premised on collaboration between different levels of government, but instead on a notion of separate responsibilities. This notion has been steadily eroded since Federation. School education, for example, is constitutionally a residual power of the states, but is an area in which federal intervention has increased in the past 50 years.

This constitutional legacy has converged in recent times with a historical anomaly that has seen Labor governments in all the states and territories, and the Coalition in power in Canberra. Together, these factors exacerbate the inherent structural tensions within our federation.

It is a matter of constitutional design, rather than a deliberate policy choice of any of our current governments, that the Commonwealth has the majority of revenue-raising capabilities and the states have the responsibilities for the majority of service delivery. In the current expression of vertical fiscal imbalance within education policy, however, we see the creation of a set of conditions that militates against collaboration in ways that are fundamentally detrimental to the creation of human and social capital in our schools.

The current dysfunction of school funding is not a matter of constitutional inevitability. The current funding and policy regimes foster the stratification of our school education system and limit positive collaboration between schools and between different levels of government.

The hard work required to make a difference for every individual child must not be confined primarily to government schools and should not be compounded by unproductive interference in the day-to-day operations of schools.

All funding provided by the Commonwealth is attached to accountability requirements that are alike for state and non-state schools. The scope of policy emanating from the federal education department has been reduced through these requirements to a series of mundane and ad hoc minutiae, such as whether every school has a regulation flagpole, displays a values poster or tests all students in a certain way at the end of Year 12.

Equally frustrating are the recent exhortations that schools should begin a dialogue with businesses. This ignores the depth of the current engagement with industry, such as I have described above in relation to Aviation High. While I accept that it is not possible to have at one's fingertips a detailed understanding of the rich tapestry of school education as it is provided across Australia, this is precisely my point. The prescriptive nature of the Commonwealth's policymaking is out of step with its knowledge of our landscape. We would prefer the Commonwealth was more aware and less prescriptive.

To borrow Wanna's words, this is a form of coercive federalism that is divorced from the lessons of day-to-day service provision, lacks the capacity to implement reforms directly and does not foster the conditions for innovation in our schools. It is a basic tenet of governance that service delivery should take place at the local level—that those closest to the ground should carry out the function, within broader policy settings that are dictated by systemic needs and priorities. The Commonwealth is ill suited to the role of micro-manager.

If we could start afresh, what roles would we assign the Commonwealth Government, and what roles would we assign the states?

We acknowledge that the Commonwealth has a broader interest in education beyond the provision of specific-purpose payments. This includes, for example, advocacy of national consistency, where appropriate. Queensland supports national consistency, where it can be shown to be in the best interests of students, parents and schools.

The states and the Commonwealth need to be able to influence and support the whole of the education sector in the service of local and national economic and social priorities. When, however, the leadership and vision that should be the role of the Commonwealth reduces to evaluating an external exam or offering prizes to teachers and students, the role of the Australian Government has been diminished.

The Commonwealth rightly seeks to exert influence over the largest provider of school education services, which remains the government school system in all states and territories. At the same time, the states are rightly wary of the stratification of schools and the imbalance in the funding regimes that serve to limit the states' capacity to influence the whole of the education sector in a time when productivity experts are telling us that it is most crucial to exert this leverage.

The Commonwealth could instead use its investment in schooling to direct the broad policy settings at the national level, in genuine collaboration with the states and territories. This would avoid the duplication of state efforts, as recently seen, for example, in the Commonwealth budget initiatives that sought to reward teacher performance by the provision of summer schools and individual incentives, or in the expansion of the $700 voucher program to address literacy and numeracy needs. Instead, we should aim to harness the collective power of Commonwealth and state resources to address these issues comprehensively.

One fruitful area in which a more collaborative partnership could begin is in relation to school funding. The Commonwealth and states could work together to design funding models for schooling that do not compromise the principle of school choice, that recognise and support differences and innovations in schools and that regulate and encourage quality in meaningful ways across sectors and systems. Above all, these new collaborative approaches could help to support all schools to provide high-quality education services and teaching to overcome disadvantage.

In the scale of collaboration that Wanna describes in his chapter of this volume, this is at the highest level and involves the highest risks. The work on the future of schooling being done by the states and territories through the newly formed Council for the Australian Federation provides a starting point for a much-needed debate with the Federal Government and with key stakeholders about the roles of respective levels of government within a federal model in charting the future of schooling.

I conclude with an invitation and an exhortation of my own. We welcome the challenge of a new federalism and the opportunity it brings to engage in high-risk but meaningful, transformative collaboration. We are passionate about the potential of creating and sustaining an education system that underpins national prosperity and has at its heart a belief in equity and a commitment to improving lives. To do so, we must dispense with recriminations and act for the sake of all students, no matter which schools they attend.

References

Holmes-Smith, Phillip 2006, *School Socio-Economic Density and its Effect on School Performance*, NSW Department of Education and Training.

McGaw, Barry 2006, 'Achieving quality and equity in education', Committee for Economic Development of Australia (CEDA), 3 August.

National Centre for Social and Economic Monitoring (NATSEM) 2006, *Indicators of Social Exclusion for Australia's Children: An analysis by state and age group*, <http://www.natsem.canberra.edu.au/publications/papers/cps/cp06/cp2006_007/cp2006_007.pdf>

Putnam, Robert 2004, Education, diversity, social cohesion and 'social capital', Meeting of Organisation for Economic Cooperation and Development Education Ministers, 18–19 March.

Wanna, John 2007, 'Governing Through Collaboration: Managing better through others', paper presented at the Australia New Zealand School of Government Annual Conference, *Governing through Collaboration: managing better through others*, held at the Hyatt Hotel Canberra, 28 and 29 June, 2007. A revised version of this paper is reproduced as Chapter 1 in this volume, 'Collaborative government: meanings, dimensions, drivers and outcomes'.

ENDNOTES

[1] This chapter was presented as a conference paper in June 2007 and, since that time, there have been some significant shifts in the landscape of Commonwealth–state relations in the area of collaboration in education, including through the Council of Australian Governments. While the chapter does not reflect these developments, the key messages are still relevant.

[2] Unpublished Australian Bureau of Statistics labour-force data; DETA Labour Market Research Unit.

[3] *Report on Government Services* 2007, School Education, Attachment 3, various tables.

[4] *Report on Government Services* 2007, Table 3A.9, Real Australian, State and Territory Government Recurrent Expenditure, 2004–05 figures.

9. From collaboration to coercion: a story of governance failure, success and opportunity in Australian Indigenous affairs

Diane Smith

The West Arnhem Shire: a story of governance success

In late June 2007, I was at the South Alligator River in Kakadu National Park attending a meeting of Indigenous leaders from local government councils and resource organisations representing communities throughout West Arnhem Land and the town of Jabiru in the Northern Territory (NT). They were meeting, as they had done regularly for the past three years, to plan the implementation of a local government shire covering the entire region of West Arnhem and Jabiru. Also present were senior officers from the NT and Federal Governments, who, under a bilateral agreement signed between the two governments in 2005, have been working closely with the Indigenous leaders on the transitional committee to facilitate the establishment of effective and culturally legitimate regionalised local government.[1]

In 2003, Aboriginal (Bininj) leaders from West Arnhem Land saw the NT Government regionalisation policy as an opportunity to secure greater authority and control for Bininj people over the things that mattered to them, and to create a strong voice that could influence government funding and service delivery to the region: 'We will get to say what we want in our communities, we will set the priorities'; 'We have control over this project'; 'We will create policies and strategies that achieve more local employment and better services'; 'We will have a much stronger voice speaking as one to government'.

Part and parcel of the regionalisation process has been the regular delivery, as an integral part of each committee meeting, of governance capacity development with the Indigenous and non-Indigenous members of the committee. This has been carried out by the same team of community-development officers from the NT Department of Local Government, with my research support, for more than three years (see Evans et al. 2006; Smith 2005, 2007). The governance work included sessions on governing roles and responsibilities, separation of powers, systems of representation, organisational structures, codes of conduct and conflict of interest, meeting procedures, human-resource management and contract conditions, and so on. Each session culminates in the committee collectively developing new governing rules—for example, in the form of written policies, agreed procedures, resolutions and a future constitution and preamble.

An important driving force behind these efforts has been the desire to create an effective regional organisation that will better reflect Bininj cultural values and institutions: 'We will have a council that respects and works with our culture.' As part of the governance capacity-building work, the Indigenous committee members routinely discuss the cultural issues involved in developing workable rules; they test proposed policies against potential community and cultural scenarios, and share practical ideas with government officers about how they might collectively and individually enforce their rules in a way that acknowledges the difficult challenges involved in working across cultures.

The result is that the community leaders on the committee have developed strong governing capacity and confidence based on the experience of working together as a team to make and enforce collective decisions. They follow up difficult issues of representation and externally imposed change with tenacity and integrity, and their relationship with the NT and Federal Government partners continues to be frank and robust.

Collaborating for good governance

Figure 9.1 Logo design for the proposed West Arnhem Shire, as endorsed by the Shire Transitional Committee, 2007.

Note: The logo for the shire was designed by Ahmat Brahim, an Indigenous man with traditional ties to the region, whose father was a member of the Transitional Committee.

The West Arnhem Shire logo endorsed by the committee demonstrates their real commitment to working as a 'joined-up' local government with the other levels of government in Australia for the benefit of Bininj and Balanda (non-Aboriginal) residents of the region. Their intention, written into their early constitution preamble and policies, is to use their traditional systems of culture and governance

> to strengthen the legitimacy of the Regional Authority [shire], and use the [shire] to strengthen traditional systems of governance. Through this vision and commitment we seek to maintain observance and respect for traditional values, and to join the responsibilities and structures of traditional authority with those of local government, to achieve a high quality of life and a wide range of opportunities and choices.

> We are developing our own rules that include our culture. In our own culture we have our own rules that are very strong and we are bringing this into the [regional local government].

The collaboration between Bininj groups across the region, and with government, hasn't all been smooth sailing by any means. The history of mutual suspicion is slowly shifting as a result of the trust and relationships being built up between the government community-development officers, community leaders and different clan groups, and as the committee members work with one another to resolve practical issues and develop shared approaches.

As one member of the committee noted in a presentation to NT Government ministers in 2005:

> When we started, people were unsure of each other. People were only interested in their own group. We had our own ideas—at the beginning we were all different. We were not used to making decisions together. Now, people have a shared commitment to the whole region. We are all working towards the one goal. Now we work through issues and make an agreed decision.

Major changes initiated in 2006 by the NT Government to its policy framework for local government have severely tested the partnership relationship. The foundation of governance capacity, however, trusted relationships with particular government officers and the growing effectiveness of Bininj decision making within the committee have built resilience in the committee and the partnership. Also, the Bininj leaders remain strongly committed to achieving real outcomes on the ground. For that purpose they continue to collaborate with government to create workable solutions that will address the entrenched backlogs in infrastructure and essential services in the region.

West Arnhem: from collaboration to coercion

On the final day of the West Arnhem Shire committee meeting in late June 2007, the Federal Government issued a media release announcing that it was taking over the administration of some 60 NT Aboriginal communities, under compulsory lease acquisition, for an estimated period of five years. The release stated that government administrators, the Army and police would be placed into each community and children would be required to undertake mandatory health checks in an effort to identify and curb child abuse. All communities located on Aboriginal inalienable freehold land under the *Aboriginal Land Rights Act (NT) 1976* would have their permit systems revoked and be subject to Australian Government leasehold conditions.

Government officers at the West Arnhem meeting were unable to shed any light on the media announcement—they had not been forewarned themselves and had to resort to the media release. Quick calls to their managers in Darwin and Canberra revealed that they were similarly uninformed.

The next day, the front-page headline of the *NT News* read 'Martial Law—Howard mobilises cops, military as he declares "national emergency" in NT communities'. The opening paragraph reported:

> The Federal Government yesterday seized control of the Territory's Aboriginal communities in the most dramatic intervention in NT affairs since self-government. Canberra in effect declared martial law over the 44 per cent of the Territory owned by Indigenous people. (Adlam and Gartrell 2007)

To say that the Bininj members of the West Arnhem committee were shell-shocked would be an understatement. In one day, without any consultation, their collaboration with the Federal Government had essentially been made null and void. Their role as the proposed local government for the entire region was thrown into question, their work in the past three years ignored and their governance roles treated with disdain. A week after the media release, the Army, police and Federal Government officials entered two communities in the region.

The West Arnhem group of Indigenous leaders had been working in partnership with the NT and Federal Governments for more than three years. Their sense of betrayal was intense, but not new. It took me back several years to 2001 when I worked with the Mutitjulu community at their request to develop a welfare-reform package for the whole community.

Mutitjulu: a litany of broken promises

In 1991, the Ngaanyatjarra, Pitjantjatjara Yankunytjatjara (NPY) Women's Council reported to government on the welfare of Indigenous (Anangu) children and families in the central Australian region that included the Mutitjulu community. The Aboriginal chairwoman of the council stated in her introduction to the report:

> We are telling this story strong about what we think about child protection…Women's law, grandmothers' law is really important one

to us…It teaches us [the] right way for children to be looked after and taught.

But a lot has changed for us on our communities. We are worried about losing our traditional means of controlling and caring for children. We are worried about our family structure breaking down. We are worried about grog and petrol sniffing and how that affects our families. And we are also worried that government and welfare mob don't understand our way and our problems.

We women have ideas about what to do to make it better. We want government and welfare mob to listen to what we say and our ideas. We want them to work with us and our organisations to get it right. (R. Forbes, NYP Women's Council, 1991)

Ten years later, after years of further inquiries and reports into their family living conditions—and little to show for it except band-aid responses from governments—the Anangu families and leaders of the Mutitjulu community had had enough.

In response to the national welfare-reform agenda of the Federal Government in 2000, the community council at Mutitjulu asked Centrelink, the Aborginal and Torres Strait Islander Commission (ATSIC) and Families and Community Services (FACS) to work with them to develop a practical strategy to address welfare dependence and related family problems in the community. Under a joint contract between ATSIC and the community council, I lived and worked in the community to ascertain what Anangu considered to be their priority welfare problems and their ideas for resolving them. In that time, I consulted with senior leaders and family members, young and old, all community organisations and service deliverers, as well as regional stakeholders and relevant government agencies (see Smith 2001).

Not surprisingly, Anangu concerns had changed little since 1991:

'Sit-down money' is killing our young people.

When the welfare money came in, it really killed the work; people started slacking off. Now young ones don't know work, they're welfare trained.

No more sit-down money, we gotta cut it out. Level 'm up, everyone gotta work.

Push all those petrol sniffers into work. Young people make everything good for family. I like them to be helping more with all the community work.

Out of the consultation process, the Mutitjulu Community Council and senior family leaders proposed a Community Participation and Partnership Agreement to be negotiated with the relevant Federal Government departments and key regional stakeholders. In 2001, it was a unique, innovative model; it came well before the Council of Australian Government (COAG) trials and before the Family Income Management pilot projects in Cape York.

The Mutitjulu Community Participation and Partnership Agreement proposed an integrated package aimed at directly attacking welfare dependence and social dysfunction in its real-life community context. Key components included the following.

- Community-wide coverage of all welfare recipients—what Anangu called the 'all-in' approach—with breaching implemented in partnership with Centrelink.
- A whole-of-community participation program based on Individual Participation Agreements that would require all welfare recipients to undertake some form of work selected from a menu of participation activities and training developed by the community.
- Tying receipt of Youth Allowance to school attendance and work participation.
- Providing intensive assistance and support to individuals to take up paid employment.
- Recognising the support role and social capital provided to families and children by older women, and creating mechanisms to ensure that welfare payments intended for the care of children were directed to the older women who invariably took care of them.
- Government agencies working alongside the community to rebuild local governance processes and provide governance capacity building to Anangu leaders and councillors to enable them to actively participate in, and manage, the implementation process.

The Mutitjulu Council proposed that the agreement should be further fleshed out and implemented in partnership with the Federal Government, FACS, Centrelink and ATSIC. Accordingly, it asked the government to:

- provide a delegation to a community officer under the *Social Security Act 1999* to enable the council (or other specific-purpose community organisations) to implement a whole-of-community approach to welfare reform
- support them in developing local Anangu breaching and enforcement rules and appeals procedures with Centrelink
- provide a consolidated block of welfare and related program funding, with a single reporting/acquittal package—what Anangu referred to as a 'one-bucket' funding strategy
- provide families with financial literacy and budgeting training, and with local banking services.

The community was not naive about the challenges for its side. Residents were adamant that they wanted a measured transition carried out in partnership with government, with sustained departmental facilitation on the ground.

Senior officers from the Federal Government visited the community and attended council meetings at which they assured local leaders that the government was listening to their proposal and would support them. That was the last the community heard of them.

What happened? Essentially, in 2001, the Federal Government and its departments walked away from Mutitjulu. Initially, the government departments involved argued that there needed to be further community consultation, and suggested that the community was in fact 'too dysfunctional' to participate in such a major reform process. (In fact, continuing consultation was an integral part of the proposed implementation process.)

In reality, the problem lay not in the community, but in Canberra. First, the key departments would not support an 'all-in' community model of welfare reform and would not support linking Youth Allowance with school attendance—even though these had been specifically requested by community members and their council. Second, Centrelink and FACS would not countenance an Indigenous community working with them to develop and implement locally relevant breaching rules. They also would not countenance a community organisation being provided with a delegation under the *Social Security Act* in order to do so ('Over my dead body,' declared one senior bureaucrat).

Third, entrenched interdepartmental turf wars in Canberra meant that the departments concerned were unable to negotiate a common position. As a result, the process inevitably became bogged down by strategic bureaucratic behaviour that led to inertia. Finally, the Federal Government was unable or unwilling to reform the chaotic state of its departmental program funding in order to streamline the pooled funding and grant-reporting arrangements that would have been required.

In 2001, the Mutitjulu community had called out in desperation to the Federal Government. It wanted decisive action, but it also wanted to be a full partner in action to address local welfare dependence and governance dysfunction. At that point, the government turned its back on the community.

As a result, it is arguable that significant responsibility for the horror of violence, abuse and despair that has since escalated at Mutitjulu can be laid fairly and squarely at the door of the Federal Government and its departments and, in more recent years, at the door of the NT Government as well.

In late June 2007, the Federal Government announced that Mutitjulu would be the first community into which it activated national emergency measures. It would do so unilaterally, not in collaboration. Ministers and some media commentators have argued that, late though it is, at least action is now being taken at Mutitjulu. Two critical elements of the community's earlier partnership proposal for welfare reform are, however, noticeably absent—namely, the implementation of a governance-building strategy right from the start, and the streamlining of related government program funding down to the community.

The new intervention policy

Clearly, we are at a watershed in terms of where the Federal Government is taking Indigenous affairs policy and practice. No-one would deny the depth of problems experienced by Indigenous families and communities in this country; Indigenous people themselves have been calling for decisive action on a whole range of social, economic and human rights issues for several decades now. After years of government failure to address deeply entrenched structural disadvantage, however, should we think that the outcomes of this hasty intervention will be any better?

The new policy approach will attempt substantial social engineering within Indigenous communities. The Federal Government appears to be undertaking another missionary phase in Indigenous affairs, one based on a well-intended desire to improve conditions for families and children, but unilaterally imposed by government using 'the full weight of its coercive power' (Scott 1998:5). The history of Indigenous affairs in Australia shows that coercion rarely leads to sustained positive outcomes. On the contrary, often it has led to unintended consequences that have exacerbated problems and created profound misery on the ground.

Since the announcement of the 'Howard–Brough–Pearson' new intervention policy, we have heard a barrage of opinion—much of it partisan and ideologically driven, with many bold assertions uninformed by empirical evidence. My concern here is not with the causal grounds for the Federal Government's action in the welfare arena, but with its logic and strategies for addressing the issues, predicated as they appear to be on a lack of analysis of why government policy has failed so badly to date, and on unproven assertions of a direct connection between the *Aboriginal Land Rights Act* permit system and child abuse. Unless these underlying issues are addressed, there is a real chance that the current intervention will simply repeat the debilitating mistakes of the past.

Implicit in the Federal Government's new intervention approach is an acknowledgment that its current whole-of-government policy has failed, even though that policy has been implemented only recently. Is this the case, and, if so, in what respects has it failed? Also, have there been any positive outcomes from that approach?

In 2002–03, COAG trials began operating in eight Indigenous sites across Australia, in a whole-of-government, partnership policy framework and with an overarching emphasis on shared responsibility. The aim of the trials was twofold: first, to build Indigenous community capacity to more effectively deliver services; and second, to strengthen the capacity of governments to work with each other in a coordinated way and deliver more streamlined funding to Indigenous communities. Important lessons for governments and communities can, and should, be derived from that practical experience. In a matter of one week, however, we seemed to go from a whole-of-government policy approach to one of coercion, in which the power of the State enforced collaboration.

To develop a more empirically informed consideration of these urgent matters, I want to describe some of the relevant research findings from a major project I have been involved with in the past four years.

The Indigenous Community Governance Project

The Indigenous Community Governance (ICG) Project is itself an innovative partnership between the Centre for Aboriginal Economic Policy Research (CAEPR) at The Australian National University and Reconciliation Australia. It is being carried out in collaboration with 11 Indigenous communities across Australia, with funding from the Australian Research Council and the Federal, NT and West Australian (WA) Governments.

The research is national in coverage and community focused. It covers a range of different types of 'communities' in remote, rural and urban locations. A team of multidisciplinary researchers has been working with the same community organisations, groups and leaders for the past three years.

The project is investigating the complex dimensions of how communities are governed—not only their cultural foundations and complex histories, but the financial, legislative and policy frameworks under which they operate—and how these impact on their effectiveness and legitimacy.

The methodology is rigorous and our research results are documented extensively on the CAEPR web site (see Hunt and Smith 2006, 2007; Smith 2005). Each researcher investigates the unique aspects of governance in the communities they are working with, and also provides extensive research data against a common project field manual that targets key governance issues and questions. The project has developed an innovative comparative analysis to identify more broadly relevant principles and common themes that appear to underlie Indigenous governance challenges and solutions across the communities.

The project is participatory and applied. Researchers work with community groups and organisations to explore best-practice solutions to their governance challenges. To assist that approach, the project is also currently working with Reconciliation Australia to develop a web-based tool kit of governance resources and diagnostic tools for use by Indigenous organisations and communities and agencies working with them. The project also aims to make the research count with governments. For that purpose, various policy, funding and program frameworks have been analysed and reported on.

The research is now starting to tell us about what works, what doesn't and why in Indigenous community governance in Australia. In particular, the evidence is consistently highlighting several conclusions that are directly relevant to the Federal Government's new intervention policy.

Project research implications for the new intervention policy

The ICG Project has thoroughly investigated and analysed the factors underlying poor governance arrangements in Indigenous communities. These are discussed in reports and case studies on the CAEPR web site. Given the current government and public focus on Indigenous dysfunction and failure, however, it is important to remember that Indigenous communities can be successful in establishing good governance and that in doing so they are securing important social, cultural and economic outcomes.

What is working

First, the research overwhelmingly confirms that the exercise of practically effective, culturally legitimate governance in Indigenous communities is critical to providing a foundation for addressing and sustaining their social wellbeing and economic development. In other words, good governance delivers a development dividend for Indigenous communities.

Second, lest we all succumb to the politics of despair about Indigenous Australia that seems to have hold of the nation at the moment, the research reports that amid the failures there are extraordinary successes in community governance.

Around the country, we are seeing Indigenous people in their organisations and communities working to address complex internal relationships and representation issues in order to develop legitimate governing arrangements that win the support of their members (for example, the West Arnhem Land Transitional Committee is developing an innovative organisational structure with a layered network of representation that will enable it to act regionally, but also recognise local community interests and decision making [Smith 2007]).

We are documenting Indigenous groups reassessing their cultural histories and geographies in order to promote greater legitimacy and accountability of leadership and decision making (for example, groups at Wadeye in the Northern Territory undertook an extensive community-wide reappraisal of the cultural underpinnings of their governance arrangements in order to create a more inclusive community council).

Project researchers have reported innovative governing structures being designed to suit changing contemporary conditions (for example, the Layhnapuy Resource Association represents the interests of a number of interrelated outstations across

East Arnhem Land and has recently restructured its governing board and management in order to better respond to changing government policy and economic opportunities for its member groups).

We are seeing direct links between the effectiveness of an organisation's governance arrangements and its ability to deliver sustained social and economic development outcomes (for example, Yarnteen Corporation in Newcastle has built up an outstanding governing board and management team who promote continuing governance training, professional development and youth mentoring. This has led to high credibility with the wider business community and investors, and has resulted in sustained success in enterprise development).

The ICG Project's research is also identifying a set of core 'design principles' that appears to underlie many of the different governance solutions on the ground. A particularly important principle is networked governance, which is applicable in remote, rural and urban communities. It is premised on a form of 'bottom-up' federalism with associated layers of power, roles and responsibilities (for example, the set of organisations and interrelated groups that now constitutes the Bunaba Corporation is a network designed to recognise the autonomy of particular groups and their economic interests, at the same time as sharing the benefits of collective representation and financial management). Models based on networked governance are seen in all the communities with which project's researchers are working.

Strong nodal leadership and succession planning are shown to make a significant contribution to the good governance of communities and organisations. Influential leaders become connecting points within networks to mobilise resources and opinions and get things done. Under their direction, the project has documented organisations undertaking the hard work of reforming their governance, creating workable rules and procedures and enforcing those in the complex inter-cultural environments in which they operate.

In particular, the research has documented innovative Indigenous processes of building practical governance capacity in the context of their daily work. When Indigenous people develop their own institutions rather than adopt externally created rules, their governance capacity and confidence appear to be significantly strengthened. In all the case studies, we are witnessing community groups and leaders using their cultural values and social relationships as assets to help them build stronger governance.

What isn't working

Many of the intractable social and economic problems confronting Indigenous Australians are, in significant part, a function of the mutually reinforcing institutional constraints and failure of governance within governments themselves. The ICG Project has documented institutional failings in policy, implementation strategies, funding frameworks, public-sector capacity and the system of fiscal federalism itself (see Westbury and Dillon 2006).

The way governments function directly affects Indigenous capacity to govern well and get things done in communities. In every case study, researchers are reporting that there is no single, whole-of-government policy approach; rather, there are several. Organisations and communities are routinely confronted with different whole-of-government policies and strategies from different departments and jurisdictions.

Departmental territorialism and inertia is rampant in Indigenous affairs. We have witnessed Indigenous initiatives to improve local governance undermined by the 'go-it-alone' attitude of particularly influential departments, which protect their niche program role and funding power and resist the efforts of other agencies to collaboratively develop program and funding coordination. The point was highlighted at one COAG trial meeting by a perceptive community leader, who asked the various departmental officers the question: 'Where is your *thamarrurr*?' He was one of the local leaders involved in the time-consuming, difficult task of getting the different clans to work together under a single regional council modelled on a traditional principle of *thamarrurr* ('coming together'). Why, he asked, couldn't governments work with each other, and why couldn't they get their departments to work together?

What hasn't been recognised—at least by governments—but what has been documented by the ICG Project and numerous reports and inquiries, is the extent to which government funding arrangements have exacerbated community and organisational dysfunction and poor governance. As Westbury and Dillon (2006) succinctly note, for Indigenous communities, 'accessing government program resources becomes a labyrinthine voyage through scores of separate programs and a sea of bureaucratic process'. This fundamentally diminishes the time, resources and capacity that community organisations can give to making their service delivery and governance more effective.

Government policy in the past 30 years has not succeeded in addressing this internal institutional failure. On the contrary, programs seem to be multiplying and grant funding and acquittal processes are becoming more onerous. In one community, at the time it began participating in a COAG trial, its representative organisation was managing 50 different buckets of government program funding. For a small community of approximately 2300 people, that in itself constituted a major administrative workload that diverted scarce human resources away from critical community governance and service issues. After three years of the trial, the same organisation was managing more than 90 different buckets of program money.

There continues to be, in Indigenous affairs, a fundamental disjunction between government policy goals and real implementation on the ground. This is compounded by a failure of engagement by governments at all levels. When governments introduced self-determination policies in the 1970s, they essentially vacated the field of community development and collaborative engagement on the ground. The result was a failure to keep up with international best practice in community development, which might have enabled a more sophisticated approach to the issues involved in the current intervention. The additional consequence has been a failure of governance capacity within an already overstretched bureaucracy reeling from one policy change after another.

A plethora of papers and reports has concluded that the institutional arrangements of fiscal federalism in Australia are fundamentally flawed and a key driver of Indigenous disadvantage, especially in remote regions. For example, the per capita allocation from Commonwealth transfers to local government in the Northern Territory makes up just more than $20 million of a $1 billion national pool of specific-purpose grants. The bizarre result is that the Northern Territory receives less in local government financial assistance than is notionally allocated for the population of Geelong in Victoria (Westbury and Dillon 2006).

The result in the Northern Territory, which covers more than one-sixth of the Australian landmass and has an Indigenous population experiencing high levels of socioeconomic disadvantage, has been to create huge backlogs in infrastructure and services in local communities. These are the very communities now being accused of not delivering much-needed basic services to children and families.

Infrastructure backlogs are not currently addressed by the Commonwealth Grants Commission (CGC), and the jurisdictional sovereignty of territory and state governments means they are not required to expend Commonwealth transfers on the Indigenous locations or service requirements against which 'disability factors' the transfers were initially assessed by the CGC (Smith 1992). As a result of the historical under-investment by governments in NT communities, CAEPR has recently estimated that to deliver on its intervention promise to spend whatever it takes to 'fix up' Indigenous communities in the Northern Territory, the Federal Government will need to allocate in the realm of $3–5 billion to achieve parity in the next five years in education, health, Community Development Employment Projects (CDEP) program transitions to work and housing alone.

We have entered a period of policy formulation in which Indigenous culture is pathologised by governments and many public commentators in much the same way as early missionaries regarded Indigenous culture as contaminating the ability of families and children to assimilate. Indigenous culture is portrayed almost as a virus, something that will undermine the effectiveness and accountability of organisations and their governance arrangements. Accordingly, policy and program solutions increasingly seek to quarantine culture to one side. The primary mode of departmental interaction with community organisations is one of managerial governance that focuses on compliance and grant acquittal. The lesson of history, however, is that Indigenous people will never leave their culture to one side; they will not be assimilated into being 'whitefellas' and their governance arrangements express cultural goals in addition to financial compliance and administrative effectiveness. Importantly, the ICG Project has documented examples of where Indigenous groups and organisations are using their cultural values, institutions and social relationships to positively support their collective efforts to rebuild their governing arrangements. In other words, cultural legitimacy can provide a powerful mechanism for accountability and effectiveness.

By and large, however, governments still do not recognise the positive developmental role of good governance, and their efforts to facilitate Indigenous governance capacity building at the local level remain ad hoc, uncoordinated, erratically funded, poorly implemented and are rarely followed up. The recommendations of numerous reports and inquiries on community governance and associated capacity building have not been implemented.

Taken together, these issues produce what Westbury and Dillon (2006) conclude is 'a fundamental failure of the nation state to govern effectively in Indigenous Affairs'. It also represents a fundamental failure of the Australian State to invest in Indigenous self-governance and related capacity, despite the mounting evidence that this can lead to significantly improved social and economic outcomes on the ground.

In many ways, an inevitable conclusion must be that the governance dysfunction within government represents at least half of the national emergency currently confronting Indigenous communities.

From coercion to collaboration?

Coercion as a policy instrument has limited developmental power for Indigenous families and communities; history has demonstrated that. Government ministers and bureaucrats often talk about the importance of developing policies and strategies on evidence-based research. The ICG Project is producing convincing comparative evidence that suggests that there are several strategies that will facilitate more effective, sustained outcomes.

First, taking genuine decision-making powers and control away from communities and organisations, and then handing them back later and expecting Indigenous people to assume 'ownership' of models and rules they have had no say in developing, will not work. In this respect at least, the ICG Project's research suggests that Noel Pearson is wrong. He has argued (Pearson 2007) that there are three policy phases to the Federal Government's decisive action: the first is unilateral intervention on the ground; the second is radical reform and innovation; the third is retreat by government and transfer of ownership to Indigenous organisations and leaders.

In fact, Indigenous self-governance and good governance lie at the very heart of positive development outcomes. Governments urgently need to provide enabling policy and legal frameworks, and integrated program guidelines, to actively promote Indigenous governance capacity and authority. Building Indigenous governance institutions and capacity should be built into any new interventions—right from the start.

Governments also need to urgently put some implementation backbone into the policy rhetoric of 'whole of government', especially in relation to funding. At the macro level, fundamental reforms to federal fiscal institutions need to be made, as they affect funding transfers to and expenditure by state and territory governments on services and programs for Indigenous people. These transfers must be allocated to the areas of substantial community need, on the bases of which they were initially determined by the CGC. Associated infrastructure/capital backlogs and cost shifting by governments to Indigenous local governments and small community organisations must be addressed at policy and institutional levels within government. Also, the CGC should be requested to include a new category that assesses Indigenous community infrastructure/capital needs (Westbury and Dillon 2006).

If we can have decisive action in Indigenous communities, presumably the same is possible within government. At a micro level, there is arguably an urgent need for the mandatory integration of program funding across departments that is relevant to community governance and capacity building. The stories presented at the beginning of this chapter and the case-study evidence of the ICG Project indicate that there are communities, organisations and leaders who want decisive action from government, but in partnership and with reform on both sides.

In conclusion, our case-study research clearly demonstrates that building governance institutions and capacity needs to be placed at the forefront of any proposed intervention from the very start, not as an afterthought. 'Governance building' should be made an integral part of every policy and its implementation on the ground. Simultaneously, the reform of governments' own governance dysfunction and bureaucratic capacity in Indigenous affairs has to be a fundamental component of any solution. Without these two parallel strategies, it is likely that the current 'decisive action' will exacerbate problems, not alleviate them.

Readers can access the CAEPR web site at <http://www.anu.edu.au/caepr/>

References

Adlam, N. and Gartrell, A. 2007, 'Martial law—Howard mobilises cops, military as he declares "national emergency" in NT communities', *NT News*, Friday 22 June 2007, Darwin, Northern Territory.

Evans, L., Appo, H. and Smith, D. E. 2006, Community development practices and principles in the development of the West Central Arnhem Regional Authority, Unpublished discussion paper, Department of Local Government, Housing and Sport, Darwin, Northern Territory.

Hunt, J. and Smith, D. E. 2006, *The Indigenous Community Governance Project. Preliminary research findings*, CAEPR Working Paper 31, Centre for Aboriginal Economic Policy Research, The Australian National University, Canberra.

Hunt, J. and Smith, D. E. 2007, *The Indigenous Community Governance Project. Phase two research findings*, CAEPR Working Paper 36, Centre for Aboriginal Economic Policy Research, The Australian National University, Canberra.

Ngaanyatjarra, Pitjantjatjara Yankunytjatjara Women's Council 1991, Looking after children grandmothers' way, Unpublished report to the Child Protection Policy and Planning Unit, Government of South Australia, Adelaide.

Pearson, N. 2007, 'Three phases of the rescue operation', *The Weekend Australian*, 23–24 June 2007, p. 22.

Scott, J. C. 1998, *Seeing Like a State: How certain schemes to improve the human condition have failed*, Yale University Press, New Haven.

Smith, D. E. 1992, *An analysis of the Aboriginal component of Commonwealth fiscal flows to the Northern Territory*, CAEPR Discussion Paper 29, Centre for Aboriginal Economic Policy Research, The Australian National University, Canberra.

Smith, D. E. 2001, *Community Participation Agreements: a model for welfare reform from community-based research*, CAEPR Discussion Paper 223, Centre for Aboriginal Economic Policy Research, The Australian National University, Canberra.

Smith, D. E. 2005, *Researching Australian Indigenous governance: a methodological and conceptual framework*, CAEPR Working Paper 29, Centre for Aboriginal Economic Policy Research, The Australian National University, Canberra.

Smith D. E. 2007, 'Networked governance: issues of process, policy and power in a West Arnhem Land regional initiative', *Ngyia Talk the Law*, Journal of the Jumbunna Centre, University of Technology, Sydney.

Westbury, N. and Dillon, M. 2006, The institutional underpinnings of Indigenous disadvantage: the failed state within, Unpublished paper, Canberra.

ENDNOTES

[1] For more information on the bilateral agreement, the process and history of the NT local government regionalisation in West Arnhem Land, see Smith (2005, 2007).

10. The PPP phenomenon: performance and governance insights

Graeme Hodge and Carsten Greve

Introduction

Public–private partnerships (PPPs) have now attracted wide interest around the world. Few people, however, agree on what a PPP really is. While they are hailed as a new collaborative way to get the best of both sectors, the definition of PPPs remains cloudy, and performance assessments are hotly disputed. This chapter presents an academic examination of this form of collaboration and looks at the global evidence of performance. It articulates just what is new in Australia's PPPs and suggests governance reforms are needed in order to overcome the legitimacy concerns of citizens and parliaments.

The public–private debate has been an important thread in history, and there has always been some degree of public-sector and private-sector cooperation (Wettenhall 2003, 2005). The fact that 82 per cent of the 197 vessels in Sir Francis Drake's fleet, which successfully conquered the Spanish Armada in 1588, were private contractors to the Admiralty,[1] Australia's long history of using private contractors for construction in huge infrastructure projects such as the Snowy Mountains Hydro-Electric Scheme, and the century-long partnership between the commercial company Falck (at one stage a part of the global company Group 4 Securicor) and the Danish public sector to deliver emergency services all attest to this. Other public–private cooperative ventures have included the successful Sydney Olympic Games and the construction of Europe's Channel Tunnel.

Viewing these arrangements as cooperative forms of partnership, however, brings with it good and bad news. On the one hand, it is true, for example, that privateer shipping underpinned the growth and dominance of the British global economic empire, and that private contracting saw the dream of the Channel Tunnel achieved. On the other hand, privateer shipping was a 'feeble and corrupt system' in which leading officials promoted partnership ventures intent on plunder, while the fragile financial position of the Channel Tunnel has now left citizens, governments and private investors with huge uncertainties. Little wonder, then, that arguments about efficiency, service quality and accountability in the two sectors have been well rehearsed.

The PPP pedigree

Scholars now view PPPs as a tool of governance, or else a 'language game' (Teisman and Klijn 2001, 2002). Turning first to partnerships as 'governance', two dimensions appear to be relevant: first, the financial arrangements between public and private actors; and second, the tightness of organisational linkages between the two actors (Hodge and Greve 2007). Formally, the Dutch public-management scholars van Ham and Koppenjan (2001:598) define a PPP through an institutional lens as 'co-operation of some sort of durability between public and private actors in which they jointly develop products and services and share risks, costs and resources which are connected with these products'. This definition emphasises durable cooperation and an equal sharing of risks and rewards in producing something jointly. This emphasis differs from the PPP notion regarding infrastructure projects, including build–own–transfer (BOT), build–own–operate–transfer (BOOT), as well as so-called sale-and-lease-back arrangements in which local governments sell their buildings and then rent them back from a financial organisation on a 20 or 30-year contract. Many other interpretations of PPPs as financial and organisational arrangements are also possible, involving at least five families of arrangements:[2]

- institutional cooperation for joint production and risk sharing—for example, the Netherlands Port Authority (van Ham and Koppenjan 2001, 2002; Klijn and Teisman 2005)
- long-term infrastructure contracts, which emphasise tight specification of outputs in long-term legal contracts—as exemplified in the United Kingdom (Osborne 2001b; Savas 2000; Berg et al. 2002; Perrot and Chatelus 2000; Ghobadian et al. 2004; Grimsey and Lewis 2004)
- public-policy networks, in which loose stakeholder relationships are emphasised (Vaillancourt Rosenau 2000)
- civil-society and community development, in which the partnership symbolism is adopted for cultural change, as in Hungary and Europe (Osborne 2001a)
- urban renewal and downtown economic development—where, in the United States, a portfolio of local economic development and urban regrowth measures is pursued (Osborne 2001a; Bovaird 2004).

These PPP families cover a wide array of different governance types and are clearly more than just the private finance initiative (PFI) experience of the United Kingdom or the current infrastructure-contracting practices of Australia.

The alternative view of PPPs is as a language game. Linder (1999) noted the 'multiple grammars' of PPPs, with governments avoiding the terms 'privatisation' or 'contracting out' in favour of speaking about 'partnerships'. This word presents a warmer and friendlier proposition than previous, more pejorative terms. It has also provided public managers with an opportunity to adopt a new buzz word or even reframe existing policies under a catchier name.

The language question is an issue of some significance, as it frames our local understanding of partnerships. Of course, language games are at the heart of all public-policy debates. Such language games in the PPP arena can, however, lead to the amusing situation in which two governments on opposite sides of the globe see PFI-type PPPs in opposite ways. Look, for example, at the long-term infrastructure-contract family of PPPs. In Victoria, Australia, such PPPs are argued as being nothing to do with privatisation and are vigorously separated from this policy. In the United Kingdom, however, the Department of Treasury and Finance sees the two as inherently connected and speaks of PPPs as being directly equivalent to privatisation (HM Treasury 2003). In other words, the same PPP phenomenon is being framed in two opposite ways for local political gain.

Another example of this language game is the very label 'partnership' for large private finance contracts. This is nonsense. Infrastructure finance deals are no more partnerships than the contract made when citizens take out a house mortgage with their local bank. Public policy language games are again being used to suit local political objectives and obscure meanings rather than to clarify and sharpen our understanding of the partnership phenomenon.

So PPPs are a broad church of many families, and it is not a simple matter to judge whether they are the next chapter in the privatisation story, another promise in our continuing attempts to better define and measure public-sector service performance,[3] a renewed support scheme for boosting business in difficult times, or a language game camouflaging the next frontier of conquering transaction merchants, legal advisors and bankers pursuing fat commissions.

Evaluating PPP performance

Several Australian states have followed the United Kingdom and, led by Victoria, have proceeded down the road of defining PPPs in terms of the PFI—that is, as a business relationship, underpinned by a long-term contract, often with private financing, for the delivery of maintenance and the operation of infrastructure and services,[4] involving large cash flows, the capacity to shift risks and rewards and potential for joint decision making.

How might we evaluate this PPP family member? There have been no meta-analyses or statistical reviews of PPP performance to date. The complexity of evaluating infrastructure arrangements is compounded by the observation that there is a wide variety of contractual and institutional options, the adoption of either public or private up-front finance and potential application across many policy areas such as transport, water, prisons, education, social and emergency services. Also critical here is the observation that we all come to such an evaluation with our own individual criteria for assessment.[5] Those involved directly in the financial transactions, not surprisingly, often speak highly of them. Of more relevance here, however, is our evaluation of PPPs against the stated objectives of PPP delivery by governments and broader policy promises being made to citizens. So, should we look at policy rhetoric, the legal contract or historical outcomes to discern partnership success (Hodge 2004b)? These outcomes vary from the weakest evidence of success at the policy rhetoric end to the strongest at the historical outcomes end.

There has been much rhetorical assessment, including colourful salesmanship and praise on the one hand, and stinging criticism on the other. PPPs are thus characterised in terms of 'yet again screwing the taxpayer', with private sponsors as 'evil bandits running away with all the loot' and as 'Problem, Problem, Problem' (Hodge and Greve 2007). The other side of the rhetoric has seen PPPs as a 'marriage made in heaven' with continued loud advocacy. Little, however, is resolved. While some analyses of contract arrangements are now available, the jury is still out given the long-term nature of these contracts.[6] How, then, have PFI-type PPPs performed according to the historical evidence of outcomes?

We ought to base our analysis on the underlying objectives of PPPs. Under John Major's government in the United Kingdom, the initial rationale was to get around formal public-sector debt levels. Private financing promised a way to provide infrastructure without increasing the public-sector borrowing ratio (PSBR). This was followed by the promise that PPPs would reduce pressure on public-sector budgets. Neither the availability of off-budget financing nor avoiding accountability for capital funding are, however, particularly valid criteria on which to evaluate PPPs. A mechanism though which governments can turn a large, one-off capital expenditure into a series of smaller, annualised expenditures has simply been provided. Like any domestic credit card or mortgage arrangement, however, this does not reduce pressure on the family budget, because all debts must be repaid in the end.[7]

The third promise of PPPs—and one with more bite to it—is that this delivery mechanism provides better value for money for taxpayers. This is a policy promise worthy of examination. Added to these promises was the implicit ethos of better accountability, improved business confidence, better on-time and on-budget delivery, as well as greater innovation. What is evident, then, is that there have been eight separate justifications for PPPs, which have altered over time and even today remain somewhat slippery.

What does the more serious evidence of the veracity of these claims say? There is a wide canvas, so we will focus only on a small number of representative evaluation findings. Looking now at the third of these eight promises—the claim of better value for money—how does the international evidence stack up?

Evidence of value for money

Early prominent estimates of efficiencies to be gained through PPPs included cost-savings figures of 17 per cent from Arthur Anderson and LSE Enterprise in their analysis of 29 business cases, 10–20 per cent based on seven empirical cases from the National Audit Office (2000) and 10–30 per cent (Shepherd 2000). Savings in these business cases were due mainly to the calculus of risk transfers assumed from the public to the private sector. The later analysis of Pollitt (2002) also summarised the findings of the National Audit Office and showed that in a sample of 10 major PFI case evaluations undertaken, the best deal was probably obtained in every case, and good value for money was probably achieved in eight of the 10 cases.

At the other extreme, the early evidence on (PFI) PPP effectiveness is not as pretty. From the United Kingdom, authors such as Pollock et al. (2002) and Shaoul (2004) have been highly critical of PFI arrangements across a wide range of services, including roads, hospitals and rail-transport infrastructure. Likewise, Monbiot (2002) launched a very public attack through the *Guardian* newspaper, labelling PPPs as 'public fraud and false accounting…commissioned and directed by the Treasury'. US commentators such as Bloomfield et al. (1998) found a Massachusetts correctional facility was 7.4 per cent more expensive through lease purchase financing than with conventional financing, with the real costs and risks camouflaged from the public. In Europe, Greve (2003) characterised the Farum PPP as 'the most spectacular scandal in the history of Danish Public Administration', resulting in raised taxes for the citizens of Farum, higher debt for its local government and a former mayor on trial in the courts. Australian PPP analyses such as Walker and Con Walker (2000) saw off-balance-sheet PPP infrastructure financing deals as 'misleading accounting trickery', which eroded accountability to parliament and to the public. In support, they cited private project consortium real rates of return, which were 10 times those expected for the public for the proposed metropolitan Sydney and Mascot Airport and Sydney's M2 Motorway (Walker and Con Walker 2000:204).[8]

Evidence continues to be mixed. At the positive end, Pollitt (2005) has shown not only the popularity of PFI—with the UK Government typically raising some 15–20 per cent of its capital budget each year through this mechanism[9] —but, through five case studies, its empirical success, notwithstanding the lengthy and costly bidding process among a small number of bidders and high-profile problems with individual PFI projects. He argues that compared with what might have happened under conventional public procurement, projects under PFI are now 'delivered on time and to budget a significantly higher percentage of the time', with construction risks 'generally transferred successfully' and with 'considerable design innovation'. Importantly, while Pollitt acknowledges that it is possible that many of the assumed benefits of PFI projects are hypothetically available through conventional procurement, the reality is that these would not be achieved without the learning and leverage provided through the PFI initiative.

Likewise, Mott Macdonald (2002) and the National Audit Office (2003) report PPPs as being delivered on time far more often than traditional infrastructure provision arrangements.[10] They found, impressively, that whereas traditional 'public' infrastructure provision arrangements were on time and on budget 30 per cent and 27 per cent of the time, PFI-type partnerships were on time and on budget 76 per cent and 78 per cent of the time, respectively. In Australia meanwhile, the Audit Office of New South Wales found 'persuasive' the business case for two PFI contracts to build 19 schools, at between 7 to 23 per cent cheaper than the traditional alternative (Auditor-General of New South Wales 2006). The Allen Consulting Group (2007), in a project funded by Australia's infrastructure suppliers, reported PPPs as being an 11 per cent cheaper alternative to traditional projects based on a sample of 54 projects.

In striking contrast is Shaoul's evidence from the United Kingdom. Countering the government's rationale, itself described as an 'ideological morass', she presents a litany of failed PFI project examples and reveals a value-for-money appraisal methodology biased in favour of policy expansion, a pitiful availability of information needed for project evaluation and scrutiny and projects in which the value-for-money case rested almost entirely on risk transfer but for which, strangely, the amount of risk transferred was almost exactly what was needed to tip the balance in favour of undertaking the PFI mechanism. Added to this apparent manipulation of the public sector comparator (PSC) process were the observations that in hospitals and schools 'the PFI tail wags the planning dog' with projects changed to make them 'more PFI-able', highly profitable investments being engineered for private companies with 'a post tax return on shareholders' funds of 86 per cent', several refinancing scandals and conspicuously unsuccessful IT projects and risk-transfer arrangements that in reality meant that risks had not been transferred to the private sector at all but had been borne by the public. Not surprisingly, Shaoul (2005) concludes that at best, PFI has turned out to be very expensive with, moreover, a lack of accountability leading to difficulty in learning from past experiences. Partnerships, in her view, are 'policies that enrich the few at the expense of the majority and for which no democratic mandate can be secured'.

Added to this criticism is the first peer review of the impressive on-time and on-budget figures reported by Mott Macdonald (2002). The review of Pollock et al. (2007) was unequivocal in its judgment of these figures, stating 'there is no evidence to support the Treasury cost and time overrun claims of improved efficiency in PFI'. The estimates being quoted were 'not evidence based but biased to favor PFI' and 'only one study compares PFI procurement performance, and all claims based on [this] are misleading'.

Other evidence lies between these extremes. Boardman et al. (2005), for instance, noted the difficulty of capturing transaction costs in any comparison of partnership and traditional project delivery and catalogued 76 major North American PPP projects. They noted that less than half included a significant private financing role. They presented five transport, water provision and waste projects, showcasing a series of 'imperfect' partnership projects with high complexity, high asset specificity, a lack of public-sector contract management skills and a tendency for governments to be unwilling to 'pull the pin' on projects once under way. They point particularly to private entities being 'adept at making sure, one way or another, that they are fully compensated for risk-taking', and to strategic behaviour such as declaring bankruptcy (or threatening to) in order to avoid large losses. There are clear tensions for governments here, having to hold their nerve and watch commercial failures materialise when risks are borne by the private sector, despite their yearning to be viewed as successfully governing a growing and vibrant market.

Similarly, English (2005) documents the failure of the Latrobe Regional Hospital case in Victoria and provides a reminder of the importance and the difficulty of value-for-money estimates. A 20-year BOO project, this arrangement failed only two years into the contract due to a commercial failure to understand the case-mix funding model as well as because of ineligibility for additional top-up funding. Importantly, English also notes that amid the appearance of full disclosure by the state government, crucial documentation in terms of PSC calculation and financial arrangements underpinning the PPPs was withheld from citizens, even after freedom-of-information requests. Imperfect PPP arrangements, indeed. The Auditor-General's line in reviewing this situation was also interesting—apparently seeing this case not only as a financial failure of the private hospital, but as a governance failure by government. English shows that the government had not behaved as an intelligent and informed buyer. It had accepted an unsustainable price bid in the first place, had not undertaken any comparative analysis to benchmark public provision and had not recognised that the government was unable, in reality, to transfer the social responsibility of hospital provision.[11]

Hodge (2005) listed 48 Australasian projects and observed that while commercial risks could have been largely well managed, the same success could not be claimed for the governance dimension. Of real importance here was evidence from eight PPP case studies in Victoria examined by Fitzgerald (2004). Two crucial observations were made.

First, the superiority of the economic-partnership mode over traditional delivery mechanisms was dependent on the discount rate adopted in the analysis. Indeed, opposite conclusions were reached when using an 8.65 per cent discount rate at one extreme (leading to the conclusion that the PPP mechanism was 9 per cent cheaper than traditional delivery) compared with an evaluation adopting a 5.7

per cent discount rate (where the PPP mechanism was apparently 6 per cent more expensive).

Second, Hodge (2005) also made the point that government had clearly moved from its traditional stewardship role to a louder policy-advocacy role. As a consequence of this, we might reflect that government now finds itself in the middle of multiple conflicts of interest, acting in the roles of policy advocate, economic developer, steward for public funds, elected representative for decision making, regulator of the contract life, commercial signatory to the contract and planner. Far more debate is now needed to discuss the optimum ways in which long-term public interests can best be protected and nurtured in the light of experience, particularly noting citizen concerns about low PPP transparency and high deal complexity as well as criticism of lack of competition in these deals.[12] In other words, in addition to scepticism about the value for money provided by PPPs, their governance seems to have been a weakness to date.

Boardman et al. (2005) from North America and Hodge (2005) from Australia conclude independently that 'caveat emptor' is the most appropriate philosophy for governments to take as we move forward with infrastructure PPPs. Learning from the global empirical experience counters the notion that 'all the evidence that I have ever read on PPPs has been positive', as recently argued by one Australasian state government minister advocating billions of more dollars in partnership investments.

Overall, it would be fair to observe that citizens have been somewhat sceptical of the political promises made for PFI-type PPPs.[13] This is hardly surprising. History provides us with plenty of examples of governments ideologically bent on applying the latest fashionable policy prescription when neither was the patient ill, nor the policy at all effective. Moreover, a range of examples, from supplying electricity in Manila[14] and the London Underground rail-transport debacle[15] to a similar recent partnership farce with Sydney's Cross-City Tunnel (Davies and Moore 2005), shows that government reforms undertaken in the name of 'partnership' can easily go wrong for a host of reasons.

As well as this evidence for and against PPPs, the question of the counterfactual is also crucial here. On the one hand, the question of the exact 'alternative' against which private finance schemes are assessed is often left cloudy. We are left uncertain about whether the alternative is the old public works department with its in-house team is assumed, or the use of competitive tendering arrangements for private contactors (already in regular use in many jurisdictions), or some other public, private or mixed arrangement. The precise details of financing are also usually unclear. On the other hand, historical empirical experience also reminds us that the London Underground (under public ownership) has had a history of completing investment projects over budget and late with, for instance, line upgrades for the Jubilee Line six years late and

30 per cent over budget, and an analysis of some 250 projects by London Underground between 1997 and 2000 revealing cost overruns averaging 20 per cent.

What might we make of all this? It seems, overall, that the economic and financial benefits of PPPs are still subject to debate and, hence, considerable uncertainty.

We noted earlier that our evaluation should include an assessment of PPP governance. There is much that might be discussed here, but before we contemplate this arena, we ought first to articulate just what is, if anything, new with Australia's trend towards PFI-type PPP arrangements.

What is new with Australia's PPPs?

In terms of providing essential public infrastructure or services through history, there is much in today's debates that is not new. Governments have always made sensitive decisions resulting in the provision of essential large-scale public infrastructure. Such decisions have often had huge, long-term financial implications. Likewise, governments have for many years employed private contractors to undertake works and services, and competitive bidding for construction contracts by private companies has been around now for decades. The PPP phenomenon ought not therefore be misconstrued as a public versus private debate or a debate about the merits of infrastructure provision. We have centuries of experience accumulated in both of these arenas, although too often this point goes unacknowledged.

There do, however, appear to be three elements that are new in Australia's PFI model of partnership:

- the preferential use of private finance arrangements
- the highly complex contractualisation of 'bundled' infrastructure arrangements
- altered governance and accountability assumptions.

Importantly, the first two new aspects of infrastructure provision—those of private finance and increased contractual complexity—have major implications for the third: governance and accountability arrangements. How well, then, do PPPs perform on these dimensions?

Governance evidence

The availability of private finance for major infrastructure projects has essentially given governments a new capacity to use a 'mega credit card' with which to sign up to infrastructure deals. These deals can be consummated through the development of large legal contracts in which projects are purchased, as if 'off the shelf'. The political incentives for government have been high: quicker promised delivery of infrastructure and more positive relationships with finance and construction businesses. These incentives have also been closely aligned with incentives for the finance industry in terms of continued business transactions, new financial deals and perhaps even policy influence and project selection priority. Each of these three dimensions deserves careful deliberation in terms of governance. For each, we also should ask what the implications are in terms of democratic legitimacy.

Preference for private finance

While in concept PPPs are not strictly dependent on the provision of private finance, the reality in Australia is that in leading jurisdictions such as Victoria, PPP activities rely almost completely on the provision of initial private finance. As we noted extensively above, however, private finance arrangements appear to come at a premium for the life of the project, and the veracity of the claim that PPPs lead to better value for money for citizens is, at best, highly contestable. In addition to the international evidence of value for money, Victoria's Fitzgerald Review estimated that Victoria's citizens had probably already paid about $A350 million more than needed for the eight Victorian projects (totalling $2.7 billion) it reviewed. Limited transparency and complex adjustment formulae for partnership financial arrangements do not give citizens confidence in the arrangements when, despite the rhetoric of risk sharing with private financing, a significant financial role for government is nevertheless often the reality.

To concerns about value for money and risks can be added the criticism that in the United Kingdom the PSC has been manipulated and planning processes have been reshaped to ensure that projects were 'more PFI-able' to access capital funds. The implications for democratic legitimacy of such matters are profound.

Complexity

The second important characteristic of Australia's PPPs has been the complexity of partnership contract deals. Of course, greater complexity was introduced through more adventurous project-management mechanisms through the 1990s before PPPs. The need for extensive legal and other contractual documentation for all financial flows and relationships between multiple parties alone is, however, a direct characteristic of the partnership phenomenon (Evans and Bowman 2005).

Complexity, however, is not simply a matter of narrow legal project concerns. It has been rare to find members of parliamentary committees who have themselves personally understood the deals being done. In states such as Victoria, there are not even any parliamentary committees overseeing such infrastructure deals. Worryingly, ministers appear to have been supporting these deals on trust. Citizens also cannot get a clear picture of their worth underneath either the veil of complexity or the cloak of 'commercial in confidence'. To date, few independent parliamentary-level reviews have been able to break through this veil. A further factor here is the need for the State to have the administrative and the intellectual capacity to understand these deals, to monitor them as they operate and to manage them as they evolve with time.

Perhaps the real issue in terms of democratic legitimacy is not the matter of complexity itself, but how complexity is handled through political and democratic processes. Public-policy decision making in government by its nature deals with multiple complex issues ranging from stem-cell research and IT privacy to intricate matters of national economic and financial importance. The real question here is whether complexity is addressed by ensuring that improved accessibility mechanisms for citizens are created or, alternatively, whether what is created is a shield behind which governments can shelter and avoid accountability. Media reports that the Victorian Government delayed numerous requests for information on PPPs that could have damaged its re-election prospects certainly do not sit well with claims that PPP arrangements are sufficiently transparent to assure legitimacy (Dowling 2006; Tomazin 2006).

Accountability and governance arrangements

PPPs encompass different accountability and governance arrangements compared with traditional procurement—indeed, these arrangements are one of the claimed advantages of this provision method. Interlinked financial incentives across a consortium of players, the sharing of risks through carefully contractualised legal relationships and more flexible decision-making processes between executive government and service providers all feature as improvements on traditional procurement arrangements. Moreover, the progressive contractualisation of the State's services and activities has been accompanied by the general assumption of increased accountability in all its forms, although this has rarely been tested. While contractualisation could have increased managerial accountability, it could have been at the expense of reduced public accountability in its various forms.

Also, while we have instituted a 'regulatory state' of independent regulators, ombudsmen and audit review bodies in order to disperse power away from political quarters after the privatisation of state businesses, this has not yet occurred with PPP deals. They have continued to be essentially two-way government–business deals rather than also involving the community or any other independent accountability body to protect the public's interests. They have also been handled on a case-by-case basis, by the government itself, in the face of multiple conflicts of interest. The potential for the interests of the advocating government and business partners to dominate the public interest is palpable here. Indeed, early drafts of Victoria's PPP guideline materials did not even mention the 'public interest' notion and treated government solely as if it were a contractual partner in a commercial deal. This is reminiscent of past centuries.[16]

Clearly, communities need far more discussion and debate about how we might better ensure that the public interest is met through PPP deals, as well as meeting the needs of the contracting parties. To the extent that new infrastructure contract-delivery arrangements have reduced existing accountability arrangements and altered longstanding governance assumptions without democratic debate, new partnership arrangements lack legitimacy (Hodge 2006).

Are such concerns just an academic obsession with an imperfect world? Three recent Australian parliamentary inquiries suggest that such concerns about PPP governance are justified and have profound implications.

Parliamentary inquiry findings

The findings of two recent high-level PPP reviews in New South Wales and Victoria[17] are striking. First, some 35 of the 46 recommendations of these two reports relate to these three governance concerns—that is, private finance preference, financial complexity, and accountability and governance matters. In other words, some 76 per cent of the changes recommended by our recent parliamentary committees have concerned these issues of governance. Second, the largest two categories of these recommendations dealt with PPP accountability and governance, and the implications of the private finance preference. Third, there is a remarkable consistency between the tone of recommendations made by the committees and the concerns expressed in this chapter. Examples of inquiry recommendations illustrating this point include recommendations for three-page summaries of contract deals and value-for-money reports, better post-implementation evaluations and audits, stronger parliamentary oversight, more precise definition of the traditional options considered and improved knowledge of discount rates.

Crucially, the very existence of these parliamentary inquiries (as well as the additional parliamentary inquiry into Sydney's Cross-City Tunnel project) is a testament to the degree to which the current legitimacy of Australian PPPs is questionable. Discussions about the legitimacy of PPPs have also moved from the cabinet table and banking boardrooms into the supermarkets and the homes of citizens through the daily media. In terms of taxpayers' interests, Tomazin (2006), for instance, stated that 'State Government secrecy surrounding billions of dollars' worth of projects done in partnership with the private sector means Victorians have no idea whether they provide value for money'. Moreover, Tomazin was concerned with 'the lock-in effect of long-term contracts [which] might have an effect on the decision making capacity of future governments'. Furthermore, traditional ministerial accountability mechanisms failed palpably when the premier and ministers of the NSW Government refused to attend the Cross City Tunnel Parliamentary Committee to explain their perspectives.[18] The illegitimacy of one government being happy to sign up the next dozen governments to multi-billion-dollar contract payments with subsequent elected representatives then not participating in a fundamental public-accountability mechanism to explain decisions marks an all-time low in our traditional democratic polity. Indeed, the fact that a significant amount of performance material was omitted from the final inquiry document in Victoria (if we believe leaks reported in the daily newspaper at the time; Tomazin 2006) suggests that there continues to be much need for legitimacy-based reforms to be instituted. The omitted information on the specific performance of PPPs in Victoria appears to have been most embarrassing for the Kennett–Stockdale state government and its ministers and the subsequent Bracks–Brumby state government. It could even be that a coalition of political interests and business interests has existed against the interests of truthful revelations to citizens.

Such sinister logic aside, there nonetheless continues to be an obvious broader confluence of interests between political interests—enjoying better party funding for elections, potentially earlier delivery of big infrastructure projects and other parties to use as scapegoats should anything go awry—and the private interests of financiers, consulting firms, advisors and infrastructure companies. This suggests that PPPs could well continue for some time yet. Having said this, the future legitimacy of PPPs will depend on the ways in which the partnership phenomenon can be reformed and these current value-for-money and governance deficits overcome.

Conclusions

The partnership ideal has a long historical pedigree. Since partnerships have always come with good and bad news, care is, however, needed in their evaluation. All assessments need to be reported, not just those results supporting one's own views. There is a huge diversity in PPP approaches around the globe today. The contemporary phenomenon of private finance dominated partnership arrangements in Australia is one important family group.

Multiple goals have been claimed for long-term infrastructure contract-type PPPs. Looking simply at the question of value for money, there is a wide range of mixed evidence. This has gone largely unacknowledged to date. In other words, there is little doubt in terms of successes and failures that some of the glowing policy promises of PPPs have been delivered. Equally, however, evaluations of such arrangements have provided contradictory evidence of value-for-money effectiveness. A further concern surrounds PPPs in terms of governance failures. Contracts can shield governments from accountability rather than enhancing it. Also, treasuries of advocating governments act with multiple conflicts of interest and are free of any independent regulator charged with protecting the public's interest. As a consequence, Australian PPPs currently lack legitimacy.

These findings are important in the midst of ideological blind spots being experienced by many PPP advocates, such as central treasury departments, who seem more intent on policy advocacy than on questions of stewardship. Governments ought operate more often with a philosophy of caveat emptor, and need now to address the significant governance shortfalls identified. PPPs promise much. Careful evaluation of who gets the biggest rewards from these schemes is, however, now needed to ensure that governments maintain their intelligence on policy effectiveness.

References

Allen Consulting Group 2007, *Performance of PPPs and Traditional Procurement in Australia*, Final Report to Infrastructure Partnerships Australia, 30 November 2007.

Arthur Anderson and LSE Enterprise 2000, *Value for Money Drivers in the Private Finance Initiative*, UK Treasury Task Force, London.

Auditor-General of New South Wales 2006, *The New Schools Privately Financed Project*, Auditor-General's Report Performance Audit, March, Sydney.

Berg, Sanford, Pollitt, Michael and Tsuji, Masatsugu (eds) 2002, *Private Initiatives in Infrastructure: Priorities, incentives and performance*, Edward Elgar, Aldershot.

Bloomfield, Pamela, Westerling, David and Carey, Robert 1998, 'Innovation and risks in a public–private partnership: financing and construction of a capital project in Massachusetts', *Public Productivity and Review*, vol. 21, no. 4, pp. 460–71.

Boardman, Anthony, Poschmann, Finn and Vining, Aidan 2005, 'North American infrastructure P3s: examples and lessons learned', in Graeme Hodge and Carsten Greve (eds), *The Challenge of Public–Private Partnerships: Learning from international experience*, Edward Elgar, Cheltenham, pp. 162–89.

Bovaird, Tony 2004, 'Public–private partnerships in Western Europe and the US: new growths from old roots', in Abby Ghobadian, David Gallear, Nicholas O'Regan and Howard Viney, *Public–Private Partnerships: Policy and experience*, London, pp. 221–50.

Davies, Anne and Moore, Matthew 2005, 'Cross City Tunnel deal: the whole bloody thing will be made public', *Sydney Morning Herald*, 19 October.

Department of Treasury and Finance 2001, *Partnerships Victoria: Risk allocation and contractual issues*, State Government of Victoria, Melbourne.

Dowling, Jason 2006, 'Bracks' secret state', *Age*, 24 September.

The Economist 2002, 'Enron-on-Thames: Railtrack and British public finance', *The Economist*, 30 March.

Edwards, Pam, Shaoul, Jean, Stafford, Anne and Arblaster, Lorna 2004, *Evaluating the Operation of PFI in Roads and Hospitals*, Certified Accountants Education Trust, London.

English, Linda 2005, 'Using public–private partnerships to deliver social infrastructure: the Australian experience', in Graeme Hodge and Carsten Greve (eds), *The Challenge of Public–Private Partnerships: Learning from international experience*, Edward Elgar, Cheltenham, pp. 290–304.

Evans, Joanne and Bowman, Diana 2005, 'Getting the contract right', in Graeme Hodge and Carsten Greve (eds), *The Challenge of Public–Private Partnerships: Learning from international experience*, Edward Elgar, Cheltenham, pp. 62–80.

Fitzgerald, Peter 2004, *Review of Partnerships Victoria Provided Infrastructure*, Growth Solutions Group, Melbourne.

Greve, Carsten 2003, When public–private partnerships fail: the extreme case of the NPM-inspired local government of Farum in Denmark, Paper for EGPA Conference, 3–6 September, Oerias, Portugal.

Ghobadian, Abby, Gallear, David, O'Regan, Nicholas and Viney, Howard 2004, *Public–Private Partnerships: Policy and experience*, London.

Grimsey, Darren and Lewis, Mervyn 2004, *Public–Private Partnerships: The worldwide revolution in infrastructure provision and project finance*, Edward Elgar, Cheltenham.

HM Treasury 2003, *PFI: Meeting the investment challenge*, The Stationery Office, London.

Hodge, Graeme 2004a, 'Conclusion', in Graeme Hodge, Valerie Sands, David Haywood and David Scott (eds), *Power Progress: An audit of Australia's electricity reform experiment*, Australian Scholarly Publishing, Melbourne.

Hodge, Graeme 2004b, 'Risks in public–private partnerships: shifting, sharing or shirking?', *Asia Pacific Journal of Public Administration*, vol. 26, no. 2, pp. 157–79.

Hodge, Graeme 2004c, 'The risky business of public–private partnerships', *Australian Journal of Public Administration*, vol. 63, no. 4, pp. 37–49.

Hodge, Graeme 2005, 'Public–private partnerships: the Australian experience with physical infrastructure', in Graeme Hodge and Carsten Greve (eds), *The Challenge of Public–Private Partnerships: Learning from international experience*, Edward Elgar, Cheltenham, pp. 305–31.

Hodge, Graeme 2006, 'Public–private partnerships and legitimacy', *University of New South Wales Law Journal, Forum*, vol. 12, no. 2, November.

Hodge, Graeme and Greve, Carsten (eds) 2005, *The Challenge of Public–Private Partnerships: Learning from international experience*, Edward Elgar, Cheltenham.

Hodge, Graeme and Greve, Carsten 2007, 'Public–private partnerships: an international performance review', *Public Administration Review*, June.

Klijn, Erik-Hans and Teisman, Geert 2005, 'Public–private partnerships as the management of co-production: strategic and institutional obstacles in a difficult marriage', in Graeme Hodge and Carsten Greve (eds), *The Challenge of Public–Private Partnerships: Learning from international experience*, Edward Elgar, Cheltenham, pp. 95–116.

Linder, Stephen 1999, 'Coming to terms with the public–private partnership: a grammar of multiple meanings', *American Behavioural Scientist*, vol. 43, no. 1, pp. 35–51.

McIntosh, Kylie, Shauness, Jason and Wettenhall, Roger 1997, *Contracting Out in Australia: An indicative history*, Centre for Research in Public Sector Management, University of Canberra, Canberra.

Monbiot, George 2002, 'Health—a challenge to the Chancellor: refute these charges, or admit that the private finance initiative is built on fraud and false accounting', *Guardian*, 18 June.

Mott Macdonald 2002, *Review of Large Public Procurement in the UK*, Mott Macdonald, London.

National Audit Office 2000, *Examining the Value for Money of Deals Under the Private Finance Initiative*, The Stationery Office, London.

National Audit Office 2003, *PFI: Construction Performance, HC 371*, The Stationery Office, London.

Osborne, Stephen 2001a, 'Introduction: understanding public–private partnerships in international perspective: globally convergent or nationally divergent phenomena?', in Stephen Osborne (ed.), *Public–Private Partnerships: Theory and practice in international perspective*, Routledge, New York.

Osborne, Stephen (ed.) 2001b, *Public–Private Partnerships: Theory and practice in international perspective*, Routledge, New York.

Perrot, Jean-Yves and Chatelus, Gautier (eds) 2000, *Financing of Major Infrastructure and Public Service Projects: Public private partnerships, lessons from French experience throughout the world*, Presses de l'Ecole Nationale des Ponts et Chaussées, Paris.

Pollitt, Michael 2002, 'The declining role of the State in infrastructure investment in the UK', in Sanford Berg, Michael Pollitt and Masatsugu Tsuji (eds), *Private Initiatives in Infrastructure: Priorities, incentives and performance*, Edward Elgar, Aldershot.

Pollitt, Michael 2005, 'Learning from the UK private finance initiative experience', in Graeme Hodge and Carsten Greve (eds), *The Challenge of Public–Private Partnerships: Learning from international experience*, Edward Elgar, Cheltenham, pp. 207–30.

Pollock, Allyson, Price, David and Player, Stewart 2007, 'An examination of the UK Treasury's evidence base for cost and time overrun data in UK value-for-money policy and appraisal', *Public Money and Management*, April, pp. 127–33.

Pollock, Allyson, Shaoul, Jean and Vickers, Neil 2002, 'Private finance and value for money in NHS hospitals: a policy in search of a rationale?', *British Medical Journal*, vol. 324, pp. 1205–8.

Savas, Emanuel Steve 2000, *Privatization and Public–Private Partnerships*, Chatham House Publishers and Seven Bridges Press, New York.

Shaoul, Jean 2004, 'Railpolitik: the financial realities of operating Britain's national railways', *Public Money and Management*, vol. 24, no. 1, pp. 27–36.

Shaoul, Jean 2005, 'The private finance initiative or the public funding of private profit', in Graeme Hodge and Carsten Greve (eds), *The Challenge of Public–Private Partnerships: Learning from international experience*, Edward Elgar, Cheltenham, pp. 190–206.

Shepherd, Tony 2000, A practitioner's perspective, Presentation to the Productivity Commission Workshop on Private Sector Involvement in Provision of Public Infrastructure, 12–13 October, Melbourne.

Teisman, Geert and Klijn, Erik-Hans 2001, 'Public–private partnerships in the European Union: official suspect, embraced in daily practice', in Stephen Osborne (ed.), *Public–Private Partnerships: Theory and practice in international perspective*, Routledge, New York, pp. 165–86.

Teisman, Geert and Klijn, Erik-Hans 2002, 'Partnership arrangements: governmental rhetoric or governance scheme?', *Public Administration Review*, vol. 62, no. 2, pp. 197–205.

Tomazin, Farrah 2006, 'Secrecy shields Bracks' deals from scrutiny', *Age*, 5 October.

Vaillancourt Rosenau, Pauline (ed.) 2000, *Public–Private Policy Partnerships*, MIT Press, Cambridge, Mass.

van Ham, J. C. and Koppenjan, Joop 2001, 'Building public–private partnerships: assessing and managing risks in port development', *Public Management Review*, vol. 4, no. 1, pp. 593–616.

van Ham, J. C. and Koppenjan, J. F.M. 2002, Partnerships passing in the night?, IRSPM 5, 8–10 April, Edinburgh.

Walker, Bob and Con Walker, Betty 2000, *Privatisation: Sell off or sell out? The Australian experience*, ABC Books, Sydney.

Wettenhall, Roger 2003, 'The rhetoric and reality of public–private partnerships', *Public Organisation Review: A Global Journal*, vol. 3, pp. 77–107.

Wettenhall, Roger 2005, 'The public–private interface: surveying the history', in Graeme Hodge and Carsten Greve (eds), *The Challenge of Public–Private Partnerships: Learning from international experience*, Edward Elgar, Cheltenham, p. 43.

Williamson, Oliver 1985, *The Economic Institutions of Capitalism*, Free Press, New York.

ENDNOTES

[1] See Wettenhall (2003), who comments that cooperative public-sector activities go back centuries and that 'there is nothing new about the mixing of public–private endeavours…whatever the new enthusiasts may think'.

[2] See Hodge and Greve (2007) for the details of these family members.

[3] The recent history of the public sector internationally has been replete with schemes aiming to better define public-sector services and measure performance. Examples of such schemes have included but are not limited to: performance indicators and targets, management by objectives, total quality management, benchmarking, contracting and outsourcing, systems analysis, zero-based budgeting, performance budgeting, output-based budgeting, results budgeting, program budgeting, program planning and budgeting systems, competitive tendering and best value in local government. While benefits have no doubt been delivered through many of these initiatives, most have also fallen well short of the promises made.

[4] Also crucial is the observation that no reviews to date have covered the political science/public policy/public administration literature (for example, Hodge and Greve 2007) and the economics/engineering literature (for example, Grimsey and Lewis 2004).

[5] One project leader explained recently that because these new PPP arrangements enabled $1 billion to be spent on infrastructure in the coming year compared with only $130 million in the previous 12 months, the new arrangements were therefore some eight times better than the old. This personal criterion is understandable and might be mirrored by others involved in these transactions, including financiers, engineers, consultants and lawyers, but it has limited relevance for the broader community.

[6] See Hodge (2004) for one such analysis.

[7] The one important exception to this is the case in which a government enters an infrastructure deal requiring users or citizens to pay directly, such as tolls on a new road. Here, such an arrangement does reduce pressure on public-sector budgets, because government has essentially purchased the infrastructure through the commitment of funds from future (private) road users rather than using its own resources.

[8] These authors nevertheless concede that 'there can be situations where BOOT schemes are good deals for both government and private sector'.

[9] The proportion of total infrastructure investments provided by private finance arrangements is unclear in developed countries, but estimates include Pollitt's figure above of 15–20 per cent of the UK capital budget, an earlier figure of about 10–13 per cent (HM Treasury 2003:128) and Pollitt's remark that this proportion is as high as 50 per cent in sectors such as transport.

[10] National Audit Office (2003) surveys also reported positive feedback from 81 per cent of organisational personnel who saw PFI projects as 'excellent' (6 per cent), 'good' (46 per cent) or 'okay' (29 per cent).

[11] Note that we also ought to keep our analysis of the commercial outcomes for government separate from our assessment of the policy-delivery mechanism here. The terms on which this hospital was transferred back to government after the 'political failure' would presumably need to be known before we assessed the relative overall success of the subsequent commercial transaction to the taxpayer.

[12] A recent example of this concern was the bidding for the Melbourne 'EastLink' project. This 39km motorway was cited as being a $2.5 billion project, and the 39-year concession was awarded after bids were made by two consortia, both of whom were owned by the same parent company.

[13] Such scepticism of policy promises seems broadly consistent with the evaluation evidence presented here. Much of the above value-for-money evaluation evidence has, as well, unfortunately been based on business case projections rather than real measurements of cash flows.

[14] See, for example, Hodge (2004b:241), who notes that after independent power producers were contracted to build greater capacity, an increase of more than 200 per cent occurred in the 'purchased power adjustment'—an additional charge remitted to private power producers for unused power. Moreover, while overall electricity bills had almost doubled, power prices were double those in neighbouring countries such as Thailand and Malaysia. This situation understandably led to outrage in the Philippines.

[15] See, for instance, The Economist (2002).

[16] Feedback to this effect resulted in the development of a 'public interest test' within the department's guidance material, which—if the boxes are ticked—guarantees (at least in terms of advocating bureaucrats) that the public interest has been 'defined' and met.

[17] Public Accounts and Estimates Committee 2006, *Seventy-First Report to the Parliament, Report on Private Investment in Public Infrastructure*; and Public Accounts Committee 2006, Inquiry into Public Private Partnerships.

[18] See Joint Select Committee on the Cross City Tunnel, *First Report, XI*, NSW Parliament.

11. Perspectives of community organisations: The Smith Family experience

Elaine Henry

In the past decade, governments have chosen to transfer the delivery of services and policy provision from the public sector to the non-government sector, involving private firms, community organisations and a range of non-governmental organisations (NGOs). For governments, this process of devolving implementation to the non-government sector has many advantages: it allows them to focus on policy formulation and core policy issues, while delivering services for pre-stipulated costs, allowing customisation of services and better quality assurance. For the non-government sector, this transfer of responsibilities places considerable strain on those organisations and the staff they employ or volunteers on whom they often rely.

From the vantage point of community organisations, therefore, there is a real need to examine this process and its impact on policy outcomes and the players involved. How does collaboration affect these organisations—and, in particular, their intended purposes, traditional roles and distinct cultures? Do contractual relationships and delivery partnerships affect the way in which these community organisations are able to fulfil their own missions, or do they displace such endeavours in exchange for government agendas and priorities? Also, how do community organisations affect the policy process—engaging deliberatively with government in the consultation process over policy design and policy implementation? This chapter addresses these questions about collaboration from the perspective of a practitioner organisation.

In 1998, The Smith Family (TSF) embarked on a journey to put its own house in order to meet the challenges of the twenty-first century—an era that would see Australia characterised as a 'knowledge society'. In March 1999, we began with a classic John Kotter comprehensive transformation from which we emerged as a national, independent, social enterprise focused on children and education. For TSF, there is value in having a national structure (which is fairly rare in the non-profit world), but to advance collaboration we found it necessary to recruit leaders or influencers at the state and territory levels, nonetheless keeping our national operational matrix.

Our attention as a charitable community organisation was on the 700 000 or so children living in jobless and often lone-parent families. We adopted a set of eight guiding principles as a working framework, among which was the idea that 'We should work with and through other organisations and individuals'—a simple phrase but one that, when brought to life, was in itself transforming. As part of our transformation, and to be able to achieve the outcomes we were seeking, we decided we also had to become champions of sectoral change in our areas of policy interest and indeed of societal change more broadly.

TSF's treasured independence as an NGO had often equated with insularity but now it had to be exercised through collaboration. We took notice of one of our governors at the time, Martin Stewart Weeks, who observed in 2000 that '[w]e are on an irreversible path away from traditional notions of government to a more complex notion of governance, one of whose defining characteristics is a reliance on networks and alliances'. The emergence of paradigms such as network governance has allowed agencies and people to work together differently across systems and, over time, it is hoped, to make significant gains in overcoming seemingly intractable social problems.

Putting such lofty ideals into practice means first and foremost treating relationships as strategic assets and managing them as such. Considine (2001) highlighted the fact that the source of rationality in network governance models was relationships. Non-profit-making or community organisations have always believed that this is their core competency and maybe this is why Considine found them more willing to embrace the model, more so than for-profit or business organisations, with governments still less ready.

I outline below examples of government–community collaboration and corporate–community collaboration, which touch on the subject of social innovation in which true collaboration between the three sectors of government, community and business might take us to the next stage.

Stronger families and communities strategy (government–community collaboration)

In 2000, I was invited by the then minister Senator Jocelyn Newman to chair the Stronger Families and Communities Partnership. It seemed to me the contemporary way of affecting social policy. I saw the strategy as an exciting empowerment model with local communities having a say in local solutions. It was apparent as time went on, however, that without an overarching framework from which local activity could be additive and produce measurable impact, no discernible difference would result. Underlying all this was a subtle but real change in the way government and community interrelated. Departmental staff saw their role as assisting with capacity building and network creation, the sharing of information and setting common standards.

We started what we called 'strategic conversations' to move collaboration beyond government and community to between different government agencies. We found that, unsurprisingly, they had arrived at the same place at the same time and were merely duplicating one another's work. Little wonder that some communities became weary of 'fly-in/fly-out clipboard research'. When the focus changed to partnerships with business, it was apparent that there was a steep learning curve ahead of us if we were to capitalise on the potential. Business was well and truly down the track of a more entrepreneurial, integrated structure to replace the old 'command-and-control' system. Government officials were in uncharted water.

TSF was ready for the challenge, but it was put on hold when a new minister and new staff put greater emphasis on managing the uncertainty and the risks than on developing the relationships. A change in tactics saw the chairs of four relevant advisory committees realise that we had a common point of reference—children—and, through collaborative effort predominantly outside government, the agenda was refocused. Papers were written and presentations given; in April 2004, phase two of Stronger Families and Communities emerged, building on the strengths of phase one and with the innovative Communities for Children (C4C) initiative as its centrepiece.

This time around government was to be even more hands-off, playing the role of enabler, with community organisations that had the necessary back-office capability taking on the role of facilitating partner. They were to be responsible for the stewardship of the government's investment in 45 disadvantaged communities, for brokering services with local providers and for leveraging the investment to garner greater resources, in an asset-building, whole-of-community approach, addressing the development needs of children from birth to five years of age.

Had the necessary cultural change started in phase one permeated community organisations sufficiently for them to adopt such new roles? More than one academic was critical of the capacity of community organisations to deliver. Therein lies a major prerequisite: true commitment to collaboration requires organisational change and tenacity. We are all aware that collaboration is not something that organisations should enter into lightly; it demands the cultivation of new resources and skill sets within community organisations and government entities if both are to come together in an effective manner, and collaboration needs to be driven from the top.

In April 2007, three years after the announcement of C4C, 44 of the 45 chief executive officers (CEOs) of facilitating partner organisations came together to workshop the various attributes of the model. The recurring theme was the positive cultural change occurring in the organisations themselves, leading to sectoral change, which had been precipitated by participation in the initiative. This was a far cry from the atmosphere on the first occasion we met. At that time, there was criticism of the burdensome contractual arrangements that were necessary for accountability purposes, the inflexibility of the funding model particularly in relation to roll-overs when implementation couldn't be rushed, and the dogged adherence to terminology and scope requiring organisations to focus rather than be all things to all people. Previous experience when community members had been relegated to the role of passive recipients rather than active collaborators had to be overcome. It took time for some to realise the potential opportunities.

Government officials had to be seen to be valuing the views of those in the practitioner community, while creating common standards and taxonomy; the community players needed resilience to challenge other perspectives and practices but in a constructive way; and both needed to question, reflect on and suggest possible alternatives. The first seven facilitating partners shared their findings with the other 38 and cooperated in overcoming the perceived power imbalance. All the players coming together periodically to share information and experiences has been invaluable.

With time, the closer relationships cultivated between the government and facilitating partners have been strengthened by numerous collaborations with other community NGOs. Of course, balancing and/or reconciling the priorities and needs of these diverse collaborators has also been challenging, but ultimately rewarding in terms of understanding how the relative strengths and weaknesses of stakeholders along the chain can interact to create a sustainable whole-of-community approach.

The engagement of the business sector is now proving extremely important for all the C4C sites around Australia, given that the political nature of government collaboration naturally generates concerns about sustainability. This is also the reason why, for example, TSF is working harder than ever to attract national and local stakeholders from the business sector to the collaboration table. Yet another major prerequisite for sustainable collaboration, then, is multi-sectoral engagement (Allen Consulting Group 2006).

The Prime Minister's Community Business Partnership (corporate–community collaboration)

A parallel endeavour with which I have been associated is the Prime Minister's Community Business Partnership (PMCBP), resulting in an increase in corporate community investment that is part of the wider issue of corporate social responsibility. A recent report by the Allen Consulting Group in conjunction with the Business Council of Australia showed the great strides that had been made since the first report on corporate community investment came out in 2000. TSF alone has more than 70 corporate partners at the national level and more than 500 business–community relationships regionally. Our business partners are major stakeholders and we use the model constructed by Austin (2000), which shows the depth of their corporate community investment: some players are still in the philanthropic mode, others have migrated to the transactional mode, while the more enlightened companies are in the integrative mode or, in other words, are into strategic investment.

The role government plays here is that of an enabler or facilitator. In particular, taxation changes have been the catalyst for accelerating the culture of giving (or giving back), which is becoming a feature of our landscape. Pre-tax payroll deductions have set up a virtuous circle of giving in the workplace involving employees and employers. Changed rules have encouraged the setting up of private prescribed funds (PPFs) that now total more than 500 and assist wealthy individuals in their endeavours. The agenda-setting role of government provides a credible backdrop to facilitate corporate–community partnerships; the skill here is not to fracture or interfere with this process, but to ensure that the activity that is engendered has some meaningful outcome. In a nutshell, we want new relationships to inspire new solutions to social problems. As we all know, these relationships take time and require nurturing. Moreover, to be successful, they require a shared vision, objectives and methodology, utilising the skills and expertise of all parties. A further prerequisite for collaboration is therefore a shared identity, which in turn requires a common language, common ground and commonsense.

Network governance (government–corporate–community collaboration)

According to Albert Einstein, 'Today's significant problems cannot be solved by the same level of thinking we were at when we first created them.' To put it another way, we now know from the ever-increasing evidence base of human development that it is no longer enough to carry on doing what we have been doing; we need to innovate as we collaborate.

It could be argued that because of the political implications of government investment strategies, governments tend to be reluctant to embrace innovation due to the potential risk involved in trying something new. Innovation, however, need not necessarily be equated with risk, particularly if it involves collaboration with credible, trusted and experienced stakeholders.

A prime example of innovative government collaboration is the Australian Research Alliance for Children and Youth (ARACY), a large, multi-sectoral network incorporating organisational and individual members, the board of which comprises predominantly businesspeople. This collaboration originated with the express intention of building and consolidating one large national network of stakeholders focused on the wellbeing of children and youth throughout Australia. The Commonwealth Department of Families, Housing, Community Services and Indigenous Affairs (FaHCSIA) is the largest source of funding for this initiative and also an active contributing partner in the network.

The governance and successful performance of ARACY depend on its capacity to promote and activate collaboration across a variety of organisational forms, across relevant knowledge domains and across the triangle of stakeholders in program delivery, research and policy development. Like many start-ups, it was initially treated with suspicion, but after a long and difficult gestation building the framework of shared principles and goals among its members, ARACY has amassed an impressive capacity and status, and is now ready to move to the next stage of its development.

Importantly, ARACY is one of the agents that have contributed to the creation of a sociopolitical climate in Australia in which collaboration can occur and be supported. At the end of 2003, it set out to develop models of best collaborative practice (ARACY 2004) and to provide advice on success factors for collaboration and the infrastructure required to support such practice (Head 2006). Because collaboration does not come naturally to organisations, we need examples such as ARACY to identify the returns to collaboration and to create incentives for collaboration rather than competition. As a member of the ARACY network, TSF has benefited from and continues to benefit from the range of resources that ARACY produces, and has access to a broader-based national collaboration in research, policy and practice than would otherwise be possible.

Finally, I would like to share a glimpse of the latest innovative form of collaboration currently being explored by TSF. While it has now been acknowledged in Australia that human-capital development is a priority in the early years of the twenty-first century, the need to accelerate social innovation to overcome in a more timely fashion seemingly intractable social issues is now emerging. Throughout 2006, the Boston Consulting Group conducted, on a pro bono basis, a feasibility study to investigate the need, and subsequently the applicable model, for a more integrative collaboration to develop innovative solutions to a number of social issues. A social incubator emerged as a possible vehicle for these collaborative outcomes.

A social incubator seeks to foster collaboration between individuals with different skill sets and backgrounds, from a range of sectors (including government) to search for innovative solutions for existing problems. It essentially provides an intensive environment in which research combines with practice to create practical initiatives and solutions, leveraging individual skills and expertise from diverse, multidisciplinary teams working together. This team environment is supported by:

- physical co-location, encouraging daily interactions between team members and the building of informal as well as formal bonds
- facilitation of teams by a project manager with responsibilities to manage interactions and promote collaboration

- a strong project process with accountabilities throughout to ensure milestones and outcomes are achieved.

Consideration is being given to developing social incubators for three areas: early childhood, youth and Indigenous people. Governments will play an important role in the design and implementation of these social incubators, but they will require collaboration from all sectors—including academia, non-profit and business—if they are to successfully develop solutions to the intractable social issues we are currently facing. Initiatives such as these therefore illustrate how collaborative efforts in the future will require increasing innovation if they are to remain relevant and effective mechanisms of support for the wellbeing of all Australians.

From a community organisation point of view, TSF is perceived as the underdog in most collaborations with governments or with business, as the last two have the money and therefore initially the power. I am inclined to say to my non-profit colleagues that we need to reject this view. We have what government and business need: local knowledge, implementation know-how and a foundation built on relationships. I counsel community organisations to know their value and not be intimidated. For collaborations with the public sector to work, we need: a) heads of departments to believe in partnerships; and b) to cultivate this as the predominant culture.

Key lessons

It was essential for TSF to address the question of our own corporate governance early in our transformation process so we could facilitate and enhance our capacity to meet the challenges and complexities of collaborating across systems and sectors. We also recognised the need to make staff changes within the organisation that built our internal capacity to initiate, manage and grow cross-sectoral relationships as a twenty-first-century currency and strategic asset for effectiveness and impact. In the case of TSF, this has meant restructuring staff responsibilities in a number of instances and recruiting leaders at the state and territory level in order to advance collaboration.

In addition to building our organisational capacity for collaboration, we have had to recognise and have the courage to grasp opportunities that we have become aware of in our environment. 'Strategic opportunism' is how we often described this particular experience of collaboration, which required us to become nimble in aligning resources to respond to emerging opportunities. We also, however, had to 'stick to strategy'—that is, clarify what we would do and would not do as collaboration partners. This lesson can be understood as the other side of the coin of strategic opportunism and is a prerequisite to ensure that we consistently increase our capacity for societal impact.

Another important lesson has been that a serious commitment to collaboration can facilitate the leveraging of resources to strengthen policy impact through demonstration and innovation. The diverse skill sets and perspectives of cross-sectoral players, who are open to doing things differently, can be powerful drivers for policy and social innovation to break through previously intractable social problems.

In summary, in order to foster successful collaboration, it is imperative that your own house is in order. The relationships that are fostered should be treated as strategic assets to be managed and to provide understanding of the needs of the various collaborators. In order to do so, a collaborating body has to be prepared to devote energy and resources to making it a success and be prepared for the long haul. A true commitment to collaboration requires innovation and organisational development, change and tenacity. It is more than simply intra-agency cooperation, and the learning experience should be shared between all partners with a touch of humility.

References

Allen Consulting Group 2006, *Stakeholder Engagement and Consultative Arrangements in Government*, Melbourne.

Austin, J. 2000, *The Collaboration Challenge*, Jossey-Boss, San Francisco.

Australian Research Alliance for Children and Youth (ARACY) 2004, *Guide to Good Collaborative Practice*, Canberra.

Considine, M. 2001, *Enterprising States: The public management of welfare-to-work*, Cambridge University Press, Melbourne.

Head, B. 2006, *Effective Collaboration*, Australian Research Alliance for Children and Youth, Canberra.

12. Collaborative approaches to 'people-based' and 'place-based' issues in Victoria

Jane Treadwell[1]

This chapter explores specific examples of collaborative approaches within the community sector, addressing issues within the broader context of the 'people-based' and 'place-based' approaches that the Department for Victorian Communities (DVC) has championed.[2] It goes on to reflect more broadly on the principles that have underpinned a successful approach to changing the way government works.

Family violence

Family violence is a major social problem in the community. It does not involve just two people, but affects the entire family, sometimes over generations. Family violence is the leading contributor to preventable death, disability and illness in Victorian women between 15 and 44 years of age. It can often start or intensify during pregnancy. It is associated with increased rates of miscarriage, low birth rates, premature birth, foetal injury and foetal death. It is a factor in more than half of the substantiated child-protection cases, and children are present at more than half the attendances for family violence.

Family violence also has a significant impact on a range of associated public services that are called on to deal with or support the people involved. These include the police, who can be called to the initial incident, the courts, where it is possible to obtain an intervention order, mental health departments and services, as well as housing services and education departments and schools, where family violence has a major impact on school attendance and learning.

In addition, there is a range of community-based services that takes an active role in supporting victims and perpetrators of family violence (because the perpetrators also need help). In 2002, as part of the Women's Safety Strategy, the Victorian Government formed a state-wide steering committee to reduce family violence. DVC took the lead role in coordinating the delivery of the strategy.

The policy was the result of the government finding different ways to listen and work. This was not just a government strategy, but a whole-of-community strategy. The idea was to link family violence services with a focus on outcomes: improving the safety of victims who experience family violence and improving the accountability of the perpetrators of violence. Initially, the government provided $35.1 million over four years for a range of strategies, which resulted in significant improvements for victims of family violence.

Several key elements led to a successful collaborative approach to improving government responses to family violence. The most important was the agreement of five ministers and three government departments, all of which wanted to make the strategy work. New resources, joined with the old, leveraged the reforms. The willingness to create regional partnerships that went beyond government boundaries and worked with communities was critical.

There were also some significant systemic and structural changes that were required. A revised police Code of Practice (in 2004) and the support of the Chief Commissioner, Christine Nixon, led to changes in the way in which intervention orders were used. The creation of a specialist court response (the Family Violence Lists in the Magistrates Courts) supported joined up approaches to helping people. In July 2006, the Victorian Department of Human Services facilitated regional partnerships with refuges, outreach services, counselling and support services and men's behavioural-change services. A common framework for risk assessment and a focus on information and communication supported these changes.

From the perspective of the person who has lived with family violence, the outcomes are now much better. There are improved counselling and support programs for women and children and, through a private rental program, additional funding and support for women who have experienced family violence. An intensive case-management system has been implemented to support women with complex needs (where there has been not only domestic violence but drug abuse and a history of broken relationships). Men's behavioural-change programs and crisis accommodation for men are also now available.

An important aspect of the program has been a willingness to look at new and more effective ways of dealing with the perpetrators of family violence—the police can now direct or detain them. This has resulted in a 34 per cent increase in the use of intervention orders and has enhanced the capacity of the police to deal with a situation before it escalates out of control, as well as improving defendant support. As ever, there is more to be done. Work is under way to link service and workflow systems so that victims experience consistent, integrated support and intervention and are not required to tell the same story over and over again.

Currently, a benchmark study across agencies is also being planned to evaluate the results achieved to date and to measure the effectiveness of new changes. The department is now scoping these additional pieces of work and working closely with government agencies to make them possible. While further work needs to be done, it is already clear that a significant impact has been made in a relatively short time, providing a coordinated government and community response that works.

Streamlining Indigenous funding agreements

In July 2004, the Minister for Aboriginal Affairs, Gavin Jennings, conducted a series of Indigenous community forums on a range of key issues relating to Victorian Indigenous affairs. In these consultations, one of the issues raised was the need for the government to look at simplifying the level of red tape involved in administering state-funded Indigenous programs. To address this issue, the government made a commitment in *A Fairer Victoria* to introduce single funding agreements for Indigenous organisations. This is part of the state government's commitment to change the way it works in an area characterised by complexity.

In 2005–06, there were agreements with 76 Indigenous organisations for 623 projects. Approximately 50 per cent of funded Indigenous organisations received funding from more than one state agency. In all, 33 Indigenous organisations received funding from state and Commonwealth agencies. Typically, they would receive funding from five to 10 different program areas to deliver more than 10 different services. Indigenous organisations have been asked to manage a large number of projects and to manage a number of funding relationships across and within government agencies.

The terms and conditions of the programs had different expectations about how funding should be managed and different rules for the management committees to abide by depending on the source of funding. Within the Victorian Government, only one department used the same set of terms and conditions for all its funding programs. More generally, there was an inconsistent use of 'plain English', which meant that terms such as 'strategy', 'objective' and 'outcome' meant different things in different agreements. Administration tasks had different payment dates, different invoicing requirements, different reporting requirements and different funding arrangements (with varying levels of flexibility and differing focuses on partnership, communication and compliance).

As a starting point to developing single funding agreements, DVC in collaboration with many other departments developed a common funding framework, illustrated in Figure 12.1. This was agreed to by all departmental secretaries. The framework captures the component parts of a funding agreement. It proposes the development of common processes and documentation for funding administration, as well as a shared sense of the way government and Indigenous organisations do business.

Figure 12.1 The single funding agreement for Indigenous organisations

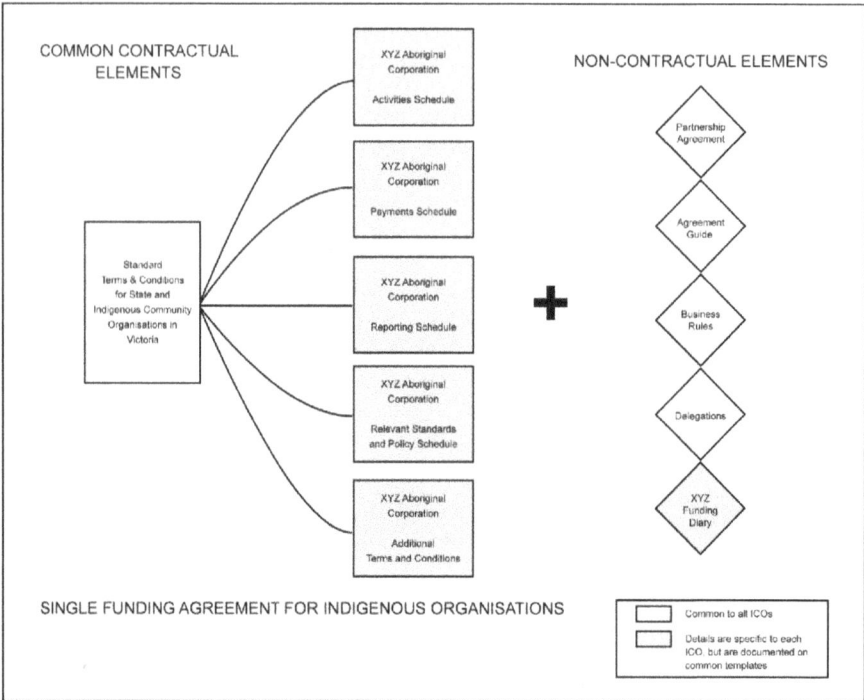

On the left of Figure 12.1 are a number of contractual elements, which will make up the funding document, with non-contractual elements on the right. Single funding agreements for Indigenous organisations display the elements that should be the same across every funding agency and these are shown in the blue or dark boxes. The elements that should be written on a common template with organisation-specific content are shown in the yellow or lighter boxes. A single core set of terms and conditions to cover circumstances that are common to all funded activities and relationships has been agreed on. Additional terms and conditions can be added for activities that have unique circumstances or specific requirements, or for unique relationships. Common 'pay days' and 'report-due' dates and work towards common reporting formats have also been agreed to. The initial impetus for single funding agreements was the need to reduce the administrative burden for Indigenous organisations. It will also, however, reduce the administrative burden for government agencies.

The improvements mean that activity specifications are better understood by provider organisations. Furthermore, the government has better awareness of each organisation's complementary and competing funding arrangements. Government agencies together can also gain a shared understanding of organisational capacities. Because of this, organisational risks are better understood and managed collectively across government.

Streamlining funding arrangements within the department supports improved transparency and better risk management. Streamlining funding arrangements across the whole of government will support the DVC's strategic directions. It will result in arrangements that are focused on community needs and outcomes, not programming silos. It reinforces the department's focus on place and people, and is a practical demonstration of running government differently.

Regional management initiatives

A key strategy of *A Fairer Victoria* was the alignment of regional boundaries of state departments into eight administrative regions so that community organisations and individuals could overcome any problems created by different regional management structures or boundaries. This simple change fostered collaboration across government agencies at a regional level. Regional Management Forums were created to provide opportunities to explore shared priorities and projects at a regional level. They comprise a regional champion (one of the departmental secretaries or chief commissioner of police) and regional managers of state government agencies and CEOs of local government. At these forums, joint recognition of the issues impacting on the provision of services and infrastructure to a shared population is generating agreement on shared priorities and projects. These forums are evidence of dynamic collaboration driven by needs and opportunities, as well as by better sharing of information and resources across agencies.

Improving information networks through 'iPlace'

Being able to access and share information across organisational boundaries is becoming a strategic enabler for competitive advantage, networked government and stronger communities. The Victorian Government's initiative 'iPlace' consolidates access to federal, state and local government information through one resource to provide 'place-based' information. It is the means by which public-sector employees (and ultimately the public) can gain easy access to thousands of government information sources about any place in the state of Victoria. It is based on a strong governance model of shared responsibilities (horizontally and vertically) across jurisdictions, and a federated model of information sharing that ensures that the information owner is able to make copies of their information available but also control who is entitled to access it.

By aggregating data from disparate sources, a platform is available for informed planning, resource management and decision making. The project, endorsed by the Victorian state coordination and management committee, is working with three regional management forums: Hume region, Northern and Western Metropolitan and the Grampians. It is an example of the value of technology in making it possible for people and organisations to share knowledge and insights, and ultimately to contribute to improving service delivery, investment mixes, policy development and local priority setting.

Conclusion

It is impossible to identify a single factor that makes effective collaboration work. Rather, many factors interact and contribute to successful outcomes. Agreement on shared goals and vision, 'branding' and communication, accountability, customers, common capabilities and individual trade-offs, clarity of governance arrangements and processes, are fundamental to successful collaboration. Experience demonstrates that relationships, the sharing of capability and building of trust take time but also create the environment for change, allowing for greater leverage and better outcomes. To ensure projects were completed and issues addressed, it was necessary for the DVC to explore various collaborative approaches. These approaches and enablers made it possible to achieve positive results and reach successful outcomes in changing the way government operated in 'people-based' and 'place-based' programs operating across the Victorian public sector.

The design principles underlying these projects were clear and simple. They included viewing the world through the lens of people, families or communities, developing a simpler or single face of government and harnessing the capacity of local leaders and entrepreneurs. Shifting from government controlling and directing the delivery of services to government playing the role of facilitator and enabler was also fundamental for successful collaboration. Devolution of service planning and service delivery to the local level meant greater awareness and cooperation between the different sectors as well as developing cross-sectoral approaches to addressing social opportunities and problems through partnerships between governments, community agencies and the corporate sector.

ENDNOTES

[1] This chapter was written when Citizen Access and Transformation was part of the former Department for Victorian Communities. After machinery-of-government changes, that department is now the Department of Planning and Community Development. Citizen Access and Transformation is now part of the Department of Innovation, Industry and Regional Development. Commitment to collaboration, joined-up government and designing services with Victorians so that their needs are met remains critical to delivering accessible and accountable government.

[2] The functions of the Department for Victorian Communities (DVC) are now incorporated in Department of Planning and Community Development following machinery-of-government changes announced in August 2007.

13. Formal collaboration, collaborative councils and community engagement

Margaret Allison

Introduction

This chapter examines the important role local government can play in the delivery of community outcomes through collaboration. It provides some examples from my own jurisdiction that illustrate the range of projects and outcomes achieved through collaboration (with a particular focus on customer and community services), and suggests some future options and possibilities for collaboration.

My central thesis is that collaboration is not merely a desirable mode of operation for local government; rather, it is fundamental to its capacity to deliver desired value for its constituents. This is especially so in Australia, where, as in many countries with federal systems of government, the *Constitution* does not recognise local government. Local government is merely a 'creature of statute' by state and territory legislatures. A roundtable meeting held in Australia in 2007 as part of a global dialogue on federalism noted that, irrespective of the size of local governments, 'What unites these institutions of state is that there is no level of government below them. That is also their strength and democratic claim: they are the government closest to the people.'

The Brisbane local government context

Brisbane City Council (BCC) is the largest local government in the Asia-Pacific region and one of the biggest anywhere in the world. Brisbane is also at the centre of the fastest-growing region in Australia, with an estimated one million additional people expected in the south-east Queensland region by 2026. Brisbane City Council's annual budget is $2.33 billion. Like any smaller council, however, it depends on a range of formal and informal arrangements, many of which are collaborative in nature.

While size makes some difference—for example, the size of infrastructure projects managed—core functions remain the same as those of our smaller neighbours. Irrespective of size, many local government functions are characterised by a visibility and immediacy and even to the most casual observer it is apparent when things are working well—or not.

Collaborative councils: areas for consideration

I would like to highlight some of the areas for consideration where remarkable outcomes can be achieved through the synergistic effects of collaboration, illustrated with examples from BCC.

Partnering and regional collaboration

Council of Mayors

The Council of Mayors (south-east Queensland) was established in September 2005 as an independent political advocacy organisation that represented the interests of the one in seven Australians who lived in south-east Queensland. It aims to influence federal and state government policies and funding priorities. With an estimated four million residents expected by 2026, the region's future growth needs to be supported by first-class infrastructure, reliable water supply, economic development and a reduction in road congestion.

An example of a current area of work for the council is responding to the state government's proposal for transfer of water assets from councils throughout Queensland. A further example of regional collaboration is the after-hours call centre services for nine neighbouring councils and a public utility provided by BCC.

Regulation Reduction Incentive Fund (RRIF)

As part of its 2004 election commitment, *Promoting an Enterprise Culture*, the Federal Government established the $50 million Regulation Reduction Incentive Fund (RRIF). Its aim was to provide local government authorities with incentives to press ahead with regulatory and compliance reforms that benefited small and home-based businesses—for example, through a reduction in the impact of regulation and associated compliance costs.

The Council of Mayors won $9.7 million to streamline development-assessment processes and provide a 'toolbox' capacity to offer customers information about local laws and licensing requirements.

Customers in all these council areas can, for example, now:

* view the city plan online, plan their development online and access the council's decision-making time frames
* lodge development applications and track their progress online according to location and development type and, in some circumstances, enable a faster turnaround
* see what different requirements various local councils might have with respect to the licensing of food premises or the display of advertising signs.

Other substantial benefits are possible in the future, such as rationalising and standardising local laws; it should be the case that the licensing requirements to establish a café are no different in Brisbane than on the Gold Coast.

RRIF projects are designed to save $90 million for small business across south-east Queensland. This project provides clear and demonstrable evidence of the benefits of collaboration in the short term and with regard to long-term sustainability in the region.

Business alliance contracts

North–South Bypass Tunnel

Between 1999 and 2007, Brisbane experienced a 34 per cent increase in private vehicle trips. Further, 250 000 motorists have to drive through the CBD every day to get to their destination. With the anticipated increases in population, the problem was expected to worsen. Brisbane City needed a solution, but clearly did not have the resources, legislation or indeed sole responsibility to overcome the problem. Collaboration with government and the commercial sector was vital.

The North–South Bypass Tunnel (NSBT), also known as RiverCity Motorway, is a $3.2 billion toll road to be built underground between the northern and southern sides of the Brisbane River, with operation expected in late 2010. It will be Australia's longest and deepest tunnel, comprising two parallel tunnels, each with two lanes, almost 5km long.

The NSBT is a partnership between BCC and a consortium of companies, including Leighton Contractors and Baulderstone Hornibrook. The total concession period is 45 years, including the construction period. At that point, the asset will be transferred to BCC. At its inception, the project required partnering with the Queensland Government, as it involved groundbreaking legislation to permit a local government to develop a PPP such as a toll road. (It is the largest PPP undertaken in Queensland to date.) Clearly, a project of this magnitude could not have been conceived and executed without collaboration with the state government and the businesses that tendered for the project.

For the Brisbane community, the major benefits will be the bypassing of 18 existing sets of traffic lights, and provision of an additional Brisbane River crossing. Associated with the project is a series of improvements to public transport and cycle/pedestrian paths, and a range of urban renewal measures.

Brisbane Water Enviro Alliance

Established in 2002 as a result of concerns about nitrogen levels in Moreton Bay, the Brisbane Water Enviro Alliance (BWEA) is an alliance between BCC and private-sector companies to upgrade four waste-water treatment plants. Benefits include:

- a new biological nutrient-removal system to treat up to nine million litres of waste water a day, removing 80 per cent more nitrogen than the previous treatment system
- environmentally friendly UV disinfection, replacing the previous chlorine-dosing method, eliminating chemicals in the discharged treated waste water.

Additionally, a thermal hydrolysis system, the first in Australia, is now in operation. It treats bio-solids to a high standard and makes them readily usable for soil and fertiliser applications. This system pressure-cooks bio-solids, breaking them down to reduce the volume and improve quality. This is the first time this process has been used in Australia, after its successful use in the United Kingdom and parts of Europe.

Methane gas produced during the treatment process assists in producing energy for the plant, reducing the need to source energy from external power suppliers. A water-tanker collection area has been established at the plant to provide the treated waste water for use in construction activities, including dust suppression.

Substantial improvements have been noted in waterway health by reducing the nitrogen content of treated waste water. From an environmental perspective, the improvement has already provided tangible benefits in Cabbage Tree Creek on Brisbane's north side, where schools of fish, large mullet and prawns, which were previously absent, are now regularly seen.

Responsive community service

Local government is taking the lead in collaboration and facilitating activities and outcomes beyond its traditional roles and responsibilities.

Homeless Connect

Homeless Connect is a program run in more than 100 US cities, bringing together local government, businesses and community groups to provide free services to homeless people for a day. These services include medical, mental health, housing, dental, legal, hairdressing, social security, food, clothing and more. Brisbane held an inaugural Homeless Connect day in November 2006 and a second in July 2007. Working with Volunteering Queensland, and through business philanthropy, we plan to hold two a year.

The two events so far saw high participation levels:

- more than 700 homeless people attended
- more than 50 services participated
- more than 400 volunteers assisted.

Services provided included:

- 150 haircuts; for some people, it was the first professional haircut they had ever had
- the council's library services waived the need for an address and signed up new members or reactivated lapsed memberships
- volunteer doctors worked to deal with a range of medical issues and also signed up people for Medicare cards.

Ninety-eight per cent of homeless people surveyed said it was a worthwhile event and they would attend again. We know from feedback from some of the volunteers who assisted on the day that they found it to be a rewarding and moving experience.

SMS and MMS service requests

One of the challenges for local government today is to meet the increasing level of community expectation that we deliver expedient and responsive services in local communities. Additionally, our research and consultation highlighted that residents also wanted to be engaged and kept informed on requests for service and council business in their suburbs.

At the same time, business units within my division, including Local Asset Services (responsible for parks, roads and drainage) and customer services (including call and contact centres), were working collaboratively to reduce follow-up calls and the necessity to make site visits to assess service requests. An opportunity was identified to use SMS technology as a simple and convenient way to contact customers.

This year, we launched the Pix-o-Gram Pilot in which residents could send an MMS to us with basic information about the nature and location of an issue to request services such as tree trimming, the filling of potholes or fixing of leaky taps in parks. This gave a clear picture of maintenance issues and reduced the time needed for site inspections. Once the work was completed, residents were advised by SMS.

The pilot has been a genuine success so far. Residents are obviously pleased to be informed of work completion. A subsidiary benefit has been the engagement with young people, who have been the primary users of the service. It has been notoriously difficult for local government to engage with the young, but the use of contemporary technologies and their preferred media has brought positive outcomes.

Kurilpa Point

Kurilpa Point is a small park just south of the city centre, adjoining a space now occupied by the Gallery of Modern Art. In 2005, it was probably the most contested public space in Brisbane. A number of older Indigenous homeless people had settled there over time. Their presence did not affect the park significantly. As the owners of public space in the city, BCC has as one of its criteria for intervention in any situation whether access by any group is being adversely impacted by the use of another group. In this case, the situation was relatively stable and peaceful.

With time, however, other people joined the original group in the park and a range of problems ensued. Complaints of assault and robbery were made to the police, the park's barbecue and toilet facilities were pretty well permanently taken over and it was clear that many former park users felt intimidated because of the atmosphere created by heavy alcohol use. Moreover, the tacit agreement between BCC and homeless people sleeping rough in parks about moving swags and sleeping gear during the day had been broken, with mattresses and other items littering the park.

At BCC's instigation, a coalition was formed with the Queensland Police and the Department of Communities (who in turn funded the NGOs providing services to homeless people) to return Kurilpa Point to its broader community use. This was not in any sense just about moving people on but about using the concerted efforts of three agencies, each of which had a unique role to play in delivering improved public space use and transition to genuine alternatives to rough sleeping.

BCC took steps to enhance the amenity of the park: lighting was improved, vegetation was trimmed to improve sight lines, toilets and barbecues were cleaned more regularly and public space liaison staff worked with people living in the park to remove mattresses and make other arrangements for storage of gear. The police increased their passive patrolling of the area—not intervening directly with park residents unless there was a specific complaint but rather aiming to improve public perceptions of the park as a safe and well-managed space. The Department of Communities, in concert with NGOs, worked to provide intensive case-management services with emphasis on assisting to other options those whose homelessness was least entrenched.

In about six months, the number of complaints recorded was reduced by more than 70 per cent and the Queensland Police Service reported fewer incidents and offences at the site. Local crime-prevention officers were advised of reduced concerns and complaints through local networks. Several of the younger Indigenous people living on the site were provided with transport home to families with additional support offered to them there. Short-term homes and shelters were provided to a small number of users who expressed a desire to move into more mainstream accommodation. Local members of the community who used the space reported increased perceptions of safety and amenity in the area.

Community engagement

Neighbourhood planning

The challenges of a rapidly growing city, along with a commitment to sustainable development, prompted BCC to start a process of neighbourhood planning. This involved a range of locally based workshops and meetings over more than six months, culminating in a City Shape workshop in August 2005 at which residents were asked to identify some preferences for the way the city should develop into the future—for example, as a multi-centred city. This input has directly shaped the city plan, and led to the establishment of a number of local neighbourhood plans.

BCC then invited interested industry and community representatives to nominate to join a Community Planning Team in their local area. These teams represented the views and interests of local communities and worked together with council officers, technical and design experts to create neighbourhood plans for the future of their local areas.

This successful collaborative planning process, involving 55 000 people, won the 2006 Australasian Award for Robust Public Participation. BCC sees it as an integral collaborative component of a planning framework that empowers the community to guide the growth of Brisbane.

Responding to the drought

South-east Queensland is in the grip of the worst drought on record, with the level of the region's significant water storages at historic lows. In mid-2007, dams were at just 18.03 per cent capacity. While this drought has extended across many parts of the state, it creates additional challenges in the south-east region, given its high population growth. The complexity and scale of the problem make it evident that only genuine and meaningful collaboration between state and local governments and residents can facilitate an effective response.

The response to the drought comprises a range of activities. BCC is drilling in more than 15 locations across the city as part of its Aquifer Project to source up to 20 million litres a day of ground water to supplement the dwindling supply. The Queensland Government in partnership with south-eastern regional councils are undertaking major infrastructure projects involving recycled water and desalination. BCC has undertaken an innovative and collaborative new venture with the international toilet company Caroma, in which BCC staff initiated and assisted in the research and development of a new toilet unit that includes a hand-wash basin and reduces water use by half.

Without significant reduction in water consumption by the community, however, these projects alone might not be enough to secure water in the region. It is clear that residents need to be genuinely engaged; they need to recognise their role in the problem as well as the solution and achieve sustained, long-term changes to water use and behaviour.

Since May 2005, when level-one water restrictions were applied, state and local governments have undertaken a major engagement program, comprising television, radio, print and electronic communication, as well as rebates and incentives to maximise water savings. The Target 140 campaign, launched in 2007, has been demonstrably effective: water savings of more than 40 per cent are playing a substantial role in preserving this precious resource while infrastructure projects are being completed.

Local government reflections on collaboration

The days of local councils being responsible only for 'roads, rates and rubbish' are well and truly over. What, then, can we learn from these examples that could be applicable more generally?

Crisis can create a wonderful engine for collaboration. Who would have thought that Brisbane residents could change their domestic water use so quickly and so profoundly? Successful partnering with the state government and directly with the community on water use brings to mind the powerful possibilities of other issues for which sustained behavioural change is essential: energy use (inextricably linked to water consumption, of course), public transport and increasing the level of people's physical activity.

The direct and genuine engagement of local governments with their constituents produces social capital that has many possibilities. The size and agility of local government can make it quick to respond to local problems, which can be advantageous in establishing partnerships with business and philanthropic interests for which dealing with bureaucratic decision-making processes can be frustrating.

True collaboration requires a mutuality of need and benefit; local government is not averse to taking on other responsibilities but resists being treated as a junior partner because of its size. From a local government perspective, there is, unfortunately, a recent history of functions and responsibilities being shifted to local government without consultation or agreement and perhaps, most importantly, without funding. Environmental regulation is an example of this.

Future directions and possibilities for collaboration with local government

The south-east Queensland Council of Mayors is currently considering the possibility of formalised resource sharing and shared service arrangements. Such a concept could go beyond organisational services such as payroll and procurement, to vegetation and pest management and regulatory services. Perhaps we need to rethink some of the traditional boundaries of responsibility between local and state and territory governments. New partnerships are possible but they require fundamental reconsideration of the limitations on local government revenue raising, such as occurred with BCC's collaboration with the Queensland Government in undertaking the legislative change necessary for the North–South Bypass Tunnel.

Just as Commonwealth funding is increasingly tied to special purposes, it is possible for the federal and state and territory governments to enter into specific partnerships with one or more local governments to 'dip their toe in the water' of a particular policy or project. Arguably, pilot arrangements such as these could be increasingly necessary to determine optimal methods for implementing large-scale programs or those with high community impact. Issues such as high-speed broadband connection and disaster-management arrangements come to mind as possibilities.

The need to embrace new technologies and media is evident. Although programs such as neighbourhood planning have demonstrated that residents are still prepared to turn out in their thousands to contribute to planning the future shape of their city, there are many others for whom a virtual relationship is sufficient. Use of these technologies is not merely a customer service imperative, it is a democratic one.

Conclusion

The prospects for collaboration among local governments and other parties are exciting. At the same time, a cautionary note needs to be sounded about the need for genuine partnerships. A further issue that needs addressing is whether the fiscal restraints on local government are commensurate with the increasingly diverse and complex nature of their responsibilities.

The report on the Global Dialogue on Federalism referred to above noted:

> In the age of globalization, where the world is getting smaller, communities have a renewed interest in the comfort zone [that the level of] government closest to them may offer. Although the majority of local governments are still to be found in small towns and villages…the majority of the population in most countries live in cities and metropolitan regions, the governance of which is not only more complex, but also affects the health of the entire country.

Local government is inherently collaborative in structure and orientation. The extent to which other government, business and community partners can leverage this capacity is exponential, and can only benefit the communities in which we live, work and play.

14. Collaborative democracy: the citizen's ability to collaborate effectively

Louise Sylvan

Introduction

Collaboration between a government and its people—not just in service delivery—is one of the most fertile areas for creating potentially successful outcomes for a society, but it remains one of the most challenging of tasks as well. Almost as challenging are collaborations between government agencies themselves.

This chapter examines some of the aspects of collaborating—the active form of the word is important given what the purposes of collaborations are—from two distinct perspectives. The first derives from a variety of experiences as a former consumer/community advocate and campaigner interacting with a number of government agencies and will focus on government–community collaboration; the second perspective is that of a government official and will highlight some of the lessons learned not only in chairing a cross-jurisdictional government task force on a new global issue affecting consumers—mass-marketed global fraud—but from a task force that has significant community and business partnerships in collaboration with its government members.

Collaborating: perspectives of a community 'collaborator'

Many positive benefits can emerge when people are involved actively in decisions that affect them. Collaboration is more than consultation; while consultation is important, collaborating implies a much more interactive process and a level of agreement on how to proceed that no consultation would entail. One key to effective collaboration is enabling (or even helping to create) the citizen, consumer or community voice that permits real collaboration to occur. That voice is often complex, diffuse, uncollected, unorganised and thus not heard successfully unless efforts are directed to ensuring that it is. The task of enabling is not a precise science and there are many examples of attempts at enabling to learn from—good examples, bad ones, honest efforts and others that would be best classed as manipulation. The cooperation that is implicit in the act of collaborating simply cannot occur if one partner cannot voice their concerns and contributions adequately.

The essential ingredients of good collaboration appear to be the relationship that is built, which is sometimes a continuing one, the development of trust within that relationship and the willingness of the public-service area involved, by definition, to give up some of its power to enable decisions to be significantly influenced by the community it is working in partnership with.

These three separate ingredients react—like the ingredients in a good cake mix—to create the end product; that end product is one that can be more easily supported by those who helped 'mix and bake it'. To develop these essential ingredients further, 'relationship' implies honest interaction: openness on all sides to listening and responding to the issues. 'Trust' implies that neither side of the relationship is controlling (control can be very hard for a bureaucracy to relinquish). 'Power sharing' implies that intelligence or wisdom is in the hands of all the participants to contribute to the result and not just some or one with the ultimate power.

While advocating such an approach for many community issues—and it is clear that not all problems or issues lend themselves to a collaborative approach—it should be noted that choosing to progress a matter collaboratively is far more time consuming and far more difficult than just advising people that a program or solution has been developed for them. It can be more difficult but collaboration is also far more likely to result in a program or solution that is people centred and effective.

Trust and power

'Talking' the rhetoric of collaboration is much easier than 'walking' it. Two of the difficult areas noted earlier are trust and power.

Trust

Table 14.1 is reproduced from the results of a global survey commissioned for the members of the World Economic Forum for its January 2003 meeting. While the information dates from 2002, the results have been replicated repeatedly in other independent surveys with similar outcomes for business, politicians, NGOs and others—although the results for the media can be quite variable in such surveys.[1] This particular survey is important because of its large size (36 000 responses from people around the globe) and its broad focus on many nations (47 developed and developing countries)—and not just Western industrialised economies. The question in the World Economic Forum survey was, 'Which institutions can be trusted to act in society's best interests?'

Table 14.1 Trust in business (World Economic Forum—global)

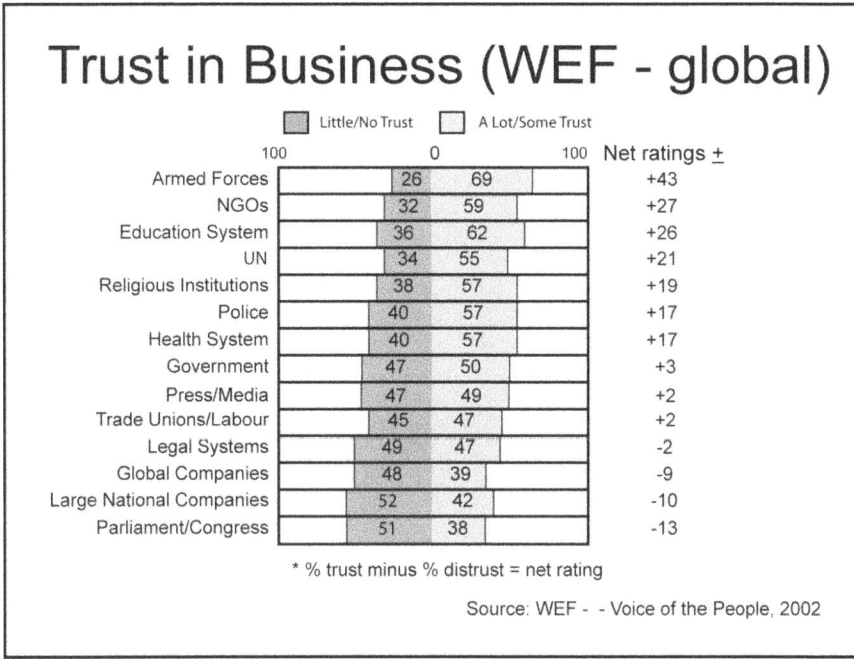

Trust in Business (WEF - global)

	Little/No Trust	A Lot/Some Trust

	100	0	100	Net ratings ±
Armed Forces		26	69	+43
NGOs		32	59	+27
Education System		36	62	+26
UN		34	55	+21
Religious Institutions		38	57	+19
Police		40	57	+17
Health System		40	57	+17
Government		47	50	+3
Press/Media		47	49	+2
Trade Unions/Labour		45	47	+2
Legal Systems		49	47	-2
Global Companies		48	39	-9
Large National Companies		52	42	-10
Parliament/Congress		51	38	-13

* % trust minus % distrust = net rating

Source: WEF - - Voice of the People, 2002

Source: World Economic Forum 2002, *Voice of the People*.

Although the point of this survey was to examine trust in business, it is worthwhile to also reflect on the position of the 'government' category. In this survey, governments—meaning the public service (clearly distinct from the parliaments or congresses of nations whose results are at the bottom of the table)—are on about the middle of the table, in positive territory. From the perspective of considering collaboration between public-service officials in general and citizens, a ranking halfway up the table is quite reasonable and encouraging. Even more encouraging for collaborative efforts are the results for crucial service-delivery people (public servants in many nations), such as health and education officials. The results show that, in contrast with the position of global businesses, for example, public-service officials are in a far more positive situation in relation to building collaboration with their citizens, which is characterised by trust in the process and the eventual outcome.

Power

Creating an incentive for power sharing is a matter for high-level leadership within public services, not only because of the difficulties involved (not least of which are the often incompatible accountability measures that fail entirely to reward collaborative effort), but as a result of two problems that often occur in these situations.

First, in service-delivery areas in particular, there can exist powerful stakeholders who have little or no interest, or in fact a contrary interest, in supporting a more community or citizen-based collaborative process. An example—by no means the only one—is a health department with very powerful provider relationships sustaining non-community-collaborative health programs. In some cases, these powerful interests are well aligned to a collaborative approach, but that will not necessarily be the case. It could be that complementary or countervailing structures or measures are necessary to enable collaboration with the community to occur successfully. Complementary structures can seek to create relationships between providers and community/consumer representatives themselves in an effort to align the goals of the two groups. Countervailing structures can also help to provide a voice to those with less power and access to the department involved. For example, the Consumers' Health Forum established a number of years ago was an organisation that was itself the result of a collaboration between about 20 community and consumer groups and was funded by the Commonwealth Health Department, in part, to expressly assist it to balance the very powerful provider interests that had much greater access to and involvement in programs and policy.

Second is a people problem: people 'feel' losses at about twice the rate that they feel gains. While this effect has been studied primarily in financial markets—and results in some very curious consumer behaviour there—the loss-aversion effects do not apply only to monetary losses; they apply more broadly. The loss effects in sharing power will therefore need to be dealt with ably within a department and the right incentives put into place to counter that strong behavioural effect.

Apart from the three ingredients identified earlier, there is a fourth important element required in the enabling of citizens' ability to collaborate effectively in governance or service delivery. The process needs to occur in a context married to the evidence and that evidence needs to be widely available to the people expected to participate. The evidence—its physical accessibility as well as its comprehensibility—grounds any collaboration and is the mutually agreed basis on which solutions and directions can be explored. While collecting and analysing the evidence is essentially part of the task of enabling collaboration and its community participants, an implication of successful collaboration is a full sharing of the fact base. In general, such availability of information is essential to a program of collaborative democracy.[2]

While there has been a considerable amount of descriptive material and evidence collected, and much analysis done, there remains a great deal to learn about citizen–government collaboration: what forms of collaboration to use for what types of problems to achieve which outcomes. The encouraging development is a growing realisation that collaboration can be a model for making real progress in a number of areas, including some formerly intractable ones, that the intelligence and learning about collaboration can be shared globally thus accelerating our learning process, and that there are technical forms of enabling evolving that were not present earlier to assist us in creating effective community voices. The key, however, remains the will and commitment of a public service to initiate and carry these collaborations through to success.

Australasian Consumer Fraud Taskforce: an example of (i) government-to-government collaboration, (ii) government-to-business collaboration and (iii) government-to-community collaboration

A task force is a particularly useful tool for collaboration, especially between governments. Task forces are specific in their focus, they are outcomes orientated and often the discipline of a time-limited task adds to their effectiveness. The Australasian Consumer Fraud Taskforce comprises 19 government agencies across the Commonwealth, states and territories and the New Zealand Government.

Table 14.2 Australian Consumer Fraud Taskforce — government members

Australian Government	State and Territory Governments
• Attorney General's Department • Australian Bureau of Statistics • Australian Communications and Media Authority • Australian Competition and Consumer Commission (Chair) • Australian Institute of Criminology • Australian Securities and Investment Commission • Australian Federal Police • Department of Communications, Information Technology and the Arts	Representative of State and Territory Police Commissioners Australian Capital Territory's Office of Fair Trading Consumer Affairs Victoria New South Wales's Office of Fair Trading Queensland's Department of Tourism, Fair Trading and Wine Industry Development South Australia's Office of Consumer and Business Affairs
New Zealand Government • NZ Commerce Commission • Ministry of Consumer Affairs	Tasmania's Office of Consumer Affairs and Fair Trading Western Australia's Department of Consumer and Employment Protection

Task-force membership is entirely voluntary. It doesn't have a line in some budget somewhere, and it isn't established by ministers requiring it; it is simply a coming together of a range of government entities to address a problem that is almost impossible to deal with separately, and it funds its activities from existing budgets.

Fraud in this instance refers quite specifically to a new phenomenon that for a few years slipped under the radar of policy and enforcement organisations. The phenomenon is 'mass-marketed global fraud'—essentially low-value, high-volume economic crime, much of which emanates from jurisdictions that are hard for enforcers to reach. Complaints were being recorded from consumers by numerous Australian agencies but the crimes involved fairly low sums (often in the hundreds of dollars only), with no assaults or weapons or public-threat dimensions to raise urgency issues.

Such acts of fraud are often better know as scams; they involve the ubiquitous advance-fee frauds such as fake lotteries, the Nigerian letters or emails, false competitions, false billing (directed particularly towards small businesses), pitches from clairvoyants and other nonsense, through to the bigger money of 'phishing'[3] and cold-call investment schemes. Organised criminals had found a new, relatively low-risk, highly lucrative way of making money, and the pattern of the approaches to consumers was similar, if not identical, globally. New technologies have made this possible and, in particular, the Internet provides such cost-effective global reach for the criminals that the losses to economies are now calculated in the billions of dollars. Research carried out in the United States and the United Kingdom found that between one in 10 and one in 13 of each population, respectively, were responding to these scams; the monies were, of course, almost invariably transmitted overseas.

It took some time too to make the links to identity-fraud attacks and money-laundering schemes (often in the form of employment scams) that abounded. The example of an employment or 'money-mules' scam reproduced here masquerades as an advertisement for a part-time job; as one can well appreciate from the language used, many vulnerable people have been caught up in this type of activity without understanding that they were becoming embroiled in international money laundering. Often these ads use familiar large company names, easily deceiving people.

Figure 14.1 Example of an emailed employment ad

> **Subject: Work For My Company And Earn A lot Monthly!!!**
>
> Would you like to work online from home/temporarily and earn constant payment? We are glad to offer you a job position in our company, XXX
>
> We permanently need new people to occupy the position of Processing Manager, able to receive and send payments between our partners' clients and our company…
>
> *** REQUIREMENTS ***
>
> —Honesty, Responsibility and Promptness in operations; PC with Internet and e-mail access; We don't work with persons under 18; Postal or Mailing address.
>
> YOUR ROLES ARE:
>
> 1. Receiving payment from our Customers
>
> 2. Cash Payments at your Bank
>
> 3. Deduct 10%, which will be your percentage
>
> 4. Forward balance after deduction of percentage/pay to any of the offices you will be instructed to send payment to.

It became clear that the problem of mass-marketed global fraud did not 'belong' obviously to any one agency; it belonged to multiple agencies and only by collaborating might consumers be successfully reached to prevent them from responding. It is also the case that sharing the problem has helped everyone with the task of dealing with these issues when they arise as consumer complaints. For example, no state police department had the time to follow up a pensioner's loss of $264, for example, to a fraudulent lottery letter, but how to convey that message in an effective way that would also help prevent future victims was not clear.[4] As with many global enforcement issues, no-one had the reach into the main jurisdictions involved (mainly in Eastern Europe) to achieve efficient enforcement action (though recently there have been a few successes). Further, no-one had a clear responsibility as the key agency for trying to 'arm' consumers, since stopping the billions of global approaches by email and letter was all but impossible.

Purposes and activities of the task force

The task force was therefore created to gain a shared understanding of what was going on in Australia in relation to mass-marketed fraud and to agree on a consistent public message and approach across all the agencies. It has commissioned and jointly funded major research by the Australian Bureau of Statistics, which is under way, into the prevalence of Australian responses and the losses involved; it has also developed a yearly campaign to raise awareness of the issues publicly. In fact, hardly a day goes by now without a major scams story in the media—and, more often than not, accompanied by the task force's advice.

The interesting aspect of this task force was that it grew organically—people in government decided that they needed to work together—though the impetus did come initially from the Australian Competition and Consumer Commission as a result of its global connections into the mass-marketed fraud work of the International Consumer Protection Enforcement Network. The other interesting aspect is the level of willingness to support the task force from the private sector and consumer and community groups, which is perhaps not surprising, as there is no inherent conflict of interest and everybody shares the problem. There are some 40 community/consumer groups involved and a similar number of private-sector businesses that support the annual campaign—and their support is real. We expect the push from the private sector to be focused outwards on its customers (such as being on the front page of their web sites) and inwards towards their employees, who are just as likely as anyone else to be responding to these frauds.

Figure 14.2 Example of message produced by the Taskforce

Conclusion

The ANZ Bank, for example, among other strategies, implemented the message in a picture on the back of its ATM receipts during the campaign. For its employees, ANZ also bought a large order of paper shredders (to prevent people facilitating identity theft by putting intact personal information in their garbage bins) and offered them at an attractive discount to staff (who, in some cases, only really understood identity theft for the first time through the task force material on their intranet and staff newsletters, and its inclusion as an agenda item in departmental meetings), achieving dramatically high take-up. This is an example of effective collaboration between government agencies and a private-sector partner. The task force has large numbers of similar stories to tell from community groups such as the Salvation Army, all the other banks, all the major telecommunications providers, and so on. The task force's government members have reiterated to all the partners that it is the repetition of the message across a variety of trusted sources that is the campaign's goal (as opposed to simply a media blitz, which alone can often fail to change consumer behaviour).

As a government group, the task force has all of the dimensions of difficulties and tensions created by working across such a large group of players, including the usual federal–state stresses. The working relationship is, however, one of strong trust, even when the agencies are nervous about their chairman or minister not necessarily being 'the lead star' out there. A 'motherhood-and-apple-pie' issue helps, but doesn't overcome the difficulties inherent in such collaborations or the time consumed in keeping the group focused on the key outcomes and time lines. It helps to ask regularly: do we want to continue this collaboration? Is it worth our time and effort? What needs to change? Each agency has to answer these questions for itself.

To conclude, it is important to collaborate but it is also important to be realistic about when to do so and to be cognisant of the substantial expectations that are raised in a collaborative setting. For agencies considering a collaborative approach, the amount of time needed to make the relationships work at all levels must be factored in. Despite the difficulties, collaboration can be a formidable tool for governments, not only in creating 'buy in' for certain social outcomes but for getting to the right outcomes in the first place.

The Australasian Consumer Fraud Taskforce is one example of the strength of successful collaboration. This task force represents the coming together of a number of government entities to tackle a growing global issue, which would be impossible to deal with separately. While mass-marketed global fraud is a continuing problem, the measures and procedures that have been put in place, and which have been outlined above, provide strong evidence that collaboration as an interactive and cross-institutional process can foster positive outcomes.

ENDNOTES

[1] The results in this survey in relation to defence forces—at the top of the table—are inconsistent with a number of other surveys. The timing of the World Economic Forum survey, conducted within a year of the 11 September attacks, could account for the particularly high ranking of the armed forces in this result.

[2] An important initiative of the Australian Government in 2006 was to make available, free on the web site, all of the statistical information produced by the Australian Bureau of Statistics.

[3] Phishing refers to an email that purports to come from a consumer's financial institution, usually carrying a warning message about security, and providing a live link to enable consumers to verify their account and password details. The email message, which in itself is usually very professional, links to a web site that mirrors almost perfectly the financial institution being 'phished'; the real web site is provided by criminals seeking passwords and accounts to defraud the consumer and possibly engage in further identity theft.

[4] High-tech crime units of the police forces were quickly on the job in terms of phishing attacks, as were the banks and credit card companies; that activity, however, was directed quite properly to closing the phishing sites. Shutting them down does not prevent the initial email attacks from occurring and continuing to reoccur, and does not deal with other types of mass-marketed frauds that abound.

Part 3. Collaboration abroad: comparative perspectives

15. Galvanising government–non-profit/voluntary sector relations: two Canadian cases to consider

Evert Lindquist[1]

Overview and challenge

This volume and the June 2007 conference on which it is based explore how collaboration can be fostered in diverse governance contexts and modes: in different policy sectors, with different types of partners and at different levels of analysis (local, state, national and international). Where collaboration with non-profit organisations was concerned, one conference panel considered intriguing collaborations between governments and local communities (for example, Eggers on the Golden Gate regional district; the Victoria Communities initiative; the Cape York initiative with Westpac, and so on), while others examined special-purpose partnerships with non-profit or charitable organisations. This chapter takes a different tack: it considers higher-order or sector-to-sector efforts to foster collaboration between government and the voluntary sector as a whole.

During the past decades, several jurisdictions have sought to foster a more productive and vibrant non-profit and voluntary sector, and to improve the relationships between this sector and governments. Examples include the United Kingdom's 'compacts', South Australia and Queensland, selected states in the United States and, more recently, several examples in Canada at the national and provincial levels (Phillips 2003b; CNPM 2004; Carter and Speevak Sladowski 2008). This chapter argues that fostering sector-to-sector relationships is an inherently complex, multi-level enterprise, embracing diverse needs and requiring considerable effort and resilience on the part of government and non-profit sector leaders alike—particularly the latter. While there are exemplars of decisive government action and engagement, particularly in the United Kingdom, launching comprehensive policy innovations is fraught with capacity and political challenges (Desveaux et al. 1994) and proceeds in fits and starts. This chapter seeks to understand the motivations of actors in engaging government–non-profit initiatives and identifies some lessons to consider.

This chapter begins by considering how government-to-non-profit-sector reform fits into the larger realm of public-management reform during the past two decades. The chapter then introduces two cases from Canada to identify some of the challenges in fostering such relationships. The first is the Voluntary Sector Initiative (VSI) formally launched in 2000 after an effective agenda-setting exercise and preliminary dialogue with government officials by several non-profit and voluntary-sector organisations. The second considers two rounds of engagement in British Columbia intended to foster improved relationships between the government and the non-profit and voluntary sector, the second still in the early phases of development. The chapter concludes with some reflections on how to design, sustain and conceive such collaborative initiatives.

Why are governments fostering collaboration with the non-profit sector?

The non-profit and voluntary sector is hardly a new phenomenon in our modern societies. Long before the emergence of the welfare state, they provided, however uneven, a social safety net, a variety of community and public goods, assistance and advocacy for special needs and innovation in the design and delivery of services. Indeed, many of the social and other government programs we take for granted can be traced back to programs that were delivered first in the non-profit and voluntary sector, and became the inspiration for or foundation on which more substantial interventions were built. While the size, scope and diversity of the non-profit and voluntary sector increased in leaps and bounds in the past century, arguably, the challenge of providing a coherent view of the sector along with the rise of the Keynesian welfare state as the acknowledged source of innovation and funding reduced its profile. Moreover, the debate during the 1980s about where to take public administration was informed largely by for-profit models and opportunities.

If this is all true, why has there been a strong expression of interest in improving the state of government–non-profit sector relations in many jurisdictions? To answer this question, it is best to begin by considering the nature and focus of public-management reforms in many OECD jurisdictions in the late 1980s and early 1990s.

A common challenge for many governments involved containing the growth of program expenditure and deficits, leading to varying combinations of policy change, program reductions or elimination and adoption of alternative ways to finance and deliver public services. Before policy and alternative delivery decisions were made, many governments engaged in across-the-board cuts and repetitive budgeting strategies, which often led to reductions in the grants and contributions to other levels of government, non-profit and private organisations as a way to protect core operations (Lindquist 1997). Some governments wondered why they were providing sustainment funding to organisations that were staunch critics. Non-profit organisations that previously received sustainment grants from governments often learned that these would no longer be forthcoming—funding was increasingly project specific and not intended to cover overhead costs.

Many governments addressed their policy, program and deficit challenges by relying on the precepts and principles of managerialism and the 'new public management'. These reform frameworks put significant emphasis on improving the quality of service, reducing or covering costs, offering flexible channels and introducing contestability, competition and contracts for service provision, performance reporting and accountability for results. Through these lenses, non-profits were seen as would-be or current 'service providers' and were often treated no differently than the for-profit sector seeking contracts and public–private partnerships (PPPs) to provide services under procurement regimes. One implication of the new procurement regimes was that non-profits found themselves not only in competition with firms but with other non-profit organisations. To compete successfully and deliver meant that many non-profits found themselves in very different operating environments, requiring the preparation of bids and competition, project management and performance monitoring and reporting. In essence, many non-profits underwent a jarring shift in focus from 'helping' key constituencies to adopting a business orientation, higher overheads and new capacities for surviving (and sometimes thriving), becoming aware of scale disadvantages and, of course, more insecurity and frustration. Non-profits had previously been entrepreneurial but rarely so directly competitive. It is not surprising that concerns emerged and were shared in various quarters of the non-profit sector and that awareness began to grow about the lack of direct representation of sector interests to governments and public-service institutions, which led to the galvanisation of action in varying degrees.

Notwithstanding these developments in the realm of public management, there emerged from an entirely different direction strong interest in the concept of social capital and the role and health of civil society, emphasising the need to maintain or rebuild the fabric and resilience of communities and citizens (for example, Putnam et al. 1994; Putnam 2000). This perspective not only recaptured the notion of 'citizens' rather than customers or clients, it implied that working with non-profit and voluntary sector organisations was about more than service delivery and performance. A bottom-up perspective led to the conclusion that non-profits worked 'in' and were often 'of' communities, that successful delivery of services often relied on building trust and understanding local developments and that non-profits, through direct contact and engagement with citizens and communities, had a role and capability as street-level delivery agents to observe on-the-ground results, issues and opportunities, and that they had a responsibility to convey them to governments and other funding organisations, which often meant challenging existing policies. The tensions between this view of the non-profit sector and new public management precepts were very real: not only were the resource outlays for building this goodwill and trust through relationships not captured in contracting and procurement regimes, many non-profits were increasingly reluctant to exercise their 'voice' when contracts and competition were at stake.

In Canada, as we will learn below, an additional dynamic has been the emergence of an environment of 'hyper-accountability' because of scandals involving the Government of Canada and how grants and contribution programs and reporting were handled (Good 2003, 2007). One outcome was that procedures for reviewing, approving, monitoring and then reporting on grants and contributions for all recipient organisations multiplied and became increasingly onerous and costly, particularly for small non-profit organisations. Although these developments arose at the federal level, the burdensome requirements had implications for other levels of government and the non-profits that dealt with several departments within and across governments. It raised the question of how well and how fairly governments dealt with the non-profit sector.

As governments became more aware of these challenges and concerns, it led to important questions about how well organised and capable governments were to engage such a diverse, sprawling and huge sector, with many different interests. Conversely, it raised questions about how capable the sector was of organising itself and articulating its concerns. With this backdrop in mind, and with the goal of exploring the dynamics of engagement within the non-profit and voluntary sector, we consider two cases from Canada.

Canada's Voluntary Sector Initiative: a few bricks in place

The Canadian Voluntary Sector Initiative (VSI), announced in 2000, is an interesting case because the momentum for engagement was built from outside government in response to the effects of successive budget decisions during the early 1990s. Several organisations representing a cross-section of the non-profit and voluntary sector formed a united front and developed a strategy to put issues on the government agenda in a credible way. Adroit agenda setting, combined with fortuitous timing with respect to national politics and the emergence of a coherent international exemplar, led to a significant process and commitment from government. The VSI was, however, sideswiped by unrelated scandals and different governments that attached less priority to it. Once again, the sector has had to work from the outside to put issues on the agenda but it now has a better base from which to exercise influence.

In the late 1980s and early 1990s, the fiscal position of the Government of Canada was worsening. This, in combination with insufficiently conservative forecasting from the Department of Finance, led to a series of restraint exercises and across-the-board cuts, sometimes several in a year (Clark 1994). These exercises and cuts, along with de-layering and reorganisations, were depicted as removing overheads, duplication and unnecessary spending. One such exercise was focused on reviewing and reducing grants and contributions from departments and agencies to all 'interest groups' receiving funding from the Federal Government. These initiatives, however, did not really address the inertia behind program spending and underlying structural issues. In anticipation of a change in government, the Canadian Public Service was significantly restructured in June 1993 (informed by the 1989 restructuring in Australia) and it was left to the incoming Liberal government after its transition to announce dramatic targets for deficit reduction and variable program cuts under the banner of the Program Review during 1994–96 (Greenspon and Wilson-Smith 1996).

Much has been written about Canada's Program Review (for example, Armit and Bourgault 1996; Paquet and Shepherd 1996), but suffice to say that departments were sent reeling (they had targets of anywhere from 17 per cent to 50 per cent over three years) and deeper cuts were piled onto the earlier cuts to the interest groups from the non-profit and voluntary sector. The effects on non-profit and voluntary organisations were significant: as governments reduced or eliminated programs, particularly social and community-orientated programs, on-the-ground non-profit and voluntary organisations were left with fewer resources when attempting to respond to the needs of recipients (the last and increasingly poorly funded line of defence for those in need) and could see first hand the cumulative effects on them. In terms of its medium to longer-term effects on the non-profit and voluntary sector, however, the Program Review also cut in other ways: it created incentives for departments and agencies at the federal level, and for provincial and local governments also feeling the squeeze of federal cuts, to look at alternative, less costly and possibly more effective ways to deliver services (Ford and Zussman 1997). This provided an opportunity for non-profit and voluntary sector organisations to receive funding, albeit of a different kind, with strings attached and under contract. In short, the entire sector found itself operating in a new institutional and economic landscape. Interestingly, however, even though there was undeniably a coercive context for these shifts, early thinking in Canada put considerable emphasis on the potential for 'collaborative governance' (Ford and Zussman 1995); it would take some time to begin 'enacting' this notion.

The non-profit and voluntary sector was not, however, a passive consumer of cuts. In 1995, 12 diverse national groups created the Voluntary Sector Roundtable (VSR) as a forum for debate and to allow mobilisation at the national level in a coherent and concerted way in response to policy changes (Phillips 2001). Described as a 'coalition of coalitions', the VSR identified priorities, such as securing more generous tax incentives from the Federal Government for charitable giving and improving accountability. The groups obtained foundation funding for an independent Panel on Accountability and Governance in the Voluntary Sector, an expert panel chaired by Ed Broadbent to explore how the sector could improve accountability and federal regulation of the sector. The Broadbent panel began its work and reported in early 1999. As Phillips (2001, 2003a) describes in considerable detail, however, the panel had influence because of serendipitous factors:

- the Deakin Commission on the Future of the Voluntary Sector had reported in 1996 and, after the June 1997 election, the Blair Labour Government in the United Kingdom began to run with its ideas on the third sector, developing its 'compacts' and attracting international attention
- Canada's Chretien Government was looking beyond the Program Review to developing a more positive policy agenda, and strengthening of the non-profit and voluntary sector found its way into its campaign commitments in the 1997 election
- the government was looking for ways to directly connect to Canadians to develop a federal presence, unmediated by provincial and territorial governments, and it sought to make contributions in the spirit of the forthcoming International Year of the Volunteer (2001).

After the election, the government established a Voluntary Sector Task Force secretariat working in the Privy Council Office to formulate an approach for the government, which tapped into the Broadbent panel's recommendations and took them to cabinet. In addition to many other discussions, three ministers with relevant responsibilities (human resources and social development, health and revenue) hosted a dinner with 10 other ministers and 20 representatives from the voluntary sector.

In March 1999, the government and voluntary sector agreed to establish three joint tables (on relationships, capacity and regulation), each with 14 members. Their mandate was to negotiate and draft a final report by August. The report, *Working Together*, then went into Ottawa's maw, first emerging as a commitment in the government's October 1999 'Speech from the Throne' and then mentioned, but not funded, in the February 2000 budget. After the creation of a Ministers' Reference Group, the VSI was announced in June 2000 with $95 million, spread over five years, to fund work in the following areas: accord development, awareness, capacity, the National Volunteerism Initiative, information management and technology and regulation.

Staffing and coordinating the elaborated joint-table process was a logistical challenge, requiring a joint table simply to keep the process on track, coordinating committees inside government (to coordinate officials and to engage relevant ministers) and independently for the sector. This intensive activity led to the adoption of a Voluntary Sector Accord in December 2001, while other reports and agreements emerged with time. For example, codes of practice for policy dialogue and funding were released in October 2002, concluding the first phase of the VSI. The second phase, from 2003 to 2005, involved additional reports emerging from first-phase activities, implementing many of the programs that had been identified and taking stock of progress and gaps that still needed to be addressed.[2] This activity was notable for the relationships it generated and the mutual understanding it fostered within and across the leadership of government and the non-profit and voluntary sector, and for the accords, codes of practice, research and specific projects it funded, as well as an agenda for action that would deepen the reach of the initiative—but it did not provide base funding for sustaining the VSI. As Phillips (2003b) and Phillips and Levasseur (2004) observe, several key issues, such as securing greater scope for funding and a different regime for charitable registration, were sidestepped. Moreover, many of the principal players on both sides were moving onto new challenges and the mix of the government's policy agenda was evolving.

By 2005, the VSI was confronted with four significant challenges. First, its sprawling agenda required consolidation and perhaps institutionalisation, or else it would dissipate. Second, the five-year funding for the VSI was coming to an end and there was concern about whether and how to renew it. Third, coming to agreement on these matters was difficult because of great uncertainty at the political level: the struggle over succession between Prime Minister Chretien and former Minister of Finance Martin, the subsequent precarious minority Martin Government, and then the minority Harper Government, which did not have the sector on its agenda. Fourth, several scandals in the early 2000s under the Chretien Government—the HRDC grants and contributions scandal,[3] the federal sponsorship affair and the federal gun-registry program cost overruns—precipitated a remarkable shift in how federal departments and agencies dealt with the non-profit and voluntary and other sectors. Ministers and officials quickly became incredibly risk averse and bureaucratic when administering grants and contributions, dramatically increasing the cost in time and administrative overheads for those outside government, as well as for other levels of government. The Martin and Harper Governments responded with many overlapping initiatives that served to increase central-agency and departmental controls and to expand audit capabilities and requirements across government, which led to the Gomery Commission and the adoption of the *Federal Accountability Act*.

The government-sector political space for moving the VSI to its next phase narrowed considerably under the Harper Government. The government was led by a disciplined prime minister focused on a few core priorities and constantly in an election-ready stance. This is not to say, however, that there were not victories for the sector: the Harper Government did approve legislation providing more favourable tax treatment of stock options as donations to charitable organisations. Moreover, the Harper Government was made aware of the increasingly widespread frustration outside and inside government over the administration of grants and contributions from the Federal Government, including higher proportional administrative costs and delays, particularly for smaller groups. In response, the government appointed a Blue Ribbon Panel on Grants and Contributions in June 2006 to review how the Federal Government managed $27 billion in spending to non-profit and voluntary organisations, universities, aboriginal organisations, businesses, international organisations and other governments.

The Blue Ribbon Panel (BRP) initially consisted of three well-known leaders from outside government and had six months in which to size up the challenge, undertake consultations and produce its final report. The BRP held extensive consultations despite the short time frames. During the consultation phases, the non-profit and voluntary sector was the best organised of the affected sectors and saw the exercise as an important 'policy window' for the sector for dealing with the Harper Government. Indeed, a key challenge for the BRP was to take advantage of the sector's expertise and connections in public-service departments but avoid having the exercise become a back-door opportunity for putting the sector back on the government agenda (this was also a risk with respect to the aboriginal and other sectors concerned). The BRP, while aware of broader concerns and ambitions, maintained its focus on improving how the Federal Government administered grants and contributions.

The report, *From Red Tape to Clear Results*, was released publicly in February 2007, though it had been completed earlier (Blue Ribbon Panel on Grants and Contributions 2006). The report called for a client-oriented, simplified and cost-effective approach to administering grants and contributions, one that recognised that recipients often received funding from multiple sources. It also suggested that the Treasury Board Secretariat build a centre of expertise for grants and contributions, work with vanguard departments and develop a government-wide training program. Among many other things, it recommended that the government act in a concerted way and monitor performance in implementing the recommendations; indeed, even before the report was published, implementation work had started at the Treasury Board Secretariat. For example, a National Task Force on Grants and Contributions, led by Imagine Canada[4] worked with the Public Policy Forum to have a follow-up consultation at a Stakeholder Forum in June 2007.

On 27 May 2008, a renewed sectoral summit with more than 250 participants invited the president of the Treasury Board to announce progress and initiatives relating to the BRP. These included overhauling the Transfer Payments Policy to be more recipient oriented and to correspond reporting requirements with the degree of risk and the track record of organisations, standards for the quality of service for grant and contribution recipients, the identification of vanguard departments (responsible for just more than half of grant and contribution spending) and pushing forward with central capabilities such as a centre of excellence and better technology for the administration of grants and contributions in the Treasury Board Secretariat. The minister's announcement was followed by a commitment to have the two BRP leaders host regional stakeholder forums in June 2008 and later in the year to discuss and report on progress from a non-profit and voluntary organisation perspective (Imagine Canada 2008).

Much has been written about the VSI and in considerable detail, often putting the Canadian approach and accomplishments in comparative perspective (Good 2001, 2003; Phillips 2001, 2003a, 2003b; Brock 2003; Brock and Banting 2003; Phillips and Lavasseur 2004). The initial publications, many written by insiders, reflect the excitement and the twists and turns of moving a significant initiative further; the later publications share more sober assessments of what was accomplished and a sense of disappointment, particularly in the wake of the HRDC grants and contributions scandal. In their broad assessment, Phillips and Levasseur (2004) use the metaphor of the game of 'snakes and ladders' to describe the non-profit and voluntary sector's experience of trying to move towards the goals many from the sector had in mind, particularly when the standard against which success was judged consisted of binding agreements with government, more substantial institutions inside and outside government to buttress those agreements and a strong associational structure in the sector. Another complication was that the core government secretariat was moved away from the centre of government to a succession of different departments, as part of broader machinery changes introduced by the Martin and Harper Governments. This, in addition to the turnover of leadership engaged directly with the VSI, has made it difficult to sustain momentum.

Much was accomplished, however, after more than a decade of effort. A coherent view developed of what a well-functioning non-profit and voluntary sector was, including how a good relationship with government might work. The Voluntary Sector Accord and the codes of practice were negotiated and foundational research was sponsored and completed to provide a good sense of the size, diversity, financial dimensions and economic impact of the sector across the country. A national learning initiative canvassed the sector to identify its needs and challenges, and the competencies and strategies required to address them, and a Human Resource Council for the Non-Profit and Voluntary Sector was established. The Canadian Centre for Philanthropy and the Coalition of National Voluntary Organisations merged capacities and respective strengths to become Imagine Canada, in part to create a more potent focal point for the sector at the national level, to animate a broader coalition of non-profit and voluntary organisations and to represent the sector on priority issues to government. The performance of Imagine Canada with the BRP process (before, during and after) demonstrated its influence, even if there were numerous other issues it concerted with other non-profit-sector organisations. There has emerged a new generation of university and think tank experts who have programs of research and who provide voices and assessments, including the National Centre for Voluntary Research and Development at Carleton University and the University of Ottawa, the Public Policy and Third Sector program at Queen's University and the Voluntary Sector Affinity Group under the auspices of the Association of Community Colleges of Canada, a Canadian offshoot of the Association for Research on Nonprofit and Voluntary Organisations (ARNOVA), to name only a few. The more general result is an enhanced network consisting of practitioners, researchers and officials who collectively have a much better ability to convey the sector's needs than 10 years earlier.

So, despite the snakes and ladders, a lot has been accomplished and there are well-developed ideas and principles waiting to be animated. Many resources were brought to the table in order to kick-start an ambitious institutional reform agenda. Much has yet to be realised from the vision first delineated as a result of the Broadbent panel process, but it is important to recall the scope of that ambition, which really should be depicted as a comprehensive policy innovation requiring institutional and cultural change. Even if there is a powerful, coherent and compelling vision for change, as with any significant restructuring of large-scale organisations, it takes time to put each of the foundational 'bricks' in place. Where the VSI is concerned, the more significant bricks will require additional and concerted political engagement, which is episodic and a matter of good timing. Many bricks have been put in place, and the non-profit and voluntary sector at the federal level is well positioned to continue making its case on the key issues it has identified. Further policy change and institutionalisation will have to await further funding and legislation, and this requires external commitment and good timing.

Recent developments in British Columbia: from Ministry of Community Development, Cooperatives and Volunteers to Government Non Profit Initiative

Efforts to improve government–non-profit sector relationships have not been confined to the national level. Several provinces have launched initiatives in the past few years, including Newfoundland, Quebec, New Brunswick, Alberta, Ontario and, most recently, British Columbia. Here, we consider recent developments in British Columbia (BC).

The BC case is interesting because it stood as an exemplar of strong government interest in strengthening the non-profit and voluntary sector during the late 1990s, but a change in government set back the gains that had been made, in part because it set in motion a fundamental restructuring of how government and the Public Service worked in the early 2000s, which put the non-profit and voluntary sector on considerably different footing, not so much by design but as a strong implication of how government generally would do business. As space was created for sector and government leaders to discuss issues of mutual concern, non-profit and voluntary sector representatives certainly had the experience of the VSI in mind (many had participated in one way or another) and they were well aware of parallel international developments in this area, including in Australia. There has been strong interest in securing change that makes a practical and direct difference to those who deliver, manage and oversee services. A distinctive feature of British Columbia is that building a more positive relationship with First Nations governments and communities is high on the policy agenda.

Before considering more recent developments, it is worth briefly acknowledging the approach taken by the New Democratic Party (NDP) government led by Glen Clark in the late 1990s. In April 1998, the Premier appointed Jenny Kwan as Minister for Community Development, Cooperatives and Volunteers, and a voluntary-sector strategy process was initiated. A supporting ministry was established in July 1999 and the next December its strategy was announced. A key initiative was InVOLve BC, $14 million for 119 seed projects that relied on a 23-person task force to assess applications. The government also used its role as chair to host the first federal–provincial territorial meeting on community development and the voluntary sector in March 2000 (Guerin 2002; Kwan 2002). This engagement was, however, on precarious footing: the NDP government was soon embroiled in a series of political crises and leadership uncertainty and succession, and the non-profit and voluntary sector in British Columbia itself was not well organised.

In May 2001, a Liberal government under the leadership of Gordon Campbell secured a landslide victory in the provincial election. The government announced a major shake-up of the ministries and structure of the Public Service and, echoing Ottawa's 1994 Program Review, launched a review of all programs as well as agencies, boards and commissions—all with the overarching goal of reining in provincial finances and making government leaner and more innovative with significant reductions in expenditure and personnel. As was the case with the Program Review, there were significant impacts on non-profit and voluntary organisations: ministry budgets were dramatically cut, often directly affecting the funding available for non-profit and voluntary organisations; the Ministry of Community Development, Cooperatives and Volunteers was eliminated, with its programs either dispersed among other ministries or phased out; and the senior management teams of ministries were consumed with meeting financial and full-time equivalent position downsizing targets for a government that valued performance and had relatively less time for cultivating relationships with non-profit and voluntary sector leaders. Coming on the heels of the federal Program Review cuts and Ottawa's increasingly risk-averse environment after the HRDC scandal, many non-profit and voluntary sector leaders found their organisations in a very difficult environment.

The governance model taking shape in British Columbia soon became apparent: in almost every policy sector, the government encouraged ministries to 'steer' rather than deliver services, and this meant either vacating certain responsibilities or relying far more heavily on for-profit, non-profit and voluntary organisations to deliver services. The government also increasingly sought to promote and rely on PPPs for the purposes of infrastructure development, establishing Partnerships BC, and aggressively pursuing the outsourcing of revenue collection and some corporate services with for-profit providers. For many non-profit and voluntary sector organisations, this meant the end of the grants they had relied on. Increasingly, however, they could secure funding through contracts for specific deliverables or compete for service-delivery contracts through the procurement system—the government's increasingly preferred vehicle for awarding work. The need to develop a results orientation and performance agreements became paramount, but overheads were typically not recognised. While the effects on various segments of the non-profit and voluntary sector varied across the waterfront of the BC Government, it is important to understand that this did not represent a deliberate policy towards furthering linkages with the sector in a certain way; rather, it was an implication of a strong push from the government under new public management and alternative service delivery principles in pursuit of higher goals as to what were the appropriate responsibilities of the Public Service. How matters shook out for the non-profit and voluntary organisations depended on their relationships with specific ministries. In short, the aggregate impacts on the sector were cumulative depending on the specific and uncoordinated decisions and styles of specific ministries.

Leaders inside and outside the sector expressed concern, although the BC non-profit and voluntary sector did not have an associational structure with as strong a voice as counterparts at the national level. That said, the Voluntary Organisations Consortium of British Columbia was established in British Columbia in 2002, and the Vancouver Foundation sponsored the start up of the Centre for Sustainable Development in Vancouver about the same time as the Centre for Non Profit Management was established on Vancouver Island. The Ministry of Public Safety and the Solicitor-General provided funding for a Centre for Non Profit Development to foster courses for non-profit and voluntary organisations in community colleges in 2003. In July 2004, the Centre for Non Profit Management (CNPM) released a discussion paper entitled *Strengthening the relationship*, calling for more dialogue between government and the sector. In October 2005, the Voluntary Organisations Consortium of British Columbia (VOCBC 2005) invited the leaders of several non-profit and voluntary organisations to discuss an approach to galvanising the sector, and it is worth noting that little was said directly about the nature of government policy towards the sector—presumably because many were concerned about how to convey their concerns without compromising fragile funding arrangements. Something was in the air.

In early 2007, with initial funding support from several ministries, CNPM and the University of Victoria's School of Public Administration published a discussion paper (CNPM 2007a) and hosted a roundtable discussion with leaders from the government and non-profit and voluntary sectors in late May 2007 on their respective challenges and perspectives, and to ascertain if there was sufficient interest in exploring a common agenda. A crucial signal was the agreement of the Deputy Minister of Public Safety and the Solicitor-General and the CEO of the Vancouver Foundation to serve as co-chairs of the event. In addition to the concerns emanating from the sector about funding, accountability, capacity and procurement, the government representatives expressed their interest in ensuring that services were well delivered by non-profit and voluntary organisations and that they were accountable and well governed.

The round table was a success and was well attended by senior representatives of both sectors (CNPM 2007b). There was widespread agreement that all parties were interested in better serving citizens and communities, and that much progress could be made without asking for significant funding increases for the non-profit and voluntary sector organisations, but rather by seeking ways to recognise their challenges, build capability, learn from success and explore the flexibilities available in procurement and other funding instruments. Out of the event came an agreement to establish a further process and another round table the next year that would focus on the priorities of fostering the relationship between the government and the non-profit and voluntary sector, building the capacity of the non-profit and voluntary sector and finding ways to better handle funding, performance measurement and accountability. The co-chairs of the May 2007 round table agreed not only to lead the next round, thereby providing continuity, but to jointly secure funding and form a core secretariat to handle coordination and logistics. In late 2007, three task forces and a steering committee were established, each co-chaired by government and sector leaders and supported by coordinating staff and researchers. It was agreed to invite participants mainly from the social-policy sectors. The process came to be known as the Government–Nonprofit Sector Initiative (GNPI). The GNPI is still very much a work in progress at the time of writing. The original goal was to have the task forces set the terms of reference for the researchers, to comment on the papers as they took shape and then for the revised versions of the papers to feed into a comprehensive discussion paper and recommendations that would feed into the second and larger round table event in late July 2008. Similar to the VSI process, however, each of the task forces saw the value of deliberation and dialogue between government and sector representatives on perceptions, definitions, concepts and frameworks, and also sought to shape the discussion papers and explore how the recommendations from each task force might link to the others. There were more requests for information, so the secretariat commissioned additional background papers. It was agreed to incorporate a broader First Nations presence into the process. With time lines sliding, it was agreed to delay wider consultations until recommendations were finalised and to use the July 2008 round table as a final meeting of the task forces, leaving the final public round table event to take place in autumn 2008. The co-chairs agreed to continue to lead the process, and it was announced that the GNPI secretariat would be transferred to the Ministry of Housing and Social Development, which was led by a deputy minister on the steering committee.

There is not the space here to delve into the working recommendations of the task forces (and there are many!) or all the considerations that have gone into drafting the report, but a few observations are in order. First, despite awareness of the models from other jurisdictions, many participants resisted focusing too much on accords, legislation and engaging politicians. Rather, there has been a desire to secure on-the-ground impacts and quick wins, and build a process that can withstand the coming and going of governments. Second, it was recognised that the government–non-profit/voluntary sector relationship proceeded at four levels (program, policy sector, horizontal initiatives and sectoral) and that, despite all of the change arising from restructuring, there were many examples of good and positive practice that relied on ingenuity, dialogue and using flexibilities to achieve better outcomes for both parties. Third, there was widespread agreement that the 'value propositions' for non-profit/voluntary organisations delivering services as well as the government-sector relationship had to be made clearly and persistently. Fourth, while the non-profit form of mobilising effort was used extensively off-reserve, particularly by the system of Aboriginal Friendship Centres in urban settings, it had not been employed by First Nations communities. With the 'new relationship' and treaty settlements in British Columbia there is the possibility that non-profits could be used more extensively. Finally, in addition to developing a jointly managed structure to continue the GNPI process, set up a web site and host future round tables or summits, it was recognised that each partner would have to deepen capabilities and structures, reaching into government and the non-profit/voluntary sector respectively, if the process were to be sustained and the envisioned gains secured.

Conclusion: some reflections to consider

This chapter has presented two Canadian cases that illustrate some of the challenges and dynamics of fostering and galvanising government–non-profit/voluntary sector relations and collaboration, recognising that many such initiatives are in progress in Australia and elsewhere in the world. Such initiatives, properly understood, are increasingly about creating a productive and equitable environment in which non-profit and voluntary sector organisations can realise their potential to innovate and meet the needs of citizens and communities—often in concert with government. This chapter has suggested that such initiatives represent efforts to find productive ground between the broad currents of new public management and strengthening civil-society approaches, and are consistent with and give expression to some of the original notions underpinning early alternative service-delivery thinking in Canada. More generally, as these initiatives unfold and take shape, they hold the promise of infusing the concepts of collaboration, transparency, risk sharing, accountability and capacity, among others, with richer meaning.

Phillips (2005), in analysing the launch of the VSI, highlighted the important role of serendipity in fostering government–voluntary sector relations. Her account shows that while chance plays an important role, shrewd strategising can also take better advantage of political opportunities as they arise. Undoubtedly, such an analytical frame can illuminate understanding of how any such collaboration emerges in different jurisdictions, but what has been made less clear is that the same dynamics are always at work, and can crowd out what was once a priority and move it quickly down a government's agenda. This happened to the VSI under the Martin Government and in British Columbia when the Campbell Government dissolved the Ministry of Community Development, Cooperatives and Volunteers. This poses an interesting challenge for officials and non-profit sector leaders seeking to improve relationships and design sustainable governance regimes.

What are the right amounts and levels of formalisation, institutionalisation and engagement between the two sectors? On one hand, while political engagement—particularly from ministers and governments—can be critical with respect to liberating resources, establishing or responding to task forces and commissions and passing legislation, such support can be fickle. Indeed, it could be prudent to not rely too heavily on political engagement at the highest levels, which can be evanescent or sideswiped by other priorities, or can be seen as being associated with the political platform of a particular government. Moreover, a sitting government could have difficulty with the advocacy of certain policy positions from certain quarters of the non-profit and voluntary sector. With this in mind, perhaps the early focus of government–non-profit sector initiatives should be on improving communication and learning across the sector, sharing innovation and experiences from all parts of the sector and those of other jurisdictions, building capacity in government and the sector to better manage contracts and relationships and finding ways to improve accountability and management. This suggests a strategy that focuses on fostering the relationship between government officials and non-profit sector representatives and keeping elected representatives of all persuasions informed and engaged as required.

The worry of elected governments and the sector about the extent to which non-profits and voluntary organisations should exercise their voice and engage in political advocacy, of course, remains. I see this, however, as a matter for the sector to deal with: it needs to develop further functional specialisation, creating or levering other organisations not involved in service delivery to undertake evaluations and studies and advocate for new or changed policies and programs. Many such organisations exist in the form of university or non-profit think tanks and provincial and national associations of one kind or another. These are the organisations that need to make the case for the sector on specific issues. When we look back to the success at the federal level in Canada and in British Columbia, we can see that the focus was on improving the context for the non-profit and voluntary sector and how it might better work with governments to improve public value, not arguing for specific substantive policies. These are crucial lessons to bear in mind.

The question of design also leads one to consider what should be the ultimate shape and content of a regime for overseeing government–non-profit/voluntary relations. Comparative analysis in the literature (for example, Carter and Speevak Sladowski 2008) has reviewed the frameworks in several jurisdictions and developed a check list for a fully elaborated system. This work focused primarily on erecting such systems and calls for heavily institutionalised and regulated systems. It tends not to examine closely what might be the best strategic approaches for building regimes in jurisdictions with different governance and sector realities, although Phillips (2003b) stands as an exception, looking closely at early phases of development in five jurisdictions. This is important because the context in which such initiatives begin can have great variation in the relative degree of coordination and capacity of the government and non-profit and voluntary sectors (Atkinson and Coleman 1989), suggesting a focus on different development paths. Moreover, closer research is required on how well such systems work, the extent to which they are sustainable across different governments or are fraught with their own challenges and whether non-profit and voluntary organisations, as well as government partners, feel well served by them. It is one thing to design and launch such regimes, and quite another to work under them. We need to know how such systems mature in a decade or two, how long it takes for cultural change to work through the partner sectors and when strategic institutional 'lifts' or step-wise investments in additional 'bricks' are made; such insight could usefully be framed with agenda-setting models as well. This suggests exciting directions for the next generation of systematic research to explore.

Finally, the literature to date does not fully recognise the complexity of the challenge of fostering government and non-profit and voluntary sector collaboration. Cultivating such collaboration is best understood as a complex policy challenge that reaches across different policy domains (each with its own unique challenges), involves fostering relationships at different levels (peak, sectoral, program and front-line), embraces diversity in the size and scope of participating organisations, works across different governments, that needs to address the evolving priorities of governments and communities, that must contend with considerable turnover in personnel and has long-term time horizons. In addition to the use of agenda-setting frameworks, it might be useful to consider these initiatives as similar to the challenges of launching and sustaining whole-of-government and joined-up government (Commonwealth of Australia 2004) and comprehensive policy interventions (Desveaux et al. 1994), and employ some of those frameworks. This should help sharpen expectations and thoughts about institutional design for government–non-profit/voluntary sector initiatives, and ascertain what is unique about them. Conversely, further accounts of government–non-profit/voluntary sector collaboration could usefully inform the whole-of-government and comprehensive policy innovation literature.

References

Alberta Municipal Affairs 2008, *Nonprofit/Voluntary Sector Initiative*, <www.municipalaffairs.gov.ab.ca/mc_volunteer_initiative.cfm>

Armit, Amelita and Bourgault, Jacques (eds) 1996, *Hard Choices or No Choice? Assessing Program Review*, Institute of Public Administration of Canada, Toronto.

Atkinson, Michael M. and Coleman, William 1989, *The State, Business, and Industrial Change in Canada*, University of Toronto Press, Toronto.

Aucoin, Peter 1996, *The New Public Management: Canada in comparative perspective*, Institute for Research on Public Policy, Montreal.

Blue Ribbon Panel on Grants and Contributions 2006, *From Red Tape to Clear Results*, December, Treasury Board of Canada, Ottawa.

Brock, Kathy L. and Banting Keith, G. (eds) 2001, *The Nonprofit Sector and Government in a New Century*, McGill and Queen's University Press, Montreal and Kingston.

Brock, Kathy L. and Banting Keith, G. (eds) 2003, *The Non Profit Sector in Interesting Times*, McGill–Queen's University Press, Montreal and Kingston.

Brock, Kathy L. (ed.) 2002, *Improving Connections Between Governments and Nonprofit and Voluntary Organizations: Public policy and the third sector*, McGill–Queen's University Press, Montreal and Kingston.

Brock, Kathy L. (ed.) 2003, *Delicate Dances: Public policy and the nonprofit sector*, McGill–Queen's University Press, Montreal and Kingston.

Canada Voluntary Sector Initiative (CVSI) 2008, *Partnering for the Benefit of Canadians*, viewed May 2008, <www.vsi-isbc.org/eng/index.cfm>

Carter, Susan and Speevak Sladowski, Paula 2008, Deliberate relationships between government and the nonprofit/voluntary sector: an unfolding picture, Draft, Centre for Voluntary Sector Research and Development, Ottawa.

Centre for Non Profit Management (CNPM) 2004, *Building Bridges: Strengthening provincial government and community voluntary sector relationships in British Columbia*, July, Centre for Non Profit Management and UVic School of Public Administration, Victoria, <http://publicadmin.uvic.ca/cpss/vsi/pdfs/bridges_v4.4.pdf>

Centre for Non Profit Management (CNPM) 2007a, *Strengthening the relationship: round table on government and non profit relations in British Columbia*, Discussion Paper, May, Centre for Non Profit Management and School of Public Administration, Victoria, <http://www.cnpm.ca/PDF%20Files/discussion_paper.pdf>

Centre for Non Profit Management (CNPM) 2007b, *Strengthening the relationship: round table on government and non profit relations in British Columbia*, Proceedings, 30 May 2007, Centre for Non Profit Management and School of Public Administration, Victoria, <http://www.cnpm.ca/PDF%20Files/Proceedings_Round_Table_30_May_clr.pdf>

Clark, Ian D. 1994, 'Restraint, renewal, and the Treasury Board Secretariat', *Canadian Public Administration*, vol. 37, no. 2, Summer, pp. 209–48.

Commonwealth of Australia 2004, *Connecting Government: Whole of government responses to Australia's priority challenges*, Management Advisory Committee, Commonwealth of Australia, Canberra.

Desveaux, James A., Lindquist, Evert A. and Toner, Glen 1994, 'Organizing for policy innovation in public bureaucracy: AIDS, energy, and environmental policy in Canada', *Canadian Journal of Political Science*, vol. 27, no. 3, September, pp. 493–538.

Evans, B. Mitchell and Shields, John 2002, 'The third sector: neo-liberal restructuring, governance, and the remaking of state–civil society relationships', in Christopher Dunn (ed.), *The Handbook of Canadian Public Administration*, Oxford University Press, Toronto, pp. 139–58.

Ford, Robin and Zussman, David (eds) 1997, *Alternative Service Delivery: Sharing governance in Canada*, KPMG Centre for Government Foundation and the Institute of Public Administration of Canada, Toronto.

Good, David A. 2001, 'A government voluntary sector accord', *ISUMA*, Summer, pp. 46–52.

Good, David A. 2003, *The Politics of Public Management: The HRDC audit of grants and contributions*, University of Toronto Press, Toronto.

Good, David A. 2007, *The Politics of Public Money: Spenders, guardians, priority setters, and financial watchdogs inside the Canadian Government*, University of Toronto Press, Toronto.

Government of New Brunswick 2008, *New Era of Partnership Between Government and Non-Profit Sector*, <www.gnb.ca/cnb/Promos/CNP/index-e.asp>

Government of New Zealand 2008, Office for the Community and Voluntary Sector,

Government of Queensland 2008,

Government of South Australia 2003, *Advancing the Community Together*, May 2003, <www.ofv.sa.gov.au/pdfs/Advancing%20the%20Community_approvedwordversion.pdf>

Government of the United Kingdom 2008a, *Giving Voice and Support to Civil Society*, England NCVO,

Government of the United Kingdom 2008b, Northern Ireland Compact, <www.grant-tracker.org/index.cfm/section/publications/key/07dec2006thecompact>

Government of the United Kingdom 2008c, *Voluntary Sector Scheme*, Welsh Assembly, <http://new.wales.gov.uk/topics/housingandcommunity/voluntarysector/publications/volsectorscheme?lang=en>

Government of the United Kingdom 2008d, *Working Together Better*, England Compact,

Greenspon, Edward and Wilson-Smith, Anthony 1996, *Double Vision: The inside story of the Liberals in power*, Doubleday, Toronto.

Guerin, Hal 2002, 'Working with the third sector', in Kathy L. Brock (ed.), *Improving Connections Between Governments and Nonprofit and Voluntary Organizations: Public policy and the third sector*, McGill–Queen's University Press, Montreal and Kingston, pp. 136–41.

Imagine Canada 2008, *Ottawa Reports*, June.

Kwan, Jenny 2002, 'Future trends in public policy and the third sector', in Kathy L. Brock (ed.), *Improving Connections Between Governments and Nonprofit and Voluntary Organizations: Public policy and the third sector*, McGill–Queen's University Press, Montreal and Kingston, pp. 163–72.

Lindquist, Evert 1997, 'The bewildering pace of public sector reform in Canada', in J. E. Lane (ed.), *Public Sector Reform: Rationale, trends and problems*, Sage, London, pp. 47–63.

Newfoundland and Labrador Community Services 2008, *Building a Voice for the Voluntary Sector*.

Nova Scotia Federation of Community Organizations 2008, *Uniting the Voluntary Sector in Halifax Regional Municipality*, viewed May 2008, <http://www.foco.ca/>

Ontario VSO 2008, *Strengthening Voluntarism in Ontario*,

Paquet, Gilles and Shepherd, Robert 1996, 'The Program Review process: a deconstruction', in Gene Swimmer (ed.), *How Ottawa Spends 1996–97: Life under the knife*, Carleton University Press, Ottawa, pp. 39–72.

Phillips, Susan 2001, 'From charity to clarity: reinventing federal government–voluntary sector relationships', in Leslie A. Pal (ed.), *How Ottawa Spends 2001–2002: Power in transition*, Oxford University Press, Toronto, pp. 145–76.

Phillips, Susan and Levasseur, Karine 2004, 'The snakes and ladders of accountability: contradictions between contracting and collaboration for Canada's voluntary sector', *Canadian Public Administration*, vol. 47, no. 4, pp. 451–74.

Phillips, Susan D. 2003a, 'In accordance: Canada's Voluntary Sector Accord from idea to implementation', in Kathy L. Brock (ed.), *Delicate Dances: Public policy and the non profit sector*, McGill–Queen's University Press, Montreal and Kingston, pp. 17–61.

Phillips, Susan D. 2003b, 'Voluntary sector–government relationships in transition: learning from international experience for the Canadian context', in Kathy L. Brock and Keith G. Banting (eds), *The Nonprofit Sector in Interesting Times: Case studies in a changing sector*, McGill–Queen's University Press, Montreal and Kingston, pp. 17–71.

Phillips, Susan D. 2007, 'Policy analysis and the voluntary sector: evolving policy styles', in L. Dobuzinskis, M. Howlett and D. Laycock (eds), *Policy Analysis in Canada: The state of the art*, University of Toronto Press, Toronto, pp. 497–521.

Putnam, Robert D. 2000, *Bowling Alone: The collapse and revival of American community*, Simon and Schuster, New York.

Putnam, Robert D. et al. 1994, *Making Democracy Work: Civic traditions in modern Italy*, Princeton University Press, Princeton.

Scottish Council for Voluntary Organisations 2008, <www.scvo.org.uk/scvo/Home/Home.aspx>

Voluntary and Non-Profit Sector Organization of Manitoba 2008, *Sustaining Manitoba's Voluntary and Non-Profit Sector*,

Voluntary Organizations Consortium of British Columbia (VOCBC) 2005, *What We Know: A roundtable for leaders in BC's voluntary/non profit sectors*, Report, 15 October 2005.

ENDNOTES

[1] Evert Lindquist is Director and Professor of the University of Victoria's School of Public Administration (SPA), which collaborated with the National Centre for Voluntary Sector Development of Carleton University on one of the many pilots associated with the much larger Voluntary Sector Initiative, the Policy Internship and Fellows (PIAF) program. He also assisted with the work of the Blue Ribbon Panel on Grants and Contributions, is a member of the ACCC Voluntary Sector Affinity Group, sits on the steering committee of the BC Government/Non Profit Sector Initiative and serves as chair of the Centre for Non Profit Management (CNPM). CNPM and SPA were catalysts for the latest effort to foster government–non-profit sector collaboration in British Columbia.

[2] For example, *Taking the Accord Forward* (December 2003); *The Journey Continues* (December 2004); *Capacity Joint Table Advisory Committee* (September 2005).

[3] See Good (2003) on the HRDC grants and contributions scandal. It is ironic that HRDC was one of the principal departments in moving the VSI forward, and David Good co-chaired one of the sectoral task forces.

[4] Imagine Canada was formed out of a merger of the Coalition of National Voluntary Organizations and the Canadian Centre for Philanthropy in the wake of the Voluntary Sector Initiative.

16. Collaboration with the third sector: UK perspectives

Ben Jupp

Introduction: a burgeoning interest in collaboration

Collaboration or partnership with the private sector and the not-for-profit sector (referred to in the United Kingdom as the 'third sector') started to become a theme for the UK Government from the mid-1990s. As with many ideas, the hype exceeded the reality for some time. By the late 1990s, however, everyone in UK policymaking was talking about partnership. It was in a way analogous to the 'dot.com' hype that reached a peak about the turn of the century. Partnerships proliferated at the national and local levels. The answer to every social problem seemed to be moving towards 'joining up' thinking, working together and harnessing the skills and resources of different sectors. And, like the dot.com crash, the more challenging reality then caught up with the rhetoric.

Partnership and collaborative relations turned out not to be as easy as people thought. Those who considered that it would be a miracle approach to addressing ingrained social problems were as disappointed as those investors who thought that every web site was inevitably going to make money. In the United Kingdom, this led to some 'partnership crashes': a number of the local collaborations on skills, health, education and housing regeneration were wound up when the tough reality of working collaboratively started to bite.

Just as with the Internet and electronic commerce, however, the underlying logic of the rise of collaborative approaches was retained throughout the oscillations of the initial over-hype and subsequent 'crash'. In the past few years, a new, more measured, but ultimately more effective agenda has been developed that has already become an enduring feature of how government works.

In this chapter, I aim to provide a brief overview of the driving forces towards greater collaboration with the not-for-profit sector, some of the main measures we have developed to enable such collaboration and my perspective on the successes and challenges associated with these approaches. This is based on my personal observations as director of the Office of the Third Sector, the part of the British Government with responsibilities for regulating and supporting the third sector.[1]

Why collaboration with the third sector?

What is driving our interest in collaboration with communities and the third sector? There are four powerful underlying drivers. Each relates to the social context and the attributes of the third sector in all its various configurations.

First, in a period of unrivalled migration and ethnic diversity, it is more important than ever for governments (and the wider community) to support those institutions that knit together the social fabric of local communities and the country as a whole. Evidence from the United Kingdom suggests that people who actively participate in community groups are far more likely to trust others. The government therefore has a significant interest in working with these groups to support their growth and to enable them to play an increasing role in strengthening the social fabric of local areas and the country as a whole.

Second, public services can benefit from collaboration with community groups and third-sector providers. Improvement can be driven partly by enabling a diverse range of suppliers, generating service effectiveness and efficiencies. Such diversity gives commissioners of services choices over the type and selection of providers to deliver effective policies. Improvements from engaging with not-for-profits can, however, be greater than those generated simply by competition. Community groups can bring uniquely strong relationships with citizens. In the United Kingdom, we still struggle to build really effective, trusted relationships between parts of our education, health and welfare services and those whom they seek to serve, particularly those suffering the greatest disadvantage. The sorts of health and welfare problems we now face, however, such as reducing obesity or the need for retraining late in adult life, require more effective relationships between the service and user than ever before. There is mounting evidence that at least some third-sector organisations are better than government at building such relationships with users and clients. The third sector has pioneered intensive projects to intervene with families or young people causing crime and 'antisocial behaviour'.

This recognition of the sector's role in delivering public services is manifested in the government's growing confidence in the sector. For instance, the government's total public expenditure through the voluntary sector more than doubled from about £5 billion ($A12 billion) in 1997 to closer to £11 billion ($A25 billion) in 2005. Almost all this growth was driven by greater public-service contracts, rather than grants. Growth has been particularly strong in areas such as child care and support for children, work with offenders, drug treatment and supported accommodation.

Third, government ministers recognise that in order to foster social change, some of the traditional collective institutions—political parties and trade unions—need more than ever to be complemented by a far wider coalition of campaigners and advocates. Although the temptation for ministers is to be defensive about campaigns and interest groups, many recognise that in addressing increasingly complex social, economic and environmental issues, neither the analysis of problems nor solutions to them can be confined to formal politics and executive government. It is often third-sector organisations that advocate social causes and provide the outlets for people to express their social conscience—whether through campaigns to reduce the debt of developing countries to enable them to invest in their own people or local environmental campaigns to increase the recycling of materials and products. They are the potential new partners for change.

Finally, and related to the third driver, it is becoming clear that people increasingly want to combine their ethical values with their work and consumption, partly as our professions and shopping habits play an increasingly important cultural role in society. Employees increasingly want to work for companies with a social edge or social conscience (employers of choice). The incidence of employee volunteering, in which employees are motivated to take on new socially responsible roles, is also rising. Consumers increasingly buy ethical goods such as environmentally friendly products or 'fair-trade' items. The ethical market in the United Kingdom was recently estimated at being worth nearly £30 billion a year (about $A70 billion). A progressive government is interested in fostering such combinations of social and economic goals, particularly by enabling the rise of social enterprises and businesses with social purposes. Again, this requires collaboration with such enterprises, from raising awareness among potential employees and investors to ensuring that government contracts lead the way in recognising the added social value that they deliver.

How have we tried to collaborate in the United Kingdom?

As head of the Office of the Third Sector, I suggest it is useful to think of our work falling along a spectrum of different types of collaboration. At one end, we have a number of programs that essentially seek to work for the sector to enable organisations to fulfil their own objectives. These have been mainly at the level of supporting the flow of various resources into the sector: encouraging and assisting volunteers, charitable giving, providing assets and organisational support and training. This is the sort of collaboration that is obviously most welcome by the sector. It enables organisations broadly to maintain their independence, but with greater resources to achieve their objectives. For example, the government has introduced citizenship education in schools, including encouraging volunteering, and developed major new programs and organisations to increase awareness and ease of volunteering, such as the development of a single national database of volunteering opportunities and the creation of 'v', a new national youth volunteering fund, which has the aim of enlisting a million new young volunteers. We now have a far more generous tax regime for gifts to charities—the value of which is up sevenfold in a decade to about £1 billion a year in income tax rebates alone—and a national program to support professional and organisational development in fields such as the use of IT and financial management. We have taken an active role in developing new forms of social investment finance, such as combined grants, development support and loans (often called patient capital) and formed partnerships to transfer local-authority assets, such as community centres, to third-sector organisations to give them a secure base from which to develop enterprise.

Our measures to build the capacity of campaigning and advocacy organisations and form collaborations with such groups are generally less well developed. We have started to invest in measures to help such organisations develop their skills, such as campaigning in new ways. The Office of the Third Sector has also developed strategic partnerships with about 50 organisations that represent parts of the diverse sector, to ensure that they can be more involved in policy development. This involves funding of three to five years (about £5 million per annum in grants) on the basis of a broad memorandum of understanding, but explicitly not seeking to determine how the resources are used.

At the other end of the spectrum are far more direct collaborations to deliver specific services or outcomes, usually through designated contracts. I noted above that total public resources going to the sector have more than doubled in 10 years. The majority of that growth has been in contracts for specific services; these, not grants, now account for more than 60 per cent of the public-sector resources going to the third sector. To promote such public-service delivery, we have sometimes obliged local agencies to shift a percentage of funding to independent providers or introduced a presumption on commissioners that they should look first to independent providers of services. That is the case with, for example, childcare services and youth programs. Generally, however, we sought to encourage local commissioners to think about service delivery by the third sector through developing a culture of commissioning for outcomes and the involvement of users, rather than designating the type of provider. We are trying to encourage a cultural change in commissioning practices to enable small organisations with few reserves to bid for contracts, such as through stipulating that contracts should be for at least three years and should take into account the full cost of providing services, such as training and overheads.

In between these enabling and direct collaborations, we have sought to improve the regulatory environment, particularly through establishing a compact between the sector and government and through modernising charity laws to create new legal forms that reflect the trading nature of many organisations and reduce regulatory burdens on small charities. The compact now covers a host of interactions, from the length and style of government consultation on policy, which has an impact on the sector, through to giving notice of the termination of grants.

What have been the outcomes of our approaches?

In broad terms, the third sector is vibrant and growing. Indeed, the number of charities registered with the Charity Commission increased from 121 000 in 1995 to more than 169 000 in 2004. There are now also about 55 000 social enterprises, and again, qualitative research indicates that numbers have been rising in recent years. In terms of the voluntary and community sector—that is, registered charities and small community groups but not all social enterprises—total turnover has risen by more than two-thirds in real terms since 1997. The total turnover of social enterprises is now estimated at £27 billion, approaching the same as registered charities. Employment has grown in the sector by more than one-fifth and the number of people undertaking regular formal or informal volunteering in England and Wales increased from 18.4 million in 2001 (the first year of the survey) to 20.4 million in 2005. Charitable giving by the community has remained broadly stable at just less than 1 per cent of gross domestic product (GDP)—or nearly £9 billion in 2005–06, or £183 per adult. While the enabling actions of government are only one factor behind these trends, and causation is often very difficult to pin down, the growth is encouraging.

There are also some encouraging signs about the positive impact of the third sector's activities. Recent research by the UK National Consumers Council suggests that users of some third-sector provider services, such as employment services, rate them better than public or private-sector providers (although they found comparable satisfaction in other fields of activity such as care for the elderly). What is more, the sector has remained at the forefront of a number of social campaigns, from healthy eating and reducing smoking to human-rights issues, such as disability rights. As noted earlier, some interesting markets are now emerging that combine social and economic returns.

There are, however, also some clear lessons. I will nominate the three most important. First, there is a risk that direct collaboration involving the contractual delivery of services leads to the creation of semi-state agencies and undermines some of the benefits of organisations being better trusted by users, which drove our interest in the first place. We have tried to avoid that through safeguards such as the compact, which seeks to protect the right of service-delivery organisations to be free to advocate and campaign. The National Consumers Council Research I noted earlier found, however, some evidence of this, such as in the area of social housing. We need more delivery mechanisms that are somewhere between generic subsidies or tax expenditures, such as tax breaks for the whole of the sector, and specific grants or contracts that run the risk of over-specifying outcomes and reducing the potential for user involvement and innovation. We are seeking to rectify this with other new initiatives such as partnership-inspired small-grant programs separate from formal contracts. This will help establish or improve local endowed foundations with broad social objectives. Such community foundations and other local endowments are able to provide independent, long-term, relatively flexible resources to local groups, but on the basis of informed funding, rather than blanket subsidies.

Second, there is a risk that government does not collaborate with the right groups on policy development. For example, in the Office of the Third Sector, we have recently been considering how the government engages with web-based and online groups—what some people describe as the 'social web'. Much of the social web is very detached from the traditional third sector and has itself only very weak organisational forms. We now recognise that our patterns of consultation and engagement tend to bypass it. There is a whole emerging civic sector that tends not to be represented through the formal channels. Instead, the task is to allow new forms of interaction—from online petitions to 'twitter' sites—and new forms of enabling support that rely as much on providing organisations with access to information as on traditional capacity building.

Third, we can be overly optimistic about the ease of creating cultural change around collaboration, among those working in the state and the third sector on partnerships and among society more generally. For example, the compact has been good in some respects, but has not penetrated much of the wider public sector. That is why we are appointing a commissioner to champion the compact among government departments, local government and the third sector and are now putting considerably more effort into incentives for local commissioners to work with the third sector, such as explicit targets for local authorities to strengthen the third sector. As in any cultural change, these incentives need to be backed up with training and support, so we are providing training for the top-2000 commissioners of local services and investing in 'bridging' organisations such as an innovation exchange that aims to link third-sector organisations with new ideas with commissioners looking for innovative solutions to local challenges.

Conclusion

Social inclusion and community wellbeing rest on an active third sector. Governments increasingly recognise the importance of this phenomenon and seek to enhance its potentialities. They have also come to realise that they cannot achieve their own goals without the active involvement of others—and indeed that such goals can be better formulated with the involvement of the third sector from the start. This does not mean that collaboration with the third sector is non-problematic or without significant downsides and risks. By giving greater emphasis to flexible, arm's-length funding, however, by better engaging with emerging civic organisations and social enterprises and by not underestimating the challenges of cultural change, sustainable collaborations can become an embedded part of the work of government in the future.

ENDNOTES

[1] The Office of the Third Sector forms part of the Cabinet Office in the United Kingdom. Most third-sector matters are devolved in Scotland, Wales and Northern Ireland and the majority of measures referred to in this chapter therefore relate to England only. This chapter is written in an entirely personal capacity and is not intended to represent the views of the UK Government.

Part 4. Collaboration: rhetoric and reality

17. Elusive appeal or aspirational ideal? The rhetoric and reality of the 'collaborative turn' in public policy

Janine O'Flynn

> Collaboration is like cottage cheese. It occasionally smells bad and separates easily.[1]

Apparently, there has been a 'collaborative turn' in public-policy circles. We have been informed that governments around the world must develop capabilities to be in a state of 'perpetual collaboration' if they are to competently face the looming challenges of the twenty-first century (Cortada et al. 2008), and that 'the future belongs to those who collaborate' (Economist Intelligence Unit 2007:4). The collaborative 'buzz' surrounding government (Wanna 2007) was even to be heard at the Australian Government's 2020 Summit in April 2008, at which the notion of collaborative governance was elevated as a 'top idea' that could propel the nation through the next decade or so (Commonwealth of Australia 2008). Prime Minister Kevin Rudd also hinted at the importance of collaboration when he addressed the Future Summit in May 2008, where he noted that there was a profound transformation afoot.[2] Clearly, collaboration is on the agenda.

What, however, is collaboration? Are we really witnessing a fundamental transformation in the way government addresses the challenges of the twenty-first century, or has collaboration become the latest fad to penetrate the Public Service? The purpose of this chapter is to reflect on the contributions to this monograph and consider such questions. My argument here is not to suggest that collaboration in government is a myth, or that collaboration is not happening on the ground. Rather, my intention is to engage in a more realistic and useful discussion of the various ways in which we might work together.

The obsession with collaboration

The attention collaboration is receiving could lead us to think that it represents a fundamental shift in how government and public-sector organisations operate and that the collaboration era has, or will soon, arrive: that a collaborative turn has occurred. A range of drivers has been identified to explain the popularity of collaboration (see Wanna, this volume), however, government interest has been summarised into three key propositions, each offering pay-offs in efficiency or effectiveness (Entwistle and Martin 2005):[3]

- collaboration can encourage trust and thus reduce conflict

- collaboration can 'unlock' the distinctive competencies of other sectors
- collaboration can deliver a transformational approach to service improvement.

Some have argued that there is a need for public-sector organisations to develop the capabilities to engage in perpetual collaboration (Cortada et al. 2008), while others have pointed to the rhetoric of collaborative governance accompanied by constant complaining about the difficulty of collaborating in practice (Huxham et al. 2000). Whether you believe collaborative governance represents the next wave of thinking or is a painful requirement for operating in the modern public service, there is no doubt that it has reached fever pitch. All this heralding of a new era, however, glosses over what many already suspect: collaboration is nothing new in the public sector even if some are positioning it at the centre of a post-new public management paradigm (for example, Denhardt and Denhardt 2000; Osborne 2006).

These ideas have been rolled in to the notion of 'collaborative public management', for example, which has been defined as 'the process of facilitating and operating in multiorganizational arrangements in order to remedy problems that cannot be solved—or solved easily—by [a] single organization' (McGuire 2006:3). Such an approach pushes collaboration front and centre and the focus on some of the seemingly intractable social problems challenging government has fuelled an interest in collaboration (see, for example, Australian Public Service Commission 2007). Interestingly, Bryson et al. (2006) have argued that the obsession with collaboration has provoked two distinct responses: 1) collaboration has become the holy grail, the 'one best way' of doing everything regardless of whether there is any evidence that it will add value; or 2) collaboration occurs where all else fails—that is, organisations fail into collaboration as a last resort when other approaches don't work. Neither, of course, provides as especially convincing basis for investing in collaborative endeavours.

With the current flurry around collaboration in public policy, we need to take time to look at what others have been doing in areas in which collaboration has been central to research and practice for decades. Reviewing a range of approaches shows that collaboration has been seen as a response to resource interdependencies, a means of pooling existing resources or of leveraging new ones, a strategy to reduce risk or enter new markets, an attempt to reduce transaction costs, a reaction to complexity or turbulent environments or a search for (re)integration in a fragmented domain (see, for example, Bryson et al. 2006; Lawrence et al. 1999; Lowndes and Skelcher 1998). There are well-established literatures on joint ventures, strategic alliances, hybrids and the like, which offer great potential, especially where we are concerned with issues such as inter-organisational trust and the costs of working together (for example, White

2005, who examines 'cooperation costs'). It would serve us well to revisit these rather than be blinded by the positive rhetoric of collaboration.

Indeed, McGuire (2006) points out that even within public policy, collaboration is nothing new. For example, in the mid-1970s, Schermerhorn (1975:846), writing in *The Academy of Management Journal*, noted that interagency cooperation was seen as the panacea to the 'coordination gap' that had emerged from duplication, overlap and fragmentation in social services in an increasingly 'turbulent environment'. Sound familiar? A similar rationale was noted in Bryson et al. (2006): collaboration was seen as the way to address complex problems in a complex world. The authors mindfully stated, however, that collaboration was no panacea. A similar point is made by Lundin (2007), who shows that inter-organisational cooperation is reasonable and beneficial in situations in which there is significant task complexity; enacting cooperative or collaborative approaches for simple-task situations is neither useful nor quantitatively beneficial. Rather, it is common to incur high costs. As Huxham has noted elsewhere: 'Collaboration is not a panacea for tackling all organizational activities. Most of what organizations strive to achieve is, and should be, done alone' (Huxham 1996:3). As the buzz around collaboration intensifies, however, it seems that such views are being sidelined.

Reviewing research on collaboration, it is clear that public-policy scholars and practitioners, for the most part, don't spend much time outside their disciplinary silos. In an ideal world, our current interest in collaboration should lead us to explore these perspectives; there has been so much written on collaboration that it seems nonsensical to start from scratch in public policy. Unfortunately, it is generally accepted that there is little cross-pollination, integration or, dare I say it, collaboration between these fields (for example, Hardy et al. 2003; Huxham and Vangen 1998, cited in Williams 2002). As the editors of a recent special issue of *Public Administration Review* noted, the idea of collaborative public management is studied largely without the benefit of examining the literature in related fields (Bingham and O'Leary 2006). In the concluding contribution to that collection, the authors suggested that 'we tend to play cooperatively each with our own set of blocks...we do not generally pool our blocks to build a common structure collaboratively' (Bingham and O'Leary 2006:161). We spend limited time looking to our colleagues in other disciplines and non-public sector worlds to help us on our way in understanding the promise and challenge of collaboration. To date, such 'collaborative' learning has been fairly limited, but great potential exists for interdisciplinary lessons.

What's in a word?

> If every galah in every pet shop was once squawking the mantra of micro-economic reform, today officials in every agency are singing the tune of collaborative harmonies. (Wanna 2007:30)

Collaboration has become so central to our conversations about public policy that few see the need to either define it or unpack what it means: collaboration has truly become part of the Zeitgeist. While many formal definitions exist, the term is used loosely by public-policy scholars and practitioners. In the Australian Public Service Commission (2007) report *Tackling Wicked Problems*, a collaborative approach is argued to be central to addressing these complex, inter-agency, inter-jurisdictional puzzles, yet collaboration itself is never defined. The Management Advisory Committee (2004:10) report *Connecting Government* similarly makes the case for the Australian Public Service (APS) to 'strive to create a "culture of collaboration"', to orient towards collaborative approaches and for secretaries to model collaborative behaviour, but it doesn't provide much in the way of telling us what collaboration really is. This relative fuzziness warrants, I believe, a discussion of the distinctive characteristics of collaboration.

As a starting point, we must accept that there is a range of means of working together, many of which are not collaborative. Further, we must also accept there is a current trend to call all forms of working together 'collaboration'. There are, however, important distinctions to make—the most important being that working together does not equal collaboration.[4] This is an important point to emphasise, not just to enable some sort of academic language game, but because collaboration has become *du jour*. A more measured analysis, drawing on the extensive existing literature, might point us to make some very different judgments about whether what we are witnessing is cooperation, coordination or, in some cases, coercion. From here, then, we can be more realistic about why organisations work together, when this might be appropriate and how they might go about really doing it. At the most basic level, understanding what we mean by collaboration is important to ensure we are talking the same language.

Collaboration has been defined as 'a process in which organizations exchange information, alter activities, share resources, and enhance each other's capacity for mutual benefit and a common purpose by sharing risks, responsibilities, and rewards' (Himmelman 2002:3). For others, it is an 'interorganizational relationship that relies on neither market nor hierarchical mechanism[s] of control but is instead negotiated in an ongoing communicative process' (Lawrence et al. 1999:481). In the public-policy world, where terms such as collaborative governance are used, the collaborative part of the term becomes fairly loose: for example, Donohue (2004:2) describes collaborative governance as an 'amalgam of public, private and civil society organizations engaged in some joint effort'. What tends to get lost is the distinctiveness of collaboration. Collaboration is not just a model of service delivery, it is something more complex, which involves sharing across a range of dimensions (for example, goal setting, risk, reward, resource, culture) a more strategic nature and autonomy (Head 2004, 2006; Axelrod 1984, 1997; Economist Intelligence Unit 2008; Shergold, this volume).

Understanding its distinctive features helps us to better see what collaboration is and what it is not.

Various typologies are available to assist in distinguishing collaboration and I will mention just a few—the common feature being that collaboration sits at the extreme end of different models of working together. Mattessich and Monsey (1992:39), for example, make clear distinctions between cooperation, coordination and collaboration. Cooperation is described as an informal relationship without a common mission in which information is shared on an as-needed basis, authority remains with each organisation, there is little (or no) risk and resources and rewards are kept separate. Coordination is seen as more formal and there are compatible missions that require some common planning and more formal communication channels. While each organisation retains authority, risk enters the equation. Collaboration is a more 'durable and pervasive relationship' (Mattessich and Monsey 1992:39), which involves creating new structures within which to embed authority, developing a common mission, engaging in comprehensive and shared planning, and in which formal communication across multiple levels occurs. Collaboration includes pooling and jointly acquiring resources, sharing rewards, but also increased risk. Clear distinctions are made here, which for our purposes help to delineate collaboration and differentiate it from other engagement strategies such as cooperation and coordination.

Similar distinctions were made by Himmelman (2002:1–5), who made the case that collaboration was just one of four common strategies for working together,[5] each representing a unique inter-organisational linkage, requiring different commitments of trust, time and turf. Each is more or less appropriate in different circumstances. In brief, the strategies are:

- *Networking* is an informal relationship in which information is exchanged for mutual benefit. This choice often reflects limited time, low levels of trust and a reluctance to share or concede turf. Himmelman uses the example of an early childhood centre and a public health department exchanging information about their approaches to supporting early childhood development. In this volume, Sylvan (Chapter 14) provides a good example with the Australasian Consumer Fraud Taskforce, which, at least in its initial stages, was an informal information-sharing forum.
- *Coordination* [6] involves a more formal linkage in which information is exchanged and activities are altered in pursuit of mutual benefit and achievement of common purpose. Compared with networking, it involves more time and higher trust, but little or no access to one another's turf. Himmelman suggests that when the two parties mentioned above then decide to alter their service schedules to provide combined support in a more user-friendly way, this constitutes coordination. A good example mentioned

in this volume and one mentioned by several authors is the Australian Government's Job Network.

- *Cooperation* involves an exchange of information, altering activities and resource sharing for mutual benefit in pursuit of a common purpose. Organisational commitments are higher, formal agreements can be used and this linkage requires higher levels of time and trust vis-à-vis networking and coordination. Each party will provide access to its turf. If the two parties Himmelman discusses now agree to share outreach services to increase the overall effectiveness of their support for early childhood development, this represents cooperation. This volume provides several examples, including the family violence strategy discussed by Treadwell (Chapter 12) and the Homeless Connect project described by Allison (Chapter 13).

- *Collaboration* is distinctive as it involves a willingness of the parties to enhance one another's capacity—helping the other to 'be the best they can be' (Himmelman 2002:3)—for mutual benefit and common purpose. In collaboration, the parties share risks, responsibilities and rewards, they invest substantial time, have high levels of trust and share common turf. Where Himmelman's two organisations now agree to provide skill-development training for the staff of the other organisation to enhance capacity and enable improved support for early childhood development, this reflects collaboration. In this volume, it was difficult to identify a case of collaboration on these terms; however, it could be argued that Carmody's (Chapter 7) discussion of crisis management comes closest.

In their work on collaboration in inter-organisational domains, Hardy and Phillips (1998) identify different engagement strategies, two of which I will note here. First, they discuss collaboration as a mutual engagement strategy in which parties participate voluntarily and, second, they contrast this with a compliance strategy in which a dominant party (for example, government) can use its power to regulate a weaker party (for example, a community group), who, essentially, has little or no choice about engaging. In other work, Hardy et al. (2003) stress the point that while collaboration can exist in many different organisational forms (for example, joint ventures, alliances, consortia, networks), it must be distinguished from cooperation, which can be purchased (for example, from a supplier) or demanded via some form of legitimate authority (for example, by a government organisation).

Power is, of course, a critical issue, and one that is remarkably absent from much of the public-policy writing to date. As Hardy and Phillips (1998) define it, genuine collaboration relies on voluntary and mutual engagement; others discuss how true collaboration involves autonomy, trust, mutual goal setting, and so on. In contrast, there are other forms of engagement that can be more, or less, voluntary and equal. The current trend, however, towards labelling all forms of interaction collaboration paints a more upbeat picture, in which collaboration is virtuous and equal. The more critical work on collaboration rejects much of this, suggesting, for example, that issues of power asymmetry, exploitation and repression (Hardy and Phillips 1998) need to be factored into our analyses of how 'real' collaboration is. Sylvan (Chapter 14) raises the issue of power and points to the challenges of power sharing, including operating in domains in which powerful stakeholders hold vested interests. Henry (Chapter 11) comes at the issue from a different perspective. She acknowledges the fact that community organisations are often seen as unequal partners in their dealings with government organisations, and to some extent this is true, because regardless of whether they hold strategic assets that the government requires, they are still heavily reliant on funding to continue, and government still remains in the position to, essentially, change its mind.

In the preceding discussion, I sought to clarify the distinctiveness of collaboration from other forms of engaging or working together. This is not a purely academic exercise, but rather a means of better analysing the contributions to this monograph. In the next section, I reflect on the general trend towards collaborative government and the more specific contributions made here to highlight this point.

Reflections on 'collaboration' in practice: what can we learn?

In reviewing the narratives captured in this monograph, it is not at all clear that 'collaboration' is evident. Rather, we have a collection of inter-organisational relationships of which few, if any, we would genuinely describe as collaboration. More likely is the case that these examples combine aspects of networking, coordination and cooperation (with some coercion or compliance in the mix). This could reflect the fact that 'surface dynamics are not necessarily an accurate description of what is going on beneath' (Hardy and Phillips 1998:217); in other words, while everyone is talking collaboration is anyone really collaborating?

Reflecting on these contributions suggests two critical things. First, government working with, or through, other parties is an increasingly popular mode of policymaking and implementation; and second, few of these relationships could rightly be described as collaborative. Just as Jupp (Chapter 16) suggested 'partnership' was the dominant rhetoric of the Blair Government in the United Kingdom, so we see that collaboration has the potential to explode in a similar way in Australia. Jupp acknowledges that there is a spectrum of engagements between government and third-sector organisations, however, even here they are all labelled as collaboration. There is, of course, nothing to suggest that government–NGO relations cannot be collaborative, but whether the use of commercial-style contracts for the delivery of public services is inherently collaborative is open to debate. In many cases, it could be more accurate to suggest that government is simply purchasing cooperation from a provider organisation (see Hardy et al. 2003). In the examples provided by Allison (Chapter 13), we can identify a range of engagement strategies between organisations and individuals, including public–private partnerships (PPPs), integrated services for the homeless, technology-based co-production of services and community-engagement forums. Based on the prior discussion, we can see that these represent a spectrum of connections and examples of working together, but it is hard to accept that these are all collaborative in the manner set out above. More likely, we have a mixed bag of co-production, coordination and cooperation. Perhaps Treadwell's (Chapter 12) example of addressing family violence comes close to collaboration, but, using Himmelman's (2002) typology, it is more likely cooperation.

If we use Hardy and Phillip's (1998) descriptors, we can see a strong case from Smith (Chapter 9) that there has been a radical departure in Indigenous affairs from collaboration towards compliance: a dominant party regulates a weaker one. Of course, interpretations depend on where you stand. Similarly, Shergold's (Chapter 2) discussion of Shared Responsibility Agreements (SRAs) is another area in which there are competing views of the extent of collaboration: are they really collaborative arrangements between government and Indigenous communities, or are they simply new compliance instruments? Shergold himself notes that while they require a commitment to consultation and negotiation, they would be much more effective if they were more genuinely collaborative. This, of course, would require ingredients such as mutual trust, shared resources, mutually agreed goals, voluntary participation and the sharing of risk and reward, for example. The practicalities of such an approach appear, at this stage in history, to be remote.

Hodge and Greve's (Chapter 10) contribution challenges the rhetoric of collaboration in PPPs; indeed, it poses a range of questions about how government and the private sector work together. The authors clearly argue that PPPs have, in many cases, been two-way deals between government and business, governed by complex, often unintelligible, commercial-in-confidence contracts. At worst, they force us to ask whether they are the outcome of the political and business interests that go against the best interests of the citizenry—a unique collaboration indeed! At the very least, we must question whether there is any collaboration happening here at all. Using the notions discussed above, at best, we might see coordination or cooperation emerging from these arrangements. Similarly, questions must be raised when we consider the issues canvassed in the education domain—and, in her contribution, Hunter (Chapter 8) points to a powerful set of institutional barriers to collaboration.

From the community sector, Henry (Chapter 11) raises questions about the effects of contractualisation on relationships between government and non-profit organisations. Is it possible that the shift towards wrapping contracts around previously grant-based relationships or inviting non-profits to enter the 'market' for services has produced a net collaborative loss in the third sector? Competition between previously collaborative non-profits in the quest for government contracting could, in fact, reduce collaboration within the sector. Smyth picks up this issue when he argues that the Job Network has been assessed as being 'overly centralised with excessive regulation'; it also ignores 'unique local circumstances and directs activity away from collaboration…and networking' (Chapter 6). This, of course, raises a broader question of just how collaborative government contracting really is. In his contribution, Shergold mentions the potential for compliance-style relationships—which have characterised the Job Network—to be transformed into more collaborative arrangements. Collaboration, he notes, will prepare the ground for 'innovation and continuing improvement in the long term' (Chapter 2). The trick, of course, will be in trying to set and shift incentives in what has been a quasi-market, where providers have competed against one another for business and for higher performance ratings. In some ways, this might represent a return to collaboration for some of the non-profit organisations, rather than some new collaborative discovery. In his discussion on developments in Canada, Lindquist (Chapter 15) notes the promise of government–voluntary sector relations, but also points to a range of challenges.

Regardless of whether we classify these examples as 'genuine' collaborations or not, there are important lessons to be drawn from the contributions about working together constructively. One of the most interesting and most novel lessons comes from Huxham and Hibbert (Chapter 5), who ask a basic yet often overlooked question: what will success look like for the parties to collaboration? Will it be the achievement of outcomes, getting processes to work, reaching milestones, gaining external recognition or a personal pride that develops from successfully championing a project? This is an important issue, because without this discussion partners will find that their measures of success will differ; success is, in the end, different things to different people.

It is also important to be realistic about the trade-off between effort and reward. As strategies for working together become more complex—that is, they move towards the collaborative end of the scale—investments and costs intensify. Our contributors remind us that there are many costs associated with inter-organisational work or working across formal boundaries and these occur regardless of whether 'success' is achieved. At the most basic, this can involve time, travel and other communication costs and participants can suffer 'partnership fatigue' (Huxham and Vangen, Chapter 4). More significantly, there can be costs to employees, clients or communities who must deal with dysfunctional experiments. As Huxham and Vangen explain, the potentiality of collaborative advantage must be weighed against the hard grind of genuine collaboration or, in their words, collaborative inertia.

Recognising the specific capabilities and strategic assets of different parties is important when engaging in different modes of operation. Henry (Chapter 11) reminds us that non-profit community organisations often hold the critical intelligence and access that government organisations need, and implies that they must learn to leverage this more fully in their relationships with governments. Within this context, especially where there are commercial contracts in place, such organisations need to be wary of becoming 'semi-state agencies', as Jupp warns (Chapter 16). This goes back to some of the basic ideas of collaboration; it involves autonomous agents working together to achieve mutual goals, not the takeover of supposed partners. Again, recognising the issue of power asymmetries is crucial in developing a more sophisticated understanding of the realities of working together; it is too easy to just assume such differentials away. Huxham and Vangen (Chapter 4), however, remind us that it is not just the 'purse strings' that produce power; there are multiple points where power is important when we work together. Power asymmetries do exist and provide the basis for, in some cases, 'collaborative thuggery' (Huxham and Vangen, Chapter 4).

It is important to consider conditions for effective joint work. Carmody (Chapter 7) points us to the power of a crisis to propel parties towards a more collaborative space—a point reinforced by Allison (Chapter 13), who argues that the water crisis has enabled radical changes in behaviour. Such situations permit a 'take-charge' attitude and set the scene for the key ingredients Carmody identifies: effective leadership, clear identification of responsibilities, common accountabilities, clear communication channels, rehearsed processes, a common agenda and depoliticised arenas in which there is no room for ideology. While such ingredients prepare the ground for an effective 'institutional architecture of crisis management', they are often missing in longer-term, non-crisis situations. Rather, as Carmody notes, they mirror common military practice and, in non-crisis situations, would go against many of the suggested models for genuine collaboration. Of course, the identification of a crisis can permit radical change in non-military situations—the NT intervention of 2007 providing a recent example.

Outside crisis situations, the sustainability of collaborative efforts is an important topic. How are these relationships cultivated, nurtured and sustained over time? How do we ensure continuity when there is turnover of people engaged in different types of 'working together'? Such questions point to the inevitable 'people issue'. When we get down to it, it is people who enable organisations to work together effectively, sometimes despite organisational barriers. Several contributors point to the importance of 'people' factors—for example, Fels (Preface) and Eggers (Chapter 3) identify the new skills needed by those who engage in more network-style arrangements, and other contributors stress a range of skills that needs to be enhanced—usually on the government side of arrangements—to enable more productive and effective engagement between parties. Sylvan (Chapter 14) cautions that we need to be aware of the people problems that can emerge when power relations change and how incentives for working together need to be carefully thought out. Clearly, collaborative capacity is a serious issue—as Fels (Preface) points out—and new thinking is required for us to enable more productive working relationships.

A final lesson is based on the cautionary messages that were included in several of the contributions to this volume. With all the hype around collaboration, it is tempting for many to see it as some panacea, as an optimal operating model in what are seen as complex and turbulent times. Prescribing collaboration as the 'one best way' to work together is, however, fraught, as Head has argued elsewhere: 'Selection of inappropriate structures and processes can be a recipe for frustration among participants, and ensures under-achievement of goals' (2004:3). Put more succinctly: '[D]on't work collaboratively unless you have to' (Huxham and Vangen 2004:200). Of course, this is more easily said than done: when and where to collaborate (and with whom) are, in practice, some of the most difficult questions of all.

Looking forward, it will be interesting to watch whether the recent change of government will provide some collaborative impetus; certainly, the noise early on revolves around how the new government will seek to 'work together' with many different groups. This is not to say that the previous government was not interested in collaboration; in fact, many of the examples provided in this monograph suggest the opposite. For some, the NT intervention showed how government agencies could come together to address social issues, and changes over time in the Job Network showed some development along the collaboration spectrum. One of the great challenges for this government will be in intergovernmental collaboration and whether it can address complex policy problems.

Concluding remarks

There appears to be little evidence from the preceding contributions that we are entering a new era. At best, we could be at the beginning of some evolutionary process that will propel us, in time, towards more genuinely collaborative approaches. This is a point made most strongly in Shergold's contribution (Chapter 2), in which he cautions us against exaggerating the speed of process or the substance of change. Strong demarcations still exist, bureaucratic barriers remain and governments retain extensive powers of control. Such factors make collaboration difficult, partially, at least, because it is always possible for government to 'trump' its supposed partners or to change its mind if it so wishes. Smith provided the perfect example of this when she told us: 'In one day, without any consultation [the Bininj leaders from the West Arnhem Shire learned that their] collaboration with the Australian Government had essentially been made null and void' (Chapter 9).

The complexity of collaboration is very real but a serious problem is emerging in the scholarly and practitioner worlds. The current trend towards labelling all forms of working together collaboration glosses over the messy, uneven world in which we operate and, if we fail to disentangle these complexities, we will never get a handle on what is really going on. Our opportunities to learn will be stymied and our ability to consider appropriate models for inter-organisational and cross-sectoral work will be hampered. The challenges and the promise make collaboration appealing indeed, but perhaps Head (2004) is right: we should consider collaboration an aspirational ideal.

References

Australian Public Service Commission 2007, *Tackling Wicked Problems: A public policy perspective*, Australian Government, Canberra.

Axelrod, R. 1984, *The Evolution of Cooperation*, Basic Books, United States of America.

Axelrod, R. 1997, *The Complexity of Cooperation: Agent-based models of competition and collaboration*, Princeton University Press, Princeton, New Jersey.

Bingham, L. B. 2006, 'The new urban governance: processes for involving citizens and stakeholders', *Review of Policy Research*, vol. 23, no. 4, pp. 815–26.

Bingham, L. B. and O'Leary, R. 2006, 'Parallel play, not collaboration: missing questions, missing connections', *Public Administration Review*, vol. 66, no. s1, pp. 161–7.

Brown, K. and Keast, R. 2003, 'Citizen–government engagement: community connection through networked arrangements', *Asian Journal of Public Administration*, vol. 25, no. 1, pp. 107–31.

Bryson, J. M., Crosby, B. C. and Middleton Stone, M. 2006, 'The design and implementation of cross-sector collaborations: propositions from the literature', *Public Administration Review*, vol. 66, no. s1, pp. 44–55.

Commonwealth of Australia 2008, *Australia 2020 Summit: Initial summit report*, April, Canberra, viewed 21 April 2008, <http://www.australia2020.gov.au/report/index.cfm>

Cortada, J. W., Dijkstra, S., Mooney, G. M. and Ramsey, T. 2008, *Government 2020 and the Perpetual Collaboration Mandate: Six worldwide drivers demand customized strategies*, IBM Institute for Business Value, IBM Global Services, New York.

Denhardt, R. B. and Denhardt, J. V. 2000, 'The new public service: serving rather than steering', *Public Administration Review*, vol. 60, no. 6, pp. 549–59.

Donahue, J. 2004, *On collaborative governance*, Corporate Social Responsibility Initiative Working Paper No. 2, John F. Kennedy School of Government, Harvard University, Cambridge, Mass.

Economist Intelligence Unit 2007, 'Collaboration: transforming the way business works', *The Economist*, London, viewed 7 April 2008, <http://www.eiu.com/site_info.asp?info_name=Collaboration_Transforming_the_way_business_works&rf=0>

Economist Intelligence Unit 2008, 'The role of trust in business collaboration', *The Economist*, London, viewed 7 April 2008, <http://www.eiu.com/site_info.asp?info_name=cisco_trust&page=noads>

Entwistle, T. and Martin, S. 2005, 'From competition to collaboration in public service delivery: a new agenda for research', *Public Administration*, vol. 83, no. 1, pp. 233–42.

Hardy, C. and Phillips, N. 1998, 'Strategies of engagement: lessons from the critical examination of collaboration and conflict in an interorganizational domain', *Organization Studies*, vol. 9, no. 2, pp. 217–30.

Hardy, C. Phillips, N. and Lawrence, T.B. 2003, 'Resources, knowledge and Influence: the organizational effects of interorganizational collaboration', *Journal of Management Studies*, vol. 40. no.2, pp. 321-347.

Head, B. 2004, *Collaboration—What We Already Know, and How to Do It Better*, Australian Research Alliance for Children and Youth, 20 January, viewed 7 April 2007, <http://www.aracy.org.au/>

Head, B. 2006, *Effective Collaboration*, Australian Research Alliance for Children and Youth, July, viewed 7 April 2007, <http://www.aracy.org.au/>

Himmelman, A. T. 2002, *Collaboration for a Change: Definitions, decision-making models, roles, and collaboration process guide*, Himmelman Consulting, Minneapolis.

Huxham, C. (ed.) 1996, *Creating Collaborative Advantage*, Sage, London.

Huxham, C. and Vangen, S. 2004, 'Doing things collaboratively: realizing the advantage or succumbing to inertia?', *Organizational Dynamics*, vol. 33, no. 3, pp. 190–201.

Huxham, Chris., Vangen, S., Huxham, C. and Eden, C. 2000, 'The challenge of collaborative governance', *Public Management Review*, vol. 2, no. 2, pp. 337–58.

Lawrence, T. B., Phillips, N. and Hardy, C. 1999, 'Watching whale watching: exploring the discursive foundations of collaborative relationships', *Journal of Applied Behavioral Science*, vol. 35, no. 4, pp. 479–502.

Lowndes, V. and Skelcher, C. 1998, 'The dynamics of multi-organizational partnerships: an analysis of changing modes of governance', *Public Administration*, vol. 76, no. 2, pp. 313–33.

Lundin, M. 2007, 'When does cooperation improve public policy implementation?', *The Policy Studies Journal*, vol. 35, no. 4, pp. 629–52.

Management Advisory Committee 2004, *Connecting Government: Whole of government responses to Australia's priority challenges*, Australian Government, Canberra.

Mattessich, P. W. and Monsey, B. R. 1992, *Collaboration: What makes it work*, Amherst H. Wilder Foundation, St Paul, Minnesota.

McGuire, M. 2006, 'Collaborative public management: assessing what we know and how we know it', *Public Administration Review*, vol. 66, no. s1, pp. 33–43.

O'Leary, R. and Bingham, L. B. 2007, *A Manager's Guide to Resolving Conflicts in Collaborative Networks*, IBM Center for the Business of Government, Washington, DC.

Osborne, S. 2006, 'The new public governance?', *Public Management Review*, vol. 8, no. 3, pp. 377–87.

Powell, W. W., Koput, K. W. and Smith-Doerr, L. 1996, 'Interorganizational collaboration and the locus of innovation: networks of learning in biotechnology', *Administrative Science Quarterly*, vol. 41, no. 1, pp. 116–45.

Rittel, H. W. J. and Webber, M. M. 1971, 'Dilemmas in a general theory of planning', *Policy Sciences*, vol. 4, pp. 155–69.

Schermerhorn, J. R. 1975, 'Determinants of interorganizational cooperation', *Academy of Management Journal*, vol. 18, no. 4, pp. 846–56.

Thomson, A. M. and Perry, J. L. 1998, 'Can AmeriCorps build communities?', *Nonprofit and Voluntary Sector Quarterly*, vol. 27, no. 4, pp. 399–420.

Wanna, J. 2007, 'Governments abuzz with collaborative harmonies', *Public Sector Informant/The Canberra Times*, 3 July, pp. 30–1.

White, S. 2005, 'Cooperation costs, governance choice and alliance evolution', *Journal of Management Studies*, vol. 42, no. 7, pp. 1383–412.

Williams, P. 2002, 'The competent boundary spanner', *Public Administration*, vol. 80, no. 1, pp. 103–24.

ENDNOTES

[1] Program director quoted in Thomson and Perry (1998:409).

[2] Keynote address by Prime Minister Kevin Rudd at the Australian Davos Connection Future Summit 2008, 11 May 2008, Hilton Hotel, Sydney.

[3] While the authors use the term 'partnership', their propositions are all linked explicitly to collaboration; collaboration is the centrepiece of partnership in the UK context.

[4] This is generally held to be the case despite a recent publication from *The Economist* stating that 'collaboration is to work together—to co-labour' (Economist Intelligence Unit 2007:7). Interestingly, in a 2008 publication from the Economist Intelligence Unit, *The Role of Trust in Business Collaboration*, the authors note that the term 'collaboration' is a misnomer and there are differences between coordination, cooperation and collaboration (see p. 2).

[5] The different strategies can also be considered as developmental stages—for example, a relationship can begin as coordination, but develop with time into cooperation.

[6] Readers will have noted that the placement of cooperation and coordination differs in the typologies offered by Himmelman and Mattessich and Monsey, with Mattessich and Monsey placing coordination before cooperation.

18. Postscript

Peter Shergold

Time moves on. Governments change. Mandarins depart (although, speaking personally, the second and third sentence are unrelated). I have had collected my Cabinet-in-Confidence files, handed back my parliamentary pass and said my fond valedictories to the Australian Public Service. In February 2008, at the end of my contract, I left. I had spent two decades as a public servant.

I have moved on (some would say, forward). I have returned to academia, taking up a position as the inaugural Professor of the Centre for Social Impact (CSI). CSI is a bold cross-university partnership between the business schools of the Swinburne University of Technology, the University of Melbourne and the University of New South Wales. It is an exciting but challenging relationship. As Chris Huxham and Siv Vangen emphasise elsewhere in this volume, 'making collaboration work effectively is highly resource consuming and often painful'. Their strongest piece of advice is 'don't do it unless you have to'.

It is my view that we have to. I can see no other way of creating a national institutional structure committed to socially responsible business management, improving the organisational capacity of not-for-profit management and making corporate citizenship more strategic. The CSI will focus on the relationship between the private, public and 'third' sectors and the potential that brings for social innovation. It will complement, I anticipate, that highly effective trans-Tasman university collaboration, the Australia New Zealand School of Government.

Generously, or perhaps provocatively, the editors have offered me the opportunity to email a brief postscript to the article I wrote when I was the Secretary of the Department of the Prime Minister and Cabinet. I sense the unstated questions. How enthused do I feel about a 'centreless society' now that I am out of the centre? How, more particularly, do I view outsourced government from the perspective of the social enterprises that win the contracts to deliver government services? Do I (perhaps) wish to eat humble pie in public?

In truth, I am relieved that my enthusiasm for the potential of shared leadership was firmly founded on the unflinching Realpolitik of the professional bureaucrat. Excited as I was by the prospect, I was realistic enough to note that the Public Service still retained positional authority at the political heart of the networks of governance.

My intuition and experience suggested that although public services, and the governments they served, needed to focus more on collaboration, they exercised their persuasive talents in an environment characterised by asymmetrical power. It was not—perhaps cannot be—a partnership of equals. Social enterprises negotiate from a position of disadvantage. The obvious question is whether not-for-profit organisations should eschew entering into contractual relationships with governments, knowing that—no matter how politically protected they are by a compact or charter of civil engagement—they will always be relatively weak when bargaining with the formidable strength of public-service agencies speaking with the authority of government.

I think not. Social enterprises will always struggle by virtue of the fact that their values-driven ambitions have an infinite capacity to outstrip the resources available. A not-for-profit organisation, committed to community benefit, will find it difficult to harness voluntary labour, raise donations, collect fees or earn interest payments on investments that are sufficient to meet its expanding goals.

The framework of charitable endeavour has changed significantly in the past generation. Whether supported by traditional philanthropy or new-age 'philanthro-capitalist' social investment, the challenge for social enterprises in dealing with individual or corporate donors is not very different from their relationship with governments. The essential challenge for community-based organisations is that, whether they depend on philanthropic foundations, business enterprises or government agencies, they usually have to negotiate financial support and partnership arrangements from a position of relative weakness.

Governments rarely use that power to threaten. The essence of the danger for not-for-profits is not 'collaborative thuggery' by public servants intent on intimidation. The exercise of power is far more subtle and, for that very reason, more pernicious.

Community-based groups define themselves in terms of the values to which they subscribe. Values underpin, although not always with adequate strategic intent, the ambitions that are articulated in organisational vision, mission, purpose and goals. Values are their reason for being. In the relentless pursuit of the resources that can make the mission manifest, however, there is a danger that collaboration with those providing the funds can progressively transform social intent.

This is true not only of their relationship with governments. Let me proffer a typical example. Not-for-profit and corporate enterprises might share a mutual interest in the provision of volunteers for community benefit. Indeed, some businesses now encourage or even require their staff to work pro bono during the course of a year. The expectations of the parties could, however, differ profoundly. Not-for-profit organisations could seek access to particular legal or financial skills from corporate executives; the corporation, in contrast, could seek to deploy voluntary labour as a form of 'do-it-yourself' team-building activity. Negotiation of such contradictory (and often unstated) expectations is required.

With governments, however, the challenges of collaboration are greater and have become larger. In aggregate, social enterprises (particularly in the area of social welfare) have become more reliant on government funding. More importantly—and often the reason for their increased financial dependence—the form of government support has changed. Governments are now relatively less likely to provide grants to not-for-profit groups to support artistic endeavour, community sport, social welfare or the environment. Conversely, governments are increasingly attracted to awarding competitive contracts for the delivery of their programs. Instead of providing funding to organisations to pursue community goals that governments agree are in the public interest, governments are now more likely to tender out to community organisations for the delivery of public services. Herein lies the potential for collaborative governance and for community discord.

The most profound danger is mission creep. It comes about in a variety of ways. The first is that, seeking to find new avenues of funding, the not-for-profit organisation widens or varies its objectives in order to meet the terms of government funding. The drift could initially seem modest: still doing things for the poor, for instance, but framing those activities in the language of successive governments (as 'mutual obligation', say, or 'social inclusion'). Almost certainly, the new mission still serves a socially beneficial purpose. The challenge, particularly if the evolution is not thought through carefully, is that the original distinctive mission is weakened. The organisation becomes diverted.

There is a second form of mission creep that can occur in a government-sponsored 'purchaser–provider' relationship. Not-for-profit values are often expressed as much in the means as in the ends. Finding someone a job, counselling a dysfunctional family, providing assistance to a homeless person or supporting an Indigenous enterprise can be tendered out by government to an experienced community organisation committed to the task. Unfortunately, the manner in which the service is to be provided can be transformed in ways that weaken the spirit—the very heart—of the community organisation. In part, this is because government contract payments are usually based on outcomes that give no acknowledgment to the processes of engagement that many not-for-profit businesses hold dear. The need to achieve outcomes, and the rigours of an imposed compliance regime, can, with time, undermine the sense of community purpose that inspires commitment.

At least in such circumstances the not-for-profit institution wins the tender with eyes wide open. Worse, by far, is when governments, although committed to outcomes payments, seek for political reasons to intervene in the approaches taken by the social enterprise. One of my worst experiences as a public servant was having to counsel a Job Network member that it should not spend public funds on paying for job-seekers' haircuts (which privately I thought represented a perfectly rational expenditure economically and socially). The cause was intense media criticism of the alleged 'misuse' of taxpayers' money. The practice had to cease in spite of the fact that the government paid only if the organisation achieved a satisfactory job placement.

There is a third variation of mission creep. This is when a government, appropriately seeking the best value for money in the purchase of services from a provider, devotes inadequate attention to the capacity of the tendering organisation to deliver—and when a not-for-profit organisation, enthused by the opportunity to expand its horizons, overestimates its ability to scale up from a local to a regional or national body. In such circumstances, both sides feel that collaborative governance has faltered. Not unusually, it is the clients (that is, the citizens) who bear the costs of failure.

Finally, there is also a more fundamental form of mission creep that extends beyond the ambit of any particular provider. For the third sector, success in winning government funding can come at a high cost. Slowly but surely a close financial relationship with government can undermine the sector's capacity for social innovation.

I was honoured, shortly after leaving the APS, to attend the 2020 Summit initiated by Prime Minister Rudd. It was a stimulating occasion, yet I was left profoundly uneasy. It seemed to me, particularly on reflection, that the community activists present too often couched their worthwhile agendas almost entirely in terms of government.

I understand that. I agree strongly with the need to set an explicit framework for the collaboration between governments and the third sector. In my view, however, such reforms are necessary but not sufficient.

The danger I see (and fear) is that in a world in which access to the levers of democratic power is palpably unequal, social enterprises could find themselves becoming minor partners in networked governance. Their wonderful strength—devising community-based, socially innovative approaches to the delivery of public benefit—could be dissipated if their potential for critical insight and new approaches is undermined not by outraged opposition but by the welcoming embrace of governments.

I am attracted now, as when I was a public servant, to forms of government that are collaborative. In an era in which party-political affiliations (and trade union membership) have declined, a robust and raucous squabble of social enterprises gives life to democratic process. In their influence on public policy, however, not-for-profit organisations need to be provocateurs as well as partners. Individually and collectively, they need the inner strength of conviction that builds a civil society. They need to preserve the knowledge and belief that they can make their own futures without government funding and irrespective of government support. It would be a tragedy if, for the very best of collaborative reasons, the capacity of social enterprises to influence governance was lost.

www.ingramcontent.com/pod-product-compliance
Lightning Source LLC
Chambersburg PA
CBHW061233270326
41929CB00027B/3446